This edition published in March 2012

Design Media Publishing Limited
20/F Manulife Tower
169 Electric Rd, North Point
Hong Kong
Tel: 00852-28672587
Fax: 00852-25050411
E-mail: Kevinchoy@designmediahk.com
www.designmediahk.com

Editing: Helen LIU
Proofreading: Qian YIN
Design/Layout: Chunling YANG

ISBN 978-988-15450-8-4

Printed in China

MODERN
BANK DESIGNS

DESIGN MEDIA PUBLISHING LIMITED

CONTENTS

BUILDING SHAPE

PUBLIC SPACE

VIP SPACE

1

ANZ Centre

Location: Melbourne, Australia
Completion Year: 2010
Designer: HASSELL and Lend Lease Design
- Architects in Collaboration
Photographer: Peter Bennetts, Earl Carter
Area: 130,000 m²

ANZ Centre, designed by HASSELL and Lend Lease Design, is one of the most open and permeable banking headquarters in the world. Rarely - if ever before - has a bank invited the public into the heart of its workplace. This "urban campus" is the next generation in design for collaboration and flexibility with most floor space dedicated to shared, interactive activity to enable the incidental connections that are so critical to today's knowledge economy. Incorporating a raft of first-time green initiatives, the building is also a global environmental and social sustainability benchmark.

Located in Melbourne's Docklands, the building's fluid forms are inspired by its riverside setting and the external colour palette is derived from nature, ranging from earth tones at ground level to light blue sky references at the upper levels. The materials, and detailing of the building architecture reflect Melbourne's urban character. Recycled timber cladding provides a link to the maritime past of the precinct and a green wall along the eastern elevation links the building to Docklands Park.

Despite its large scale, ANZ Centre provides an opportunity to make small-scale engagements with its local community. The building form steps down to engage with the waterfront and operate as a permeable extension of the existing urban precinct. Large floors at lower levels with smaller floors at upper levels allow for changing floor-to-floor character within the building.

This '"urban campus" design concept is focused around a central publicly accessible daylight-flooded "common". The scale and complexity of the space allow it to operate like a microcosm of the city itself - with plazas, laneways, streets and formal and informal meeting places. Cafés, public art, a visitor centre and community event spaces all contribute to creating a lively community hub. The use of timber evokes the metaphor of driftwood on river banks, echoing the external façades. Bluestone paving on the common echoes Melbourne's famous bluestone paved laneways and further helps to bring the city's public realm into the interior.

1. The façade is in recycled timber cladding
2. The design uses earth tones at ground level and light blue sky references at the upper levels

3

3. The use of timber inside echoes the external façades
4. Atrium
5. Informal meeting space
6. View to 'Grow' hub

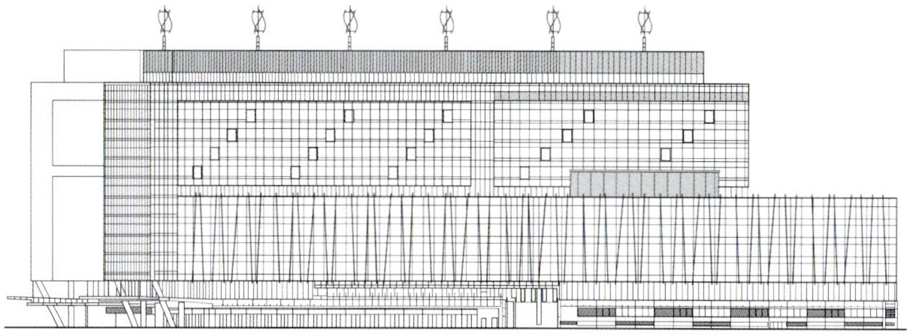

South Elevation

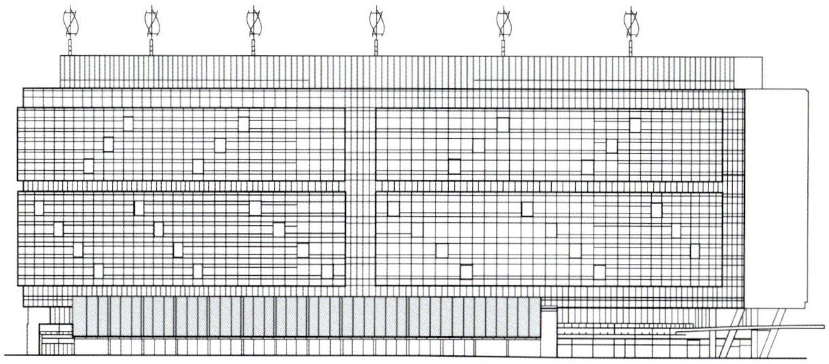

North Elevation

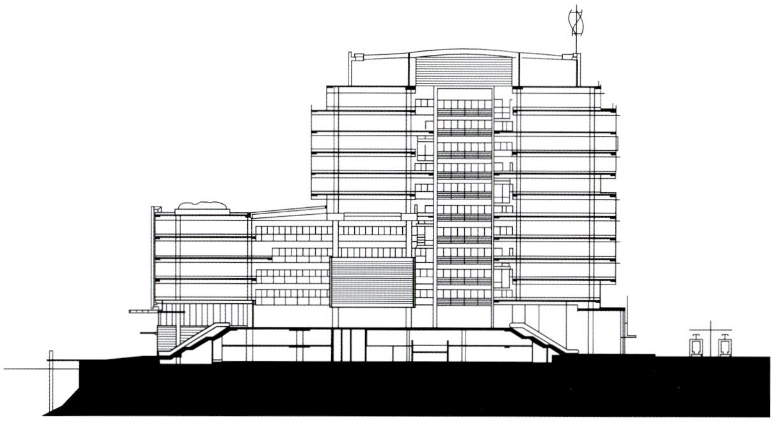

Section

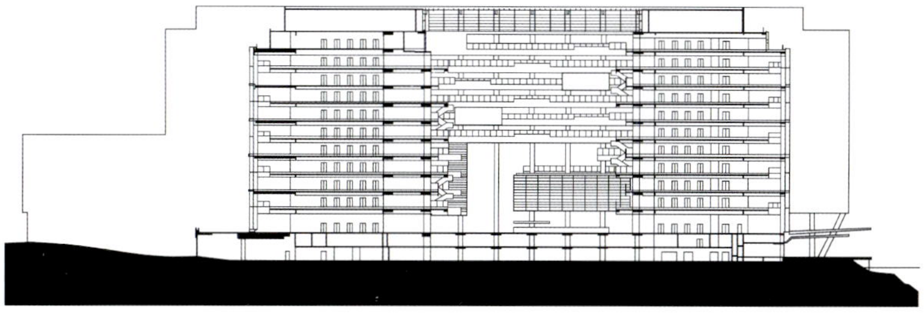

Section

5

1
2
2
2
3
4
4
5

Ground Floor Plan
1. Reception
2. ANZ Meeting Suites
3. Wellness Centre
4. Retail
5. Visitors Centre

7

8

9

7. Work space
8. 'Create' hub environment
9. View to 'Play' hub

DnB NORD
DnB NORD
DnB NORD

1

DnB NORD
DnB NORD

DnB NORD Office Building in Riga

Location: Riga, Latvia
Completion Year: 2010
Designer: Audrius Ambrasas Architects
Photographer: Audrius Ambrasas Architects
Area: 14,445 m²

DnB NORD Bank building is situated along Skanstes Street in a newly developed multifunction area to the north of Riga's Old Town. Bank building is the first office building in the newly shaped block and individually interprets planned urban/architectural block conception. Angular location suggested the building should be a clear boundary/ corner formant of the block. But at the same time the building was created as an open, inviting and involving inside for both visitors and workers.

The building consists of two separate 10-storey volumes connected by a transparent vertical communication unit. Volumes are covered by a rectangular one-storey roof slab on the top. Free area under the roof creates a new type of space. Using this space is seeking to blur the boundaries between buildings' inside and outside, to create cosy surroundings and a comfortable and smooth entry way to the bank from outside space to inside space. Also, the outdoor space of Skanstes Street is kind of "sucked in" under the roof plane and in spite of the short front side of the building creates a spatial connection with main Skanstes Street. Building façades are covered by dark stone slabs with mat finish surface, a series of aluminium profile glazing, aluminium panels and white frosted glass lines with integrated lighting.

The building is accessed through the following two entrances under the roof. One entrance is set for the visitors of bank branch on the ground floor, the other for the bank's employees working in the building. Mainly bank floors are planned as open type office working spaces for the bank employees. Also planned are a dining hall, training classrooms, meeting rooms, a server room and meeting rooms, exposition spaces in the console roof floor. A small amount of parking places are planned in the basement; rest of the cars are planned to store in common parking building in the middle of block, which is going to be built in the future.

1. General view from the southeast side
2. View of the north façade

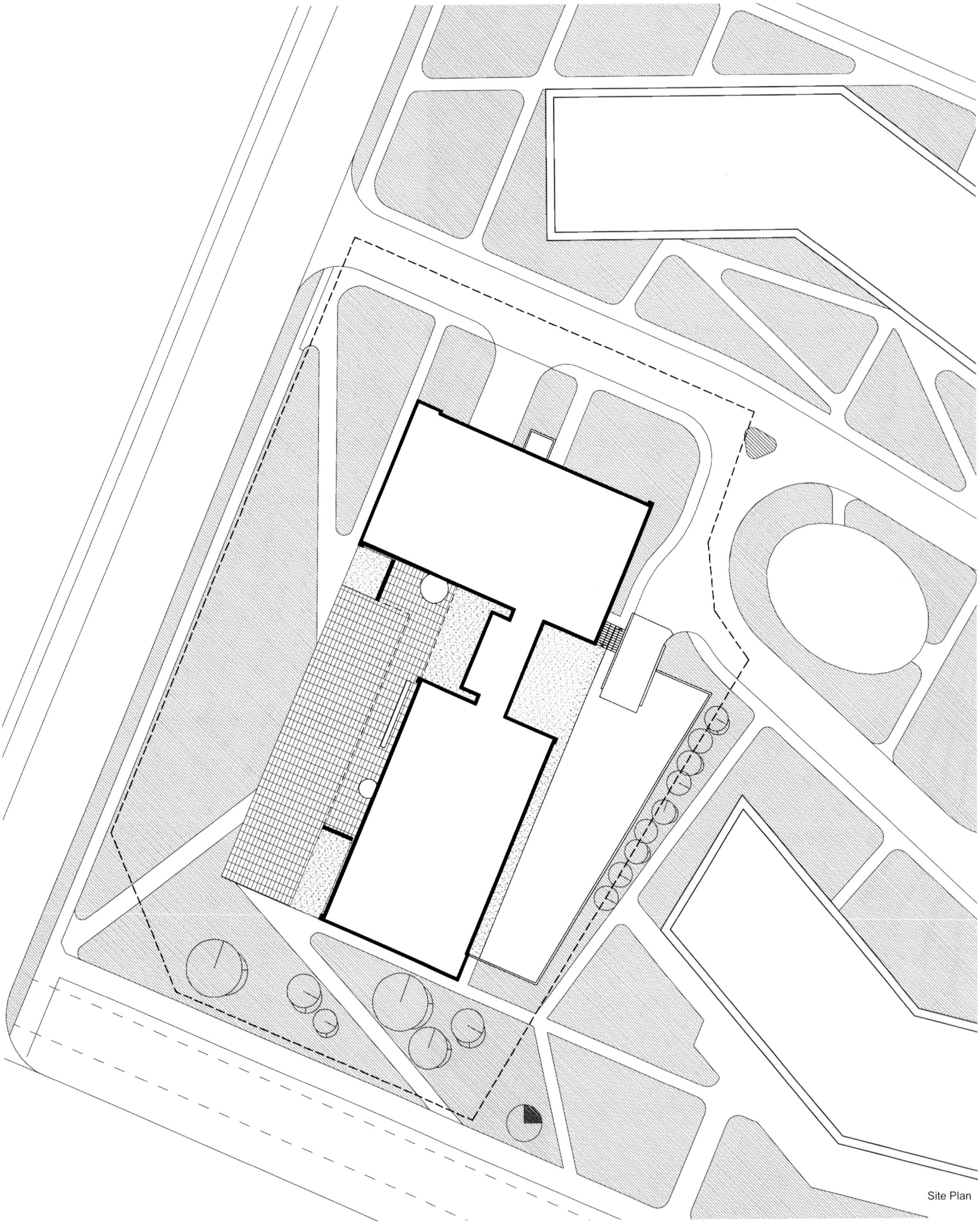

Site Plan

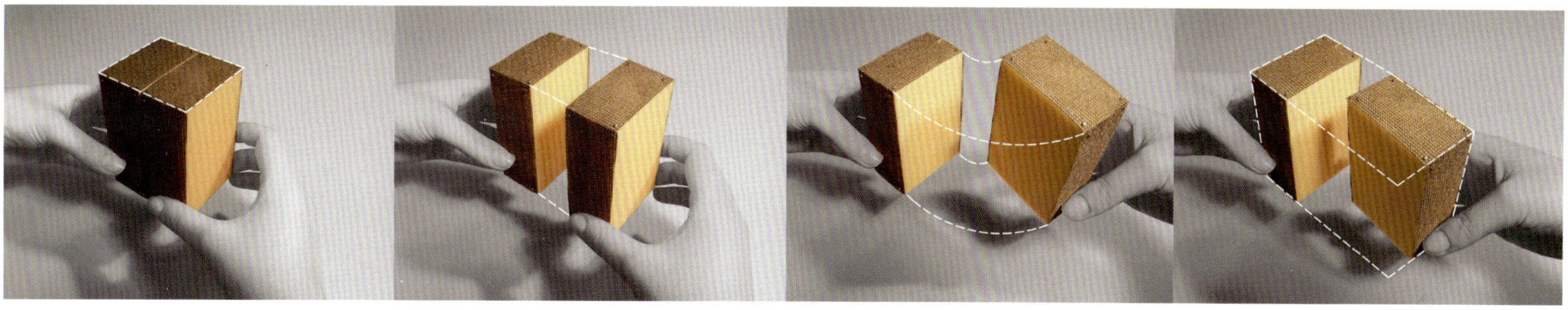

Concept

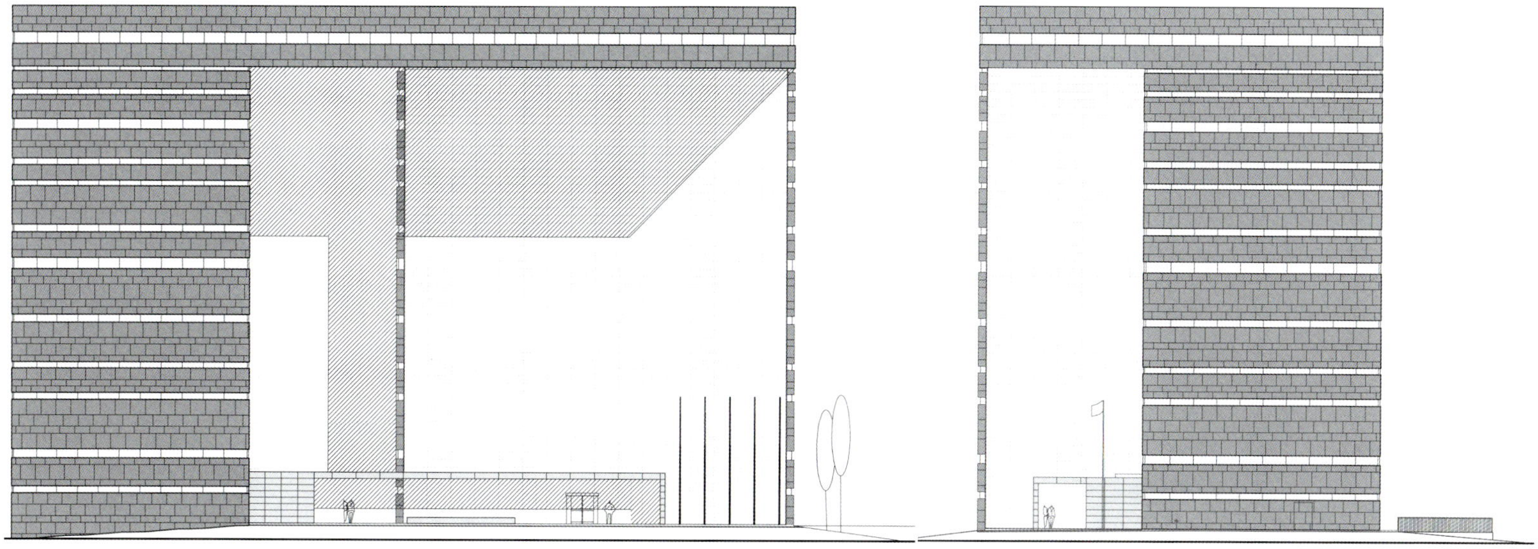

Elevations

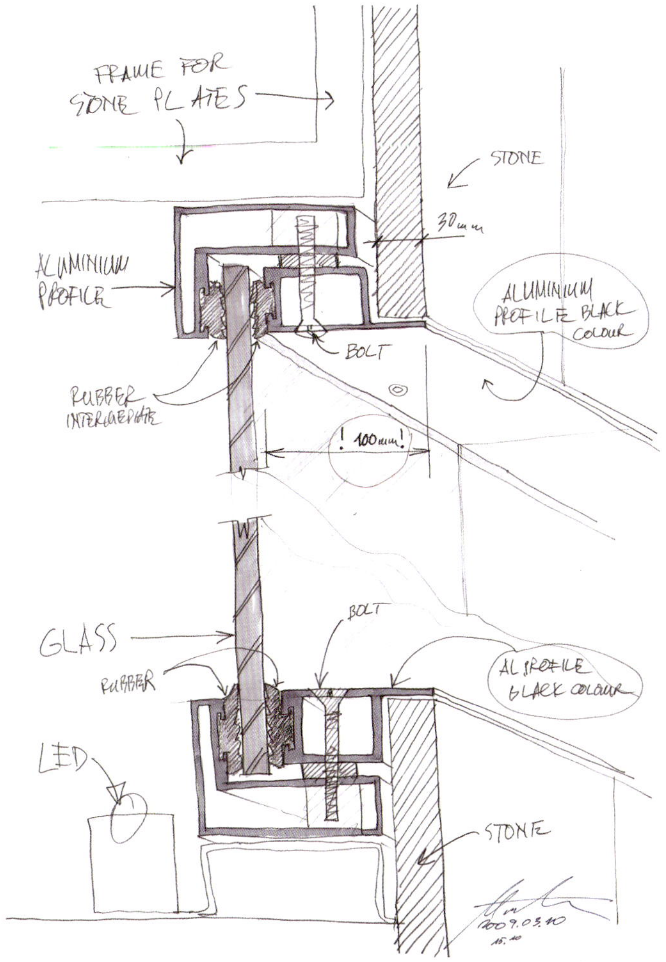
FRAME FOR
STONE PLATES
STONE
30mm
ALUMINIUM
PROFILE
ALUMINIUM
PROFILE BLACK
COLOUR
BOLT
RUBBER
100mm!
GLASS
RUBBER
BOLT
AL PROFILE
BLACK COLOUR
LED
STONE

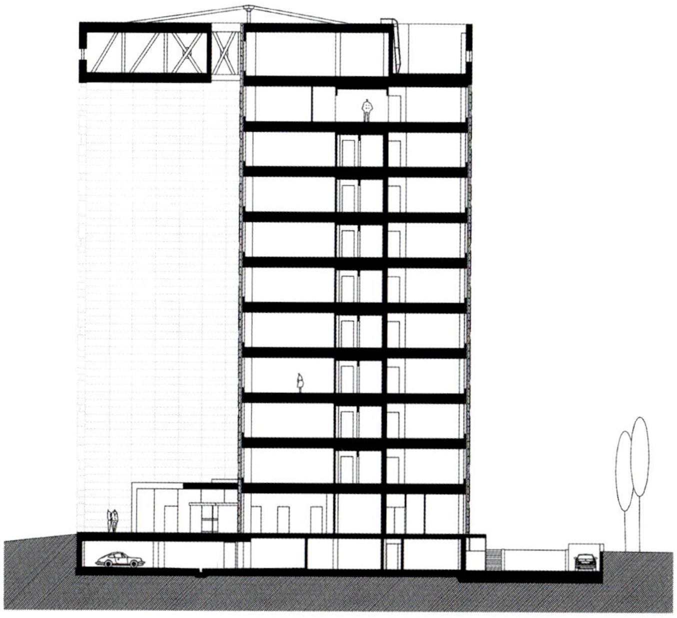

Section

DnB
3

4

3. Entrance roof
4. Employees entrance hall
5. Main staircase

Functional Scheme

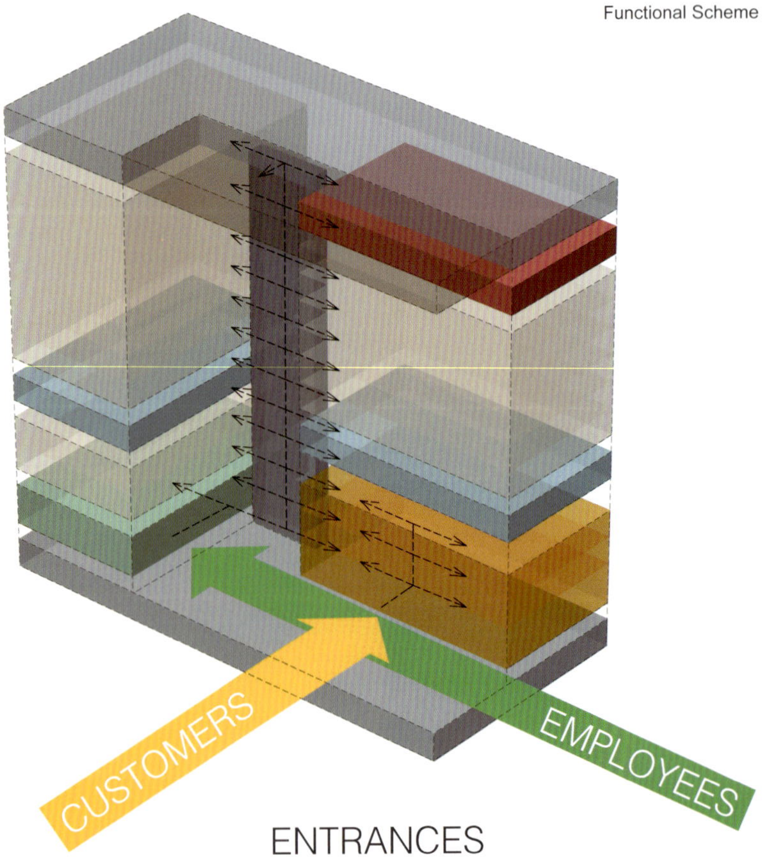
CUSTOMERS
EMPLOYEES
ENTRANCES

5

Ground Floor Plan (Right)
1. Employees Entrance
2. Customers Entrance
3. Employees Entrance Hall
4. Customers Relax Area
5. Board Meeting Room
6. Customers Service Centre
7. Canteen

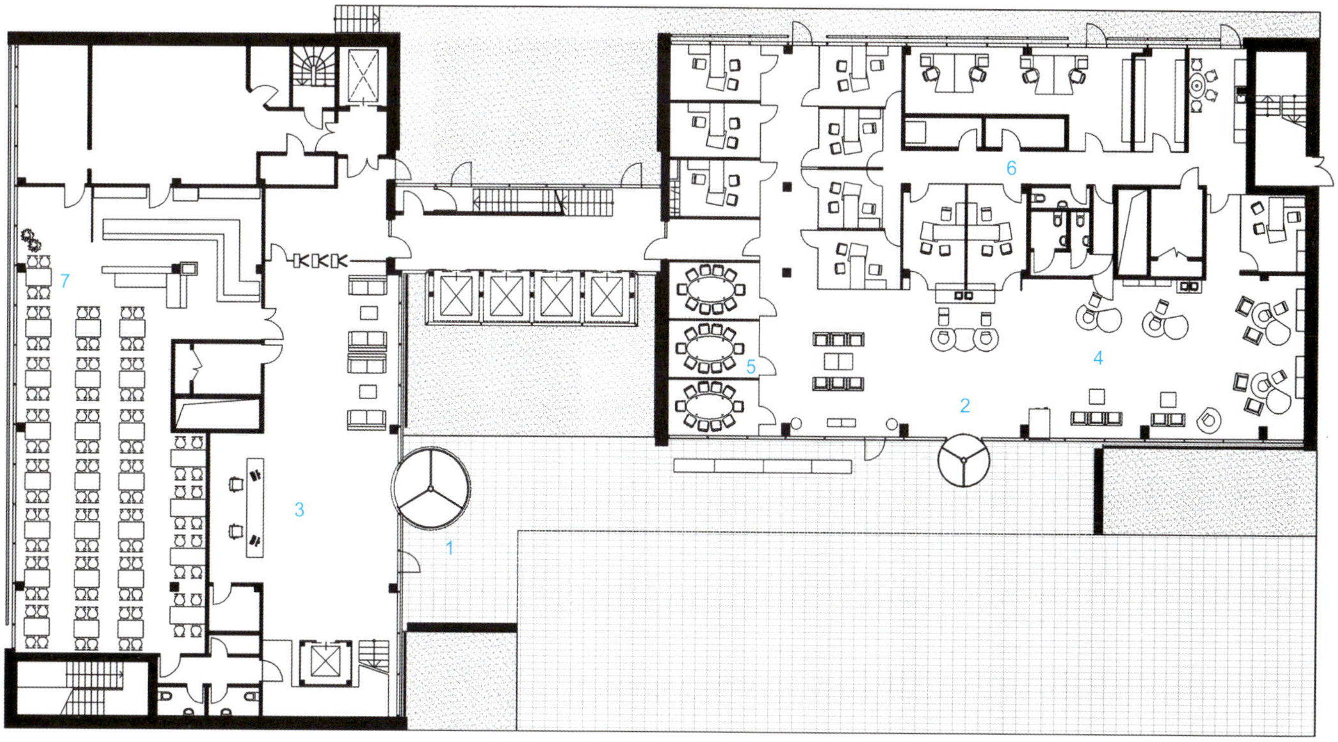
1
2
3
4
5
6
7

6. Employees entrance space
7. Top floor hall
8. Typical secretary desk at floor entrance

DnB NORD

7

8

A
916

9. Console structure inside view
10. Ground window in a console floor
11. Conference hall
12. Board meeting room

11

12

Raiffeisen

Raiffeisen Headquarters

Location: Sarajevo, Bosnia-Herzegovina
Completion Year: Headquarters 2009,
The second building 2011
Designer: Christoph Karl and Andreas Bremhorst
Photographer: Rupert Steiner
Area: 25,250 m²

A new landmark arises in the civil war ruined area of Sarajevo. The modern architecture rises in the middle of a bombed site: an office-complex with an integrated training centre. This architecture is seen as a restart, promising chance and visible sign.

The settlement of international companies leads to the establishment of jobs and future-perspective. The atrium-tower represents the Raiffeisen headquarters of Bosnia-Herzegovina.

An over-12-storey-high atrium contains the entrance hall, space for representation, as well as the vertical and horizontal flow. It brings light into the elegant and cubistic building and creates an impressive indoor-dimension. Bridges are well placed in every floor and crossing the atrium, so there are very interesting views. Transparent and mirrored glass creates a maximum of transparency and offices of high quality. Insights and outsights enable space and illusion.

The other building is orientated towards the river Miljacka and houses the public functions, a training centre, as well as a restaurant. It can be seen as a link to the city of Sarajevo, a place of future and perspective.

1. Back view
2. Atrium

isen BANK
Info pult

3

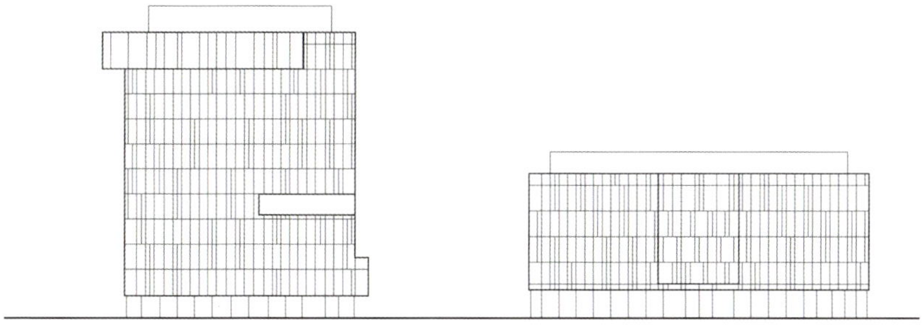

West Elevation

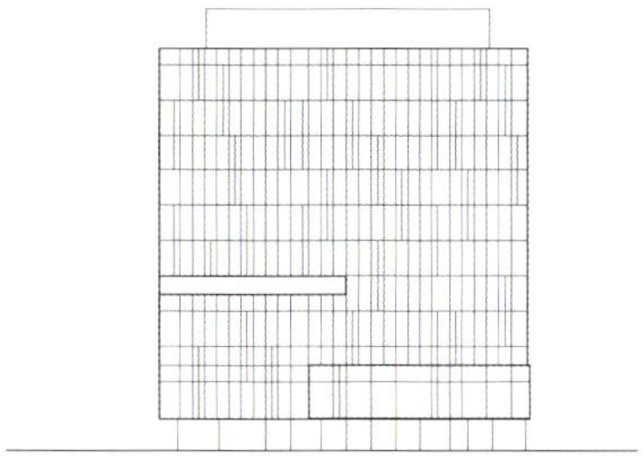

South Elevation

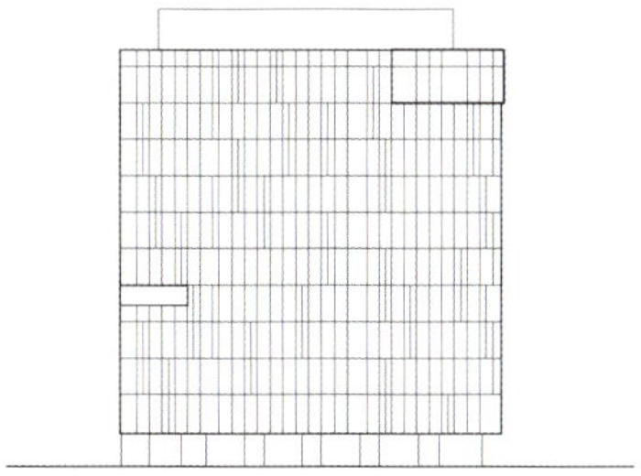

North Elevation

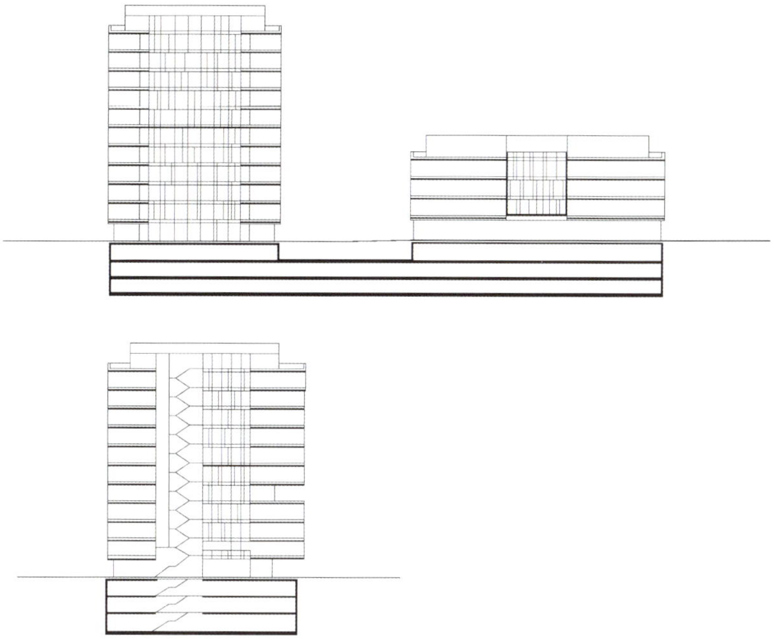

Sections

3. Entrance hall
4. Frontage
5. Hall way

EXIT

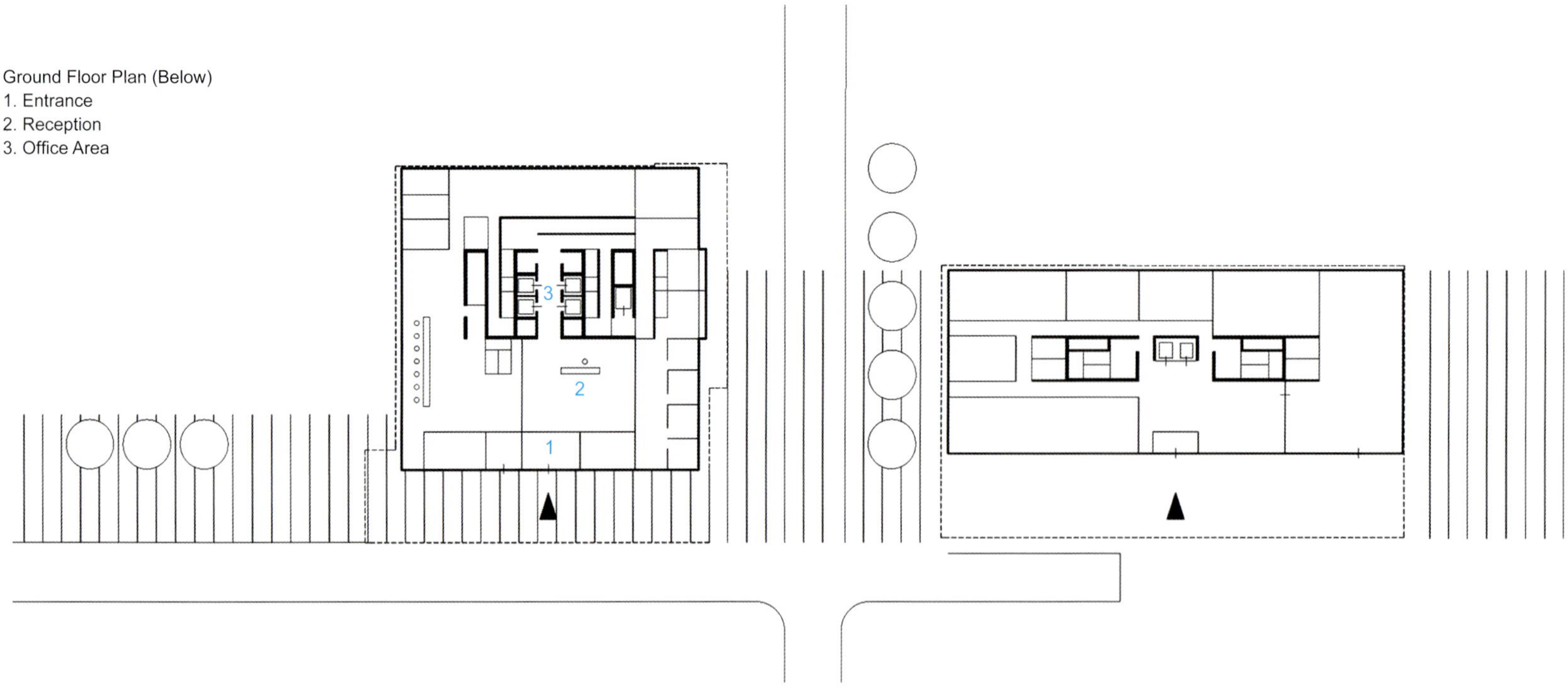
3
2
1

Ground Floor Plan (Below)
1. Entrance
2. Reception
3. Office Area

7

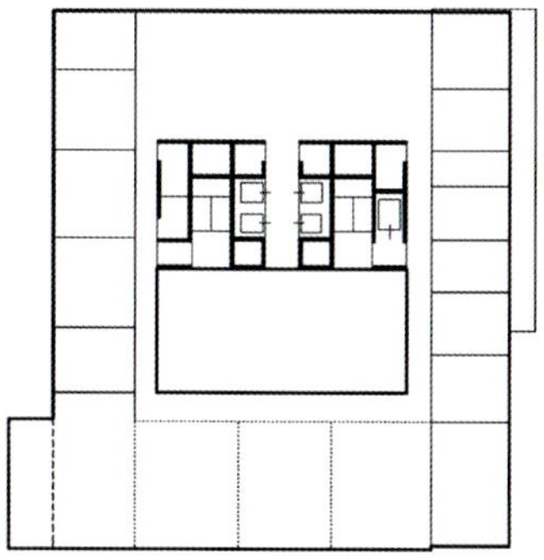

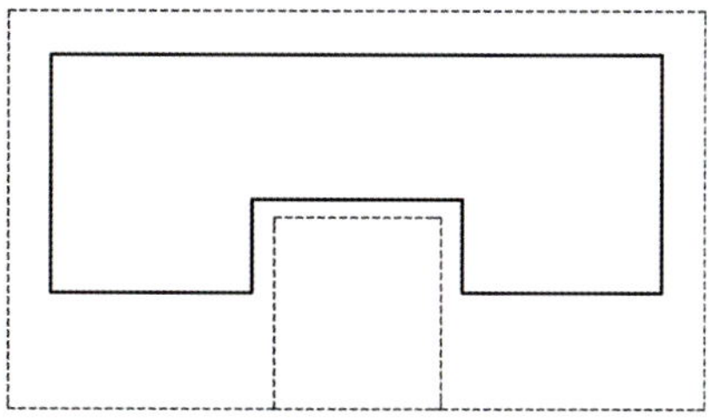

Top Floor Plan

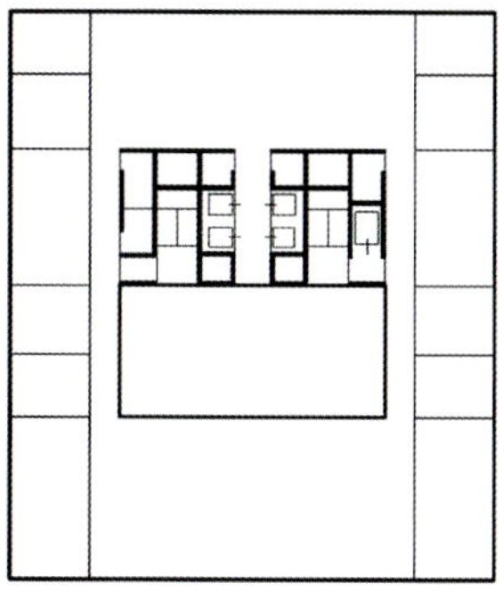

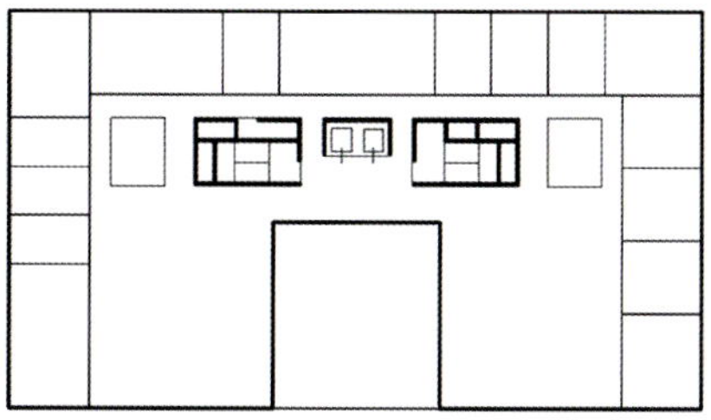

Typical Floor Plan

6. Atrium bridge
7. Conference room

Swedbank

Swedbank
2

Swedbank Head Office Building

Location: Vilnius, Lithuania
Completion Year: 2009
Designer: Audrius Ambrasas Architects
Photographer: R.Urbakavicius, A.Ambrasas, K.Satunas
Area: 23,700 m² (Over ground)
19,400 m² (Underground)

A distinctive feature of the new head office building is its openness and accessibility by the public. The site for the bank building is being developed on the old Ukmerges Street which becomes the main axis of the building's composition. The internal pedestrian street (the old Ukmerges Street) and the flowing spaces on the building's ground floor are planned as an public urban space. The building consists of two parts: high-rise part of two 15 and 16 storeys high structures and the lower part comprises two more blocks: the broken-lined parterre and the regular four-storey administrative part. The highlight of the building is the over-4,500-square-metre terrace, constructed on the stylobate part and offering excellent views of the river bank.

The ground floor, under the terrace, opens a wide one-piece space. This artfully crafted part of the complex seeks to become an important public attraction centre even during cold seasons of the year. It comprises a café for 150 visitors, both employees and guests of the bank, and also an auditorium for an audience of 150 persons and a reading room, in addition to the customer servicing centre and the business centre.

The developers and the designers demonstrate their respect to the public by using high-quality, long lasting and aesthetic materials and details. The most important finishing of the blank façade walls used stainless-metal plates polished in different directions. The ornamental effect was obtained by varying the plate brushing direction what makes the façade look multi-coloured.

1. Northeast perspective
2. View from the southeast, upper viewpoint

3

3. General view from west side
4. Inner street view
5. Meeting rooms in atrium
6. Auditorium

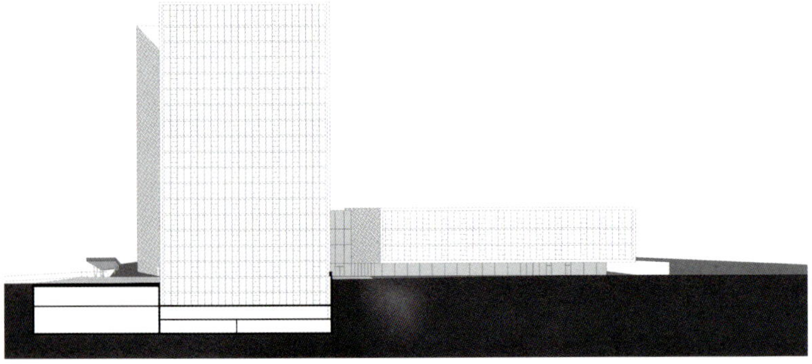

Elevation

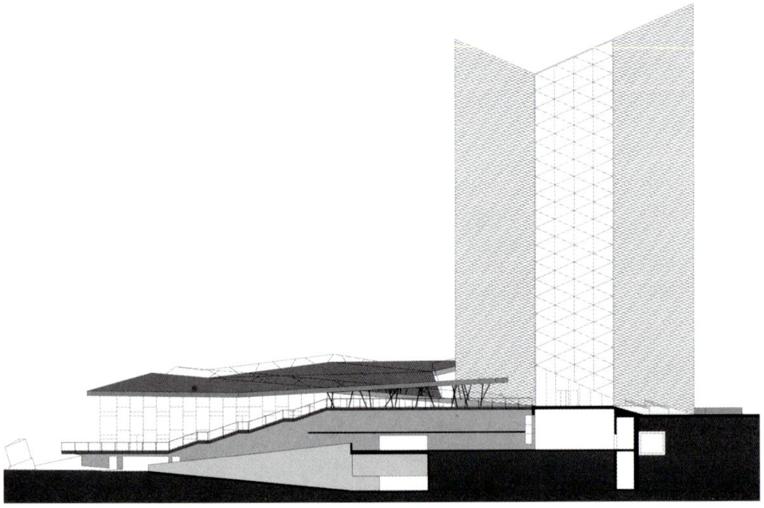

Elevation

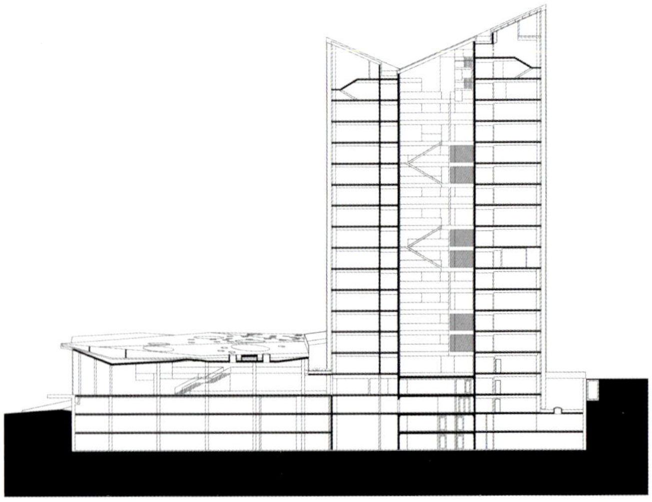

Section

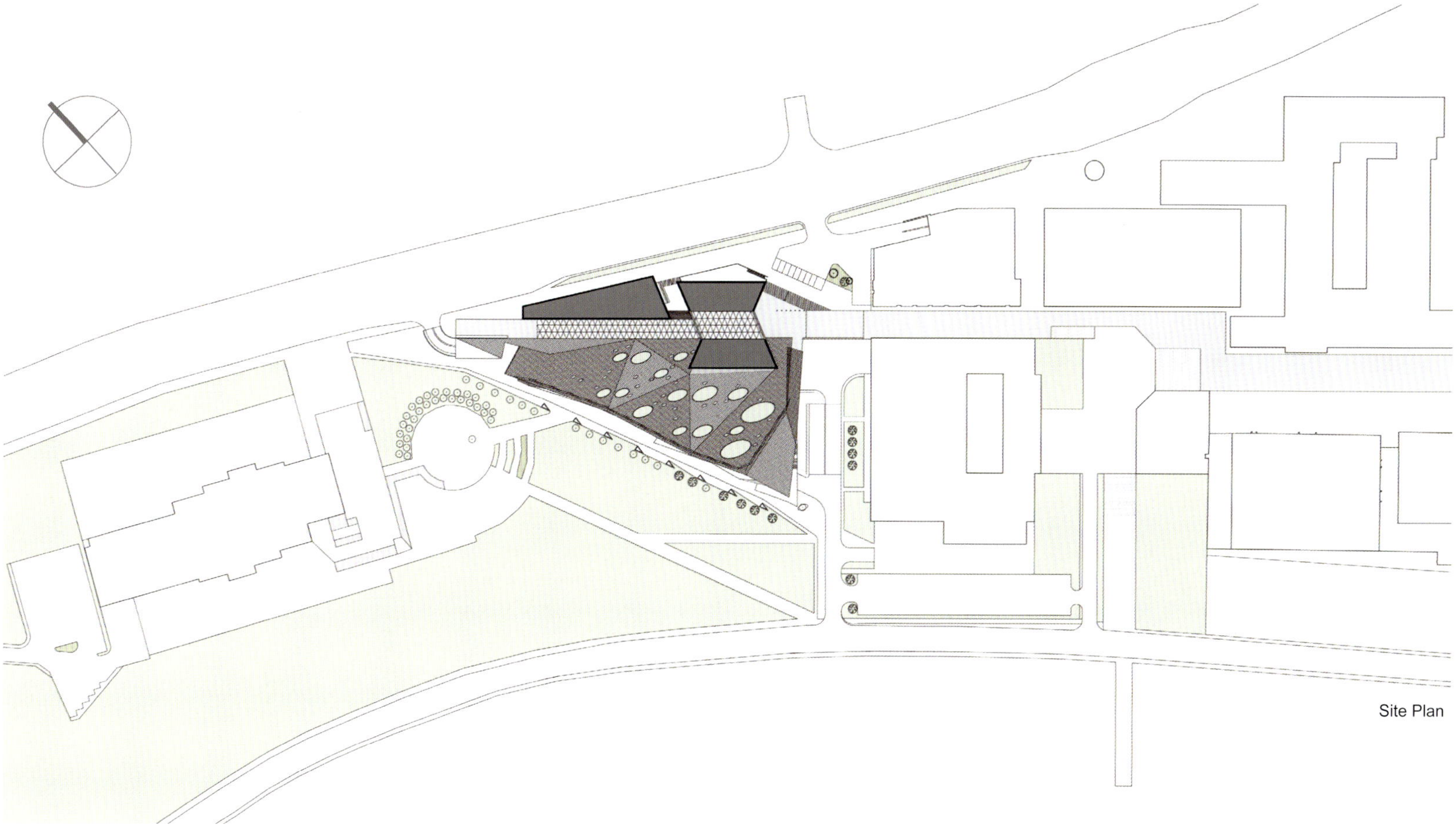

Site Plan

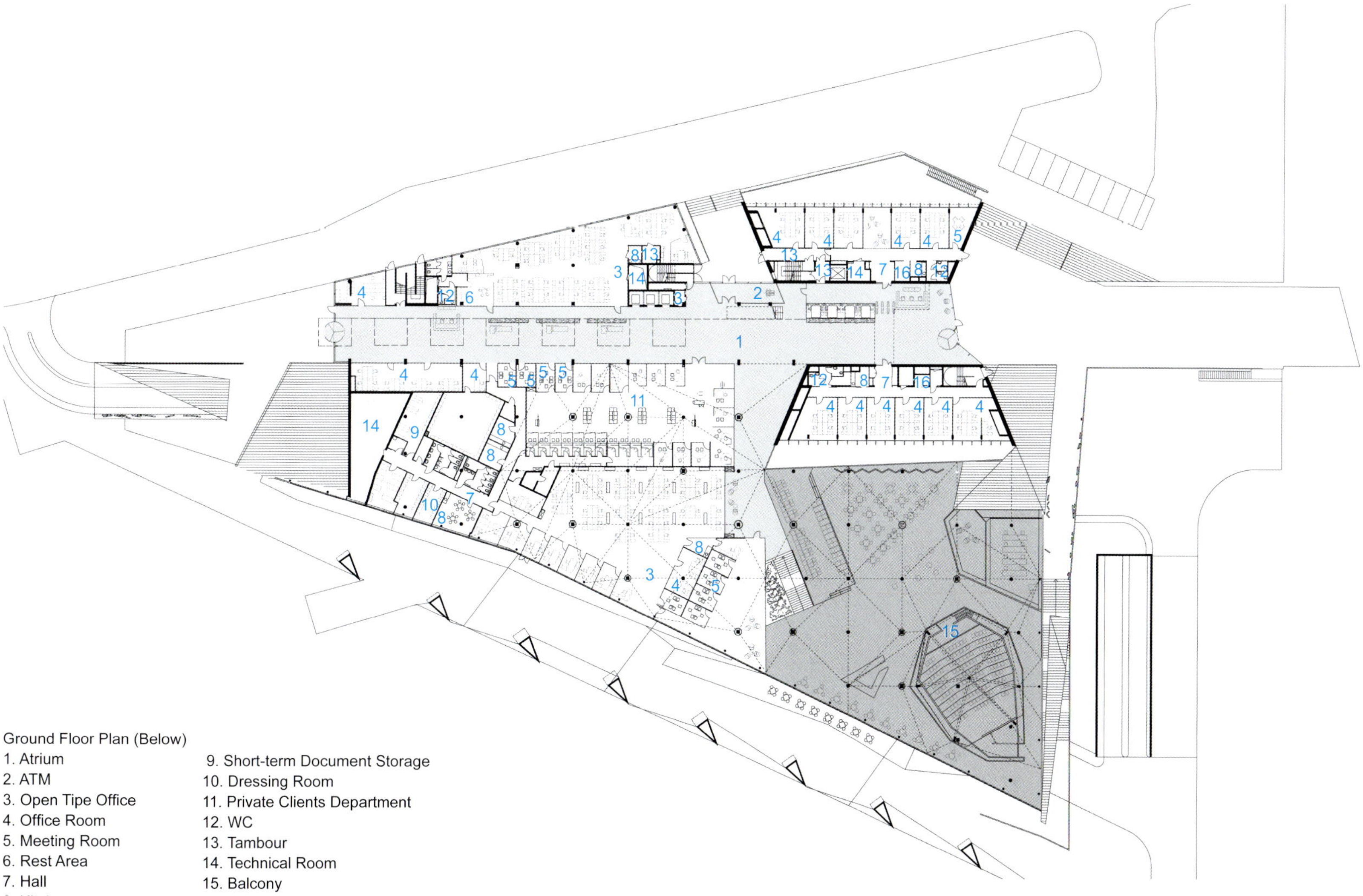

Ground Floor Plan (Below)
1. Atrium
2. ATM
3. Open Tipe Office
4. Office Room
5. Meeting Room
6. Rest Area
7. Hall
8. Kitchen
9. Short-term Document Storage
10. Dressing Room
11. Private Clients Department
12. WC
13. Tambour
14. Technical Room
15. Balcony
16. Copy Room

4

5

6

7

8

9

7. Cafeteria under terrace
8. Space under terrace
9. Cafeteria interior detail

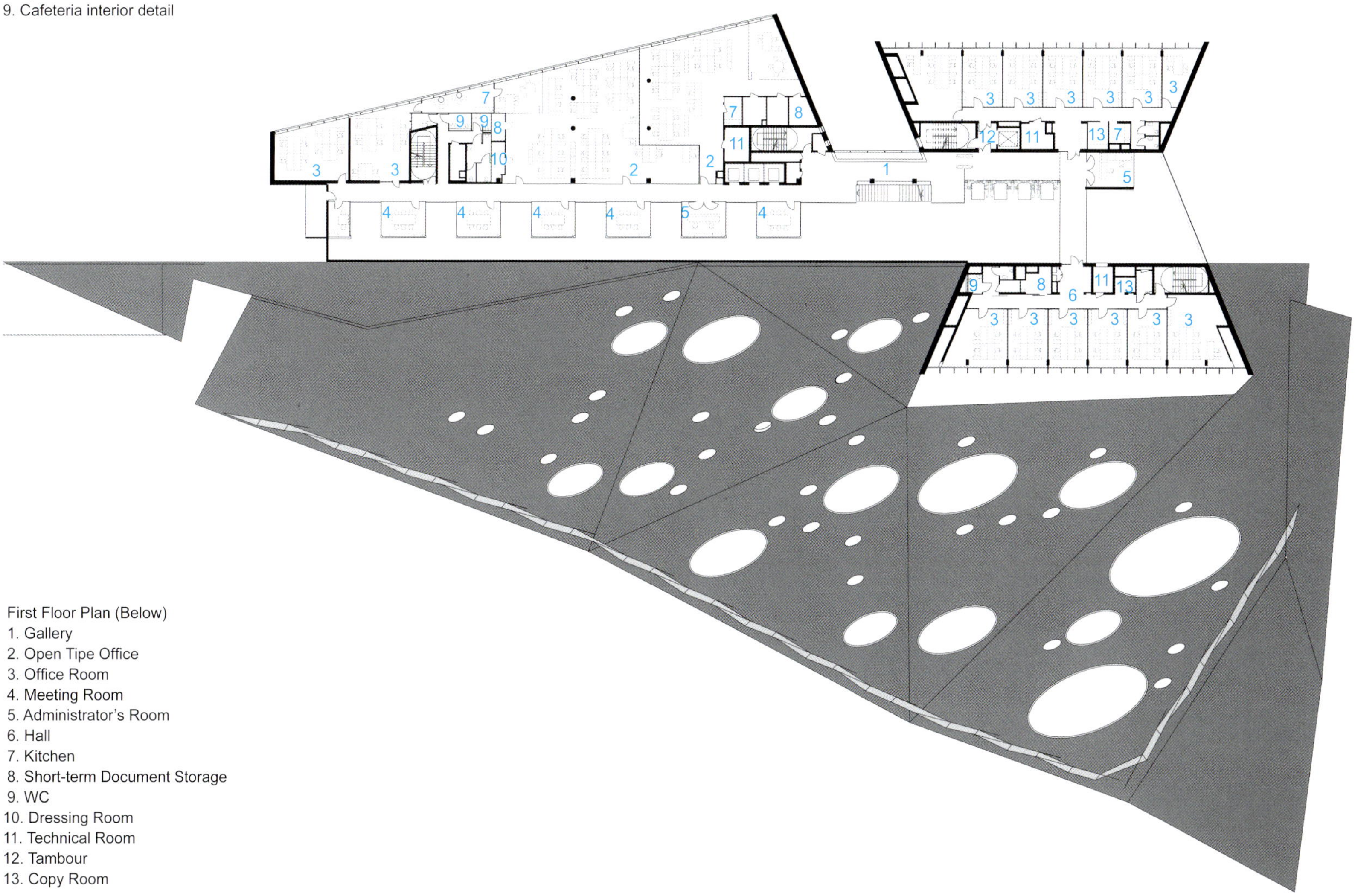

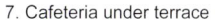

First Floor Plan (Below)
1. Gallery
2. Open Tipe Office
3. Office Room
4. Meeting Room
5. Administrator's Room
6. Hall
7. Kitchen
8. Short-term Document Storage
9. WC
10. Dressing Room
11. Technical Room
12. Tambour
13. Copy Room

exciting point of
living on the
noisy scene.
extremely popular
Ladies' Baths,
pens on both sides.

2

Bendigo Bank (Stage 1)

Location: Bendigo, Australia
Completion Year: 2009
Designer: Gray Puksand
Photographer: John Gollings, Dianna Snape
Area: 25,000 m²

Sense of community, transparency of operations, staff interaction and user control were key drivers in the development of the new Bendigo Bank Headquarters. The Bank clearly understood that its staff were its core asset and enabled staff to tailor their immediate environment, enabling an empowerment of the individual to contribute to the culture of the organisation.

Bendigo Bank was aware it was embarking upon the most significant building in Bendigo in 100 years. A key criterion was to raise the standard of all buildings in Bendigo and Regional Australia. The Bank's culture is based upon the model, whereby a successful and prosperous village (or community) will by consequence, result in a successful and prosperous bank. The building was designed to be part of the community, not to corporatist the community.

The intention of the design was quite simple: providing a sense of community or place; maximising daylight penetration; encouraging interaction informally and providing a variance of workpoint; maximising the human capital of the Bank; providing a building with a small ecological footprint.

The design revolved around an internal street and two atriums. These elements provided the "glue" that bound the various "fingers" of the building. Each finger or component of the average 3,500-square-metre floor plate was designed to be a self sufficient "neighbourhood" within the metropolis. Each neighbourhood has its own distinction, aspect and identity to provide a sense of place so as not to be lost within the large floor plate. The neighbourhoods are linked physically by the atriums, the internal streets and bridges, to provide a sense of the overall metropolis that is the building itself. Ensuring the individual is not consumed by the whole is vital in any successful workplace design.

The street and atrium combine all tea/meeting points, formal and informal meeting rooms and casual seating. Colour and finish selection effectively designed itself out of the desire to create identity.

1. Entrance
2. Night view of the exterior

3

4

Ground Floor Plan (Below)
1. Entrance
2. Entrance Hall
3. Meeting Room
4. Quiet Room
5. Main Street
6. Toilet
7. Lounge

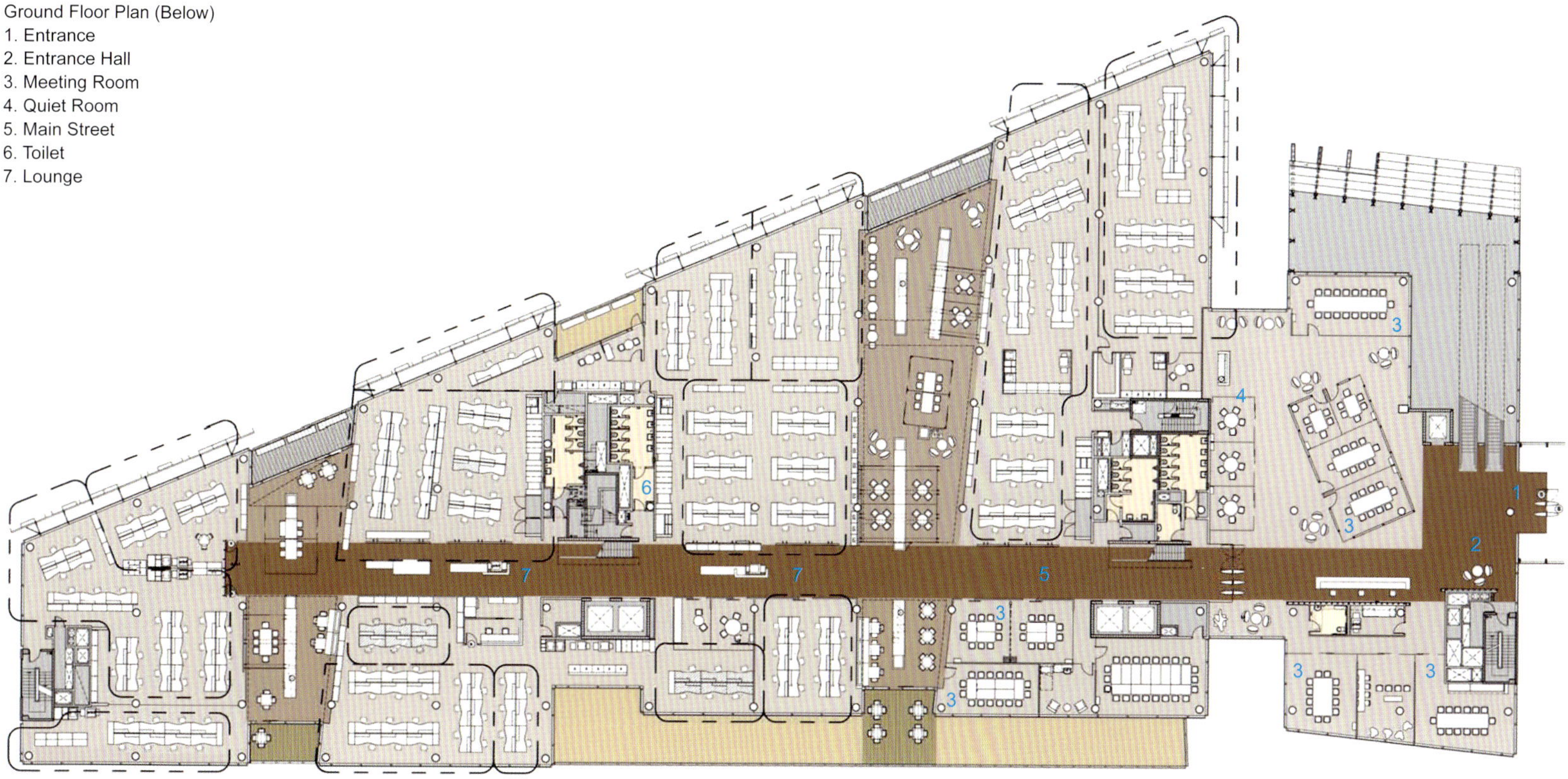

1
2
3
3
4
5
6
7
7
3
3
3
3
3

3. The rich colours provide the building with an outstanding feature
4. Exterior details
5. Divisions of various work spaces
6. Rest area
7. Meeting room
8. The colours of atrium echo with the exterior colours
9. Relax area
10. Kitchenette

5

6

EXIT

7

First Floor Plan (Below)

1. Waiting Area
2. Reception
3. Meeting Room
4. Kids Zone
5. Quiet Room
6. Parenting Room
7. Lounge
8. Project Room
9. Toilet

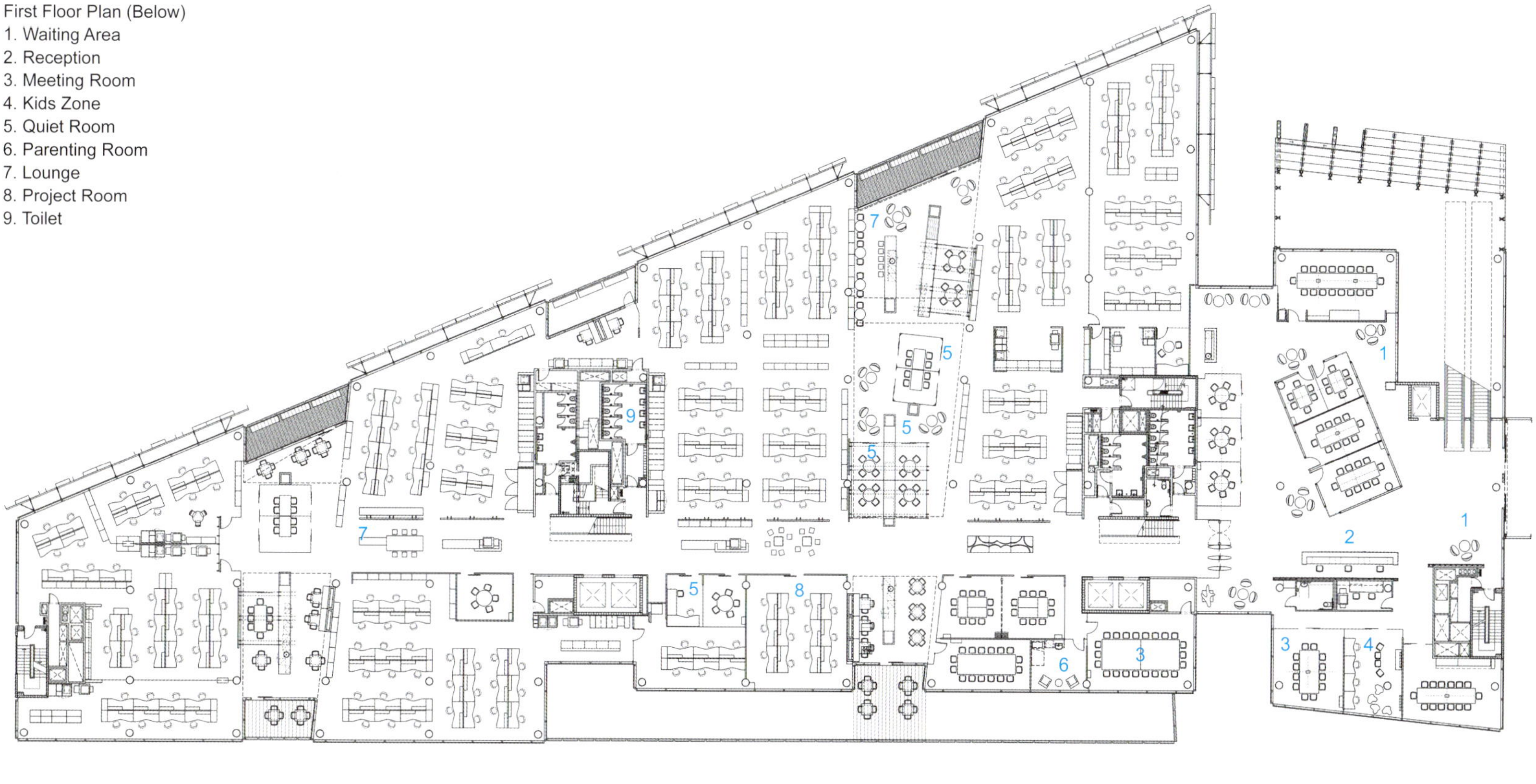

8

Second Floor Plan (Below)
1. Meeting / Training Room
2. Quiet Room
3. Tea Prep
4. Lounge
5. Meeting Room
6. Test Area
7. Console Room
8. Toilet

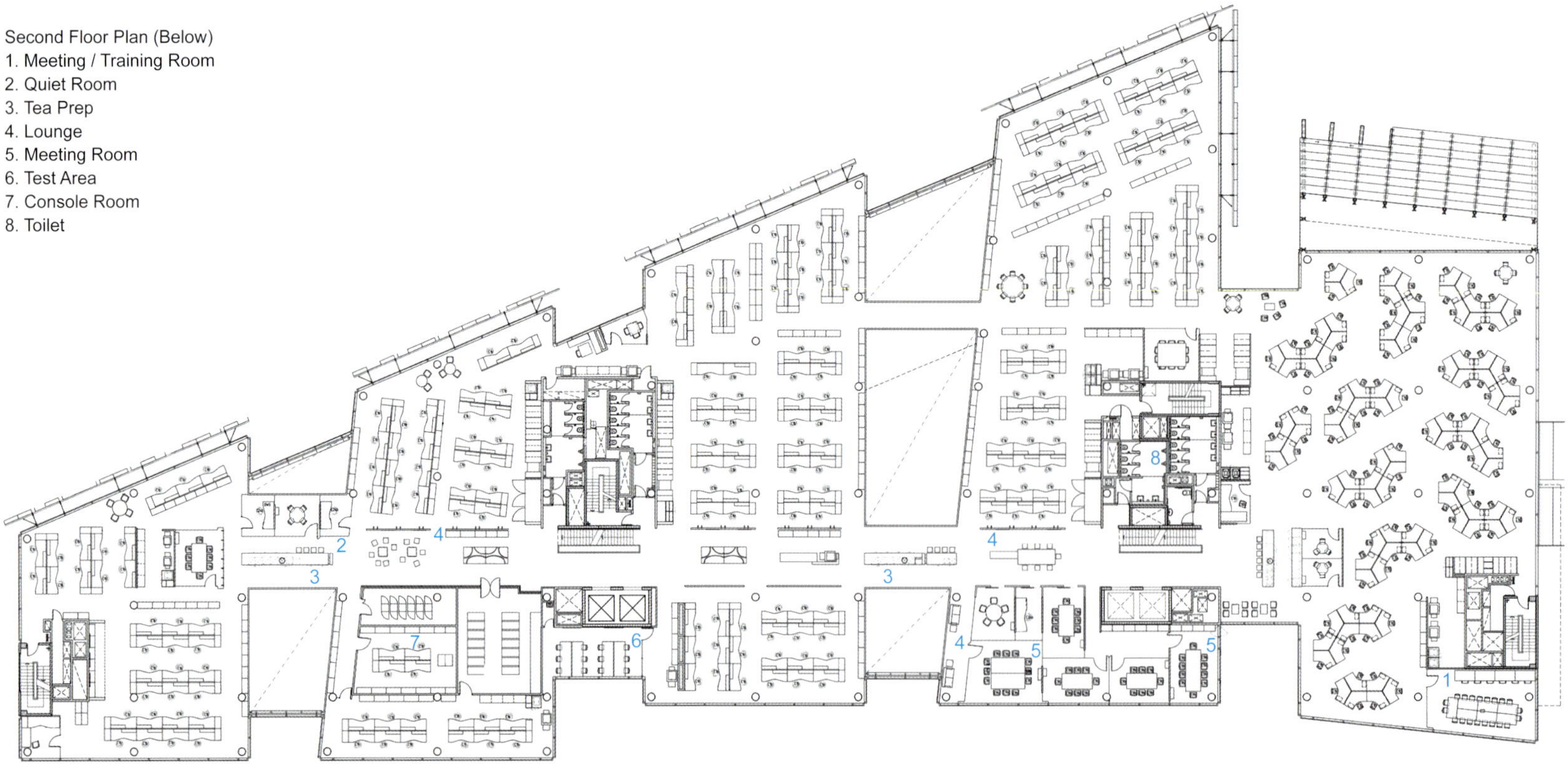

1
2
3
4
3
4
4
5
5
6
7
8

9

10

Raiffeisen

Raiffeisen Finanz Centre, Eisenstadt

Location: Eisenstadt, Austria
Completion Year: 2010
Designer: Pichler & Traupmann Architekten ZT GmbH
Photographer: Paul Ott, Lisa Rastl
Area: 2,561 m²

The design of the building playfully responds to the restrictions imposed by the building regulations as well as to the schedule of accommodation for the different floors, and develops an encasing figure that encloses all the activities of the bank in a continuous form. The continuity of the building envelope conveys a sense of identity to both staff and customers, while the building's volumetric shaping ensures it a striking role in the appearance of the town. It is made of aluminium sandwich panels whose colouring might awaken associations with coins or the bank's corporate identity. Narrow window openings at calculated positions in the façades respond to the need to screen people who work at computers from glare.

The interior is formulated as a regulated system of reference on various levels of meaning: firstly, in terms of spaces and materials it forms a single entity with the building's external form. The material used for the external shell provides the starting point for the concept of materials used in the interior. Secondly, in directing the relationship between indoor and outdoor space. The office walls onto the corridor zones are, in principle, to be made as a system of glass partitions. This means that views inside, outside and through the building can be directed as required, transparency and spatial depth can be experienced, and indeed outdoor space and the landscape are brought into the innermost area of the building. Thirdly, as a depiction of the company's internal organisation, the structural layout of the building and the articulation of the façade on a basic grid of 1.30 metres allows the office partition walls to be positioned flexibly within the given grid system. This allows rooms of different sizes to be made that respond to various functions and needs and, where necessary, can be easily altered. Fourthly, as an articulated body of rules of communication. The partitions between the individual offices are made of glass or have a high-level strip of glazing that varies in height. The different amounts of glazing articulate the different amount or degree of communication required.

1. The façade is made of aluminium sandwich panels
2. Exterior, narrow window openings screen staff from glare

1

Site Plan

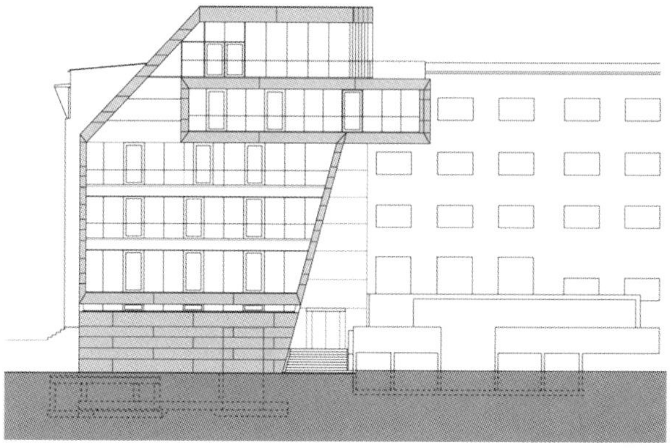
South Elevation

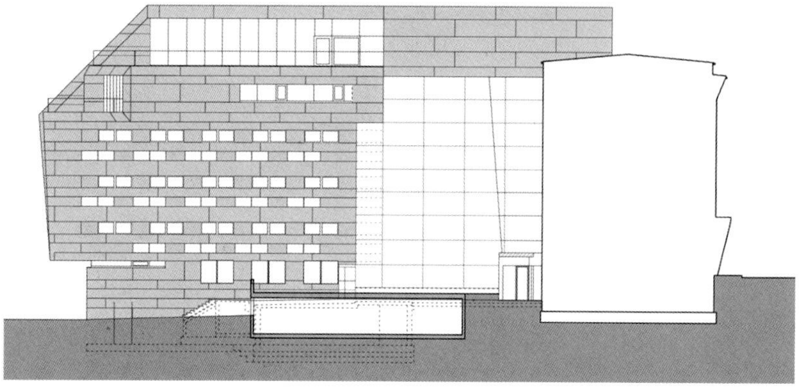
East Elevation

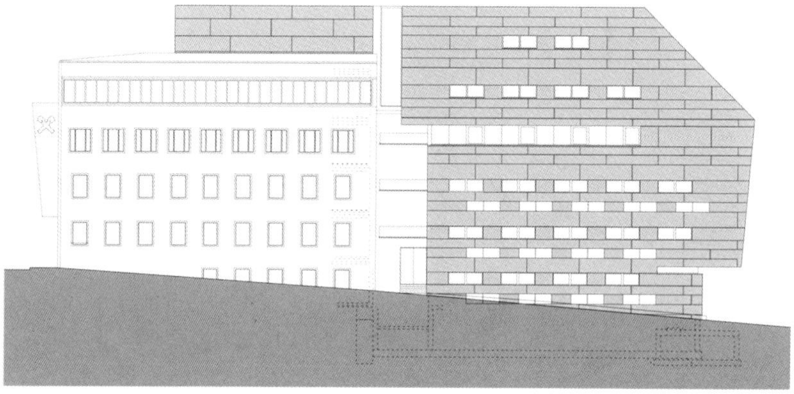
West Elevation

Cross Section

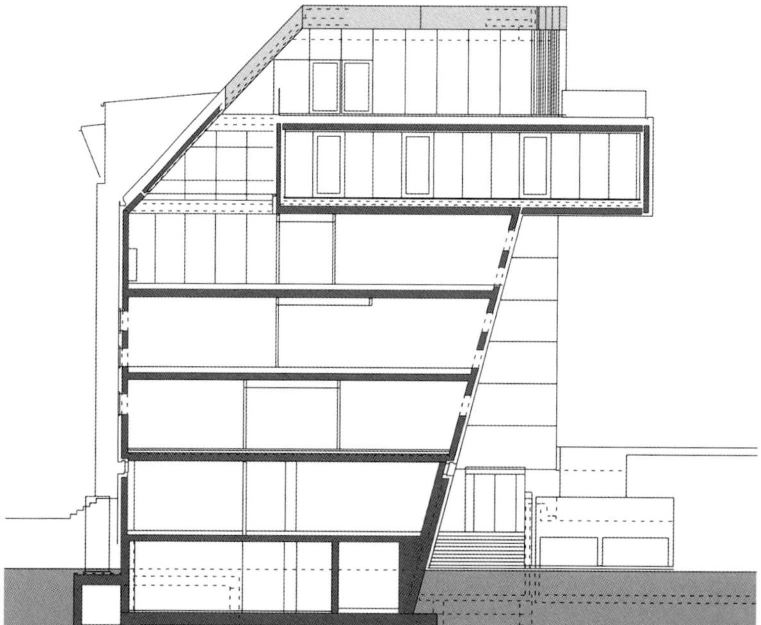
Cross Section

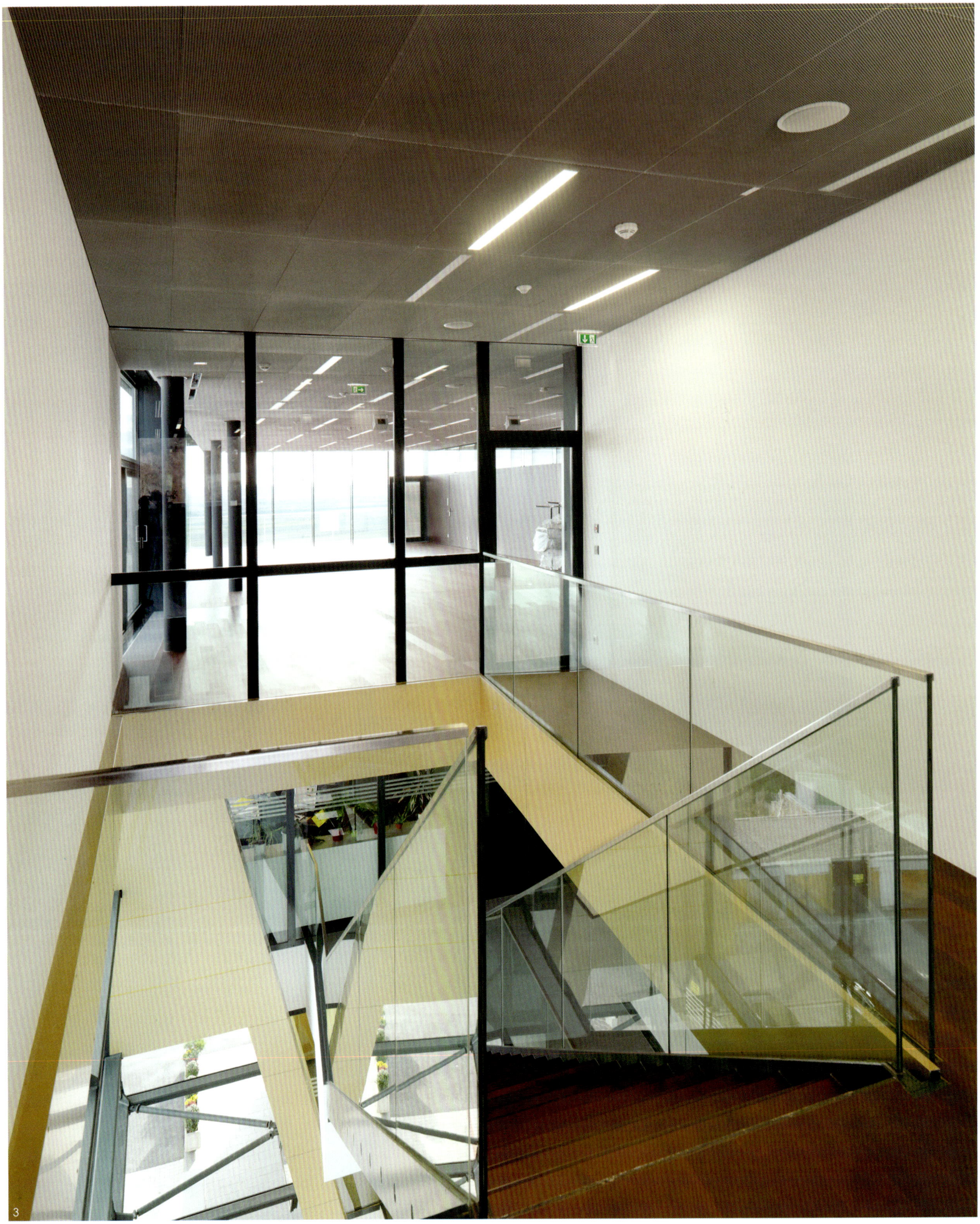

3

3. Corridor and staircase
4. The glass walls ensure the work space with depth and openness

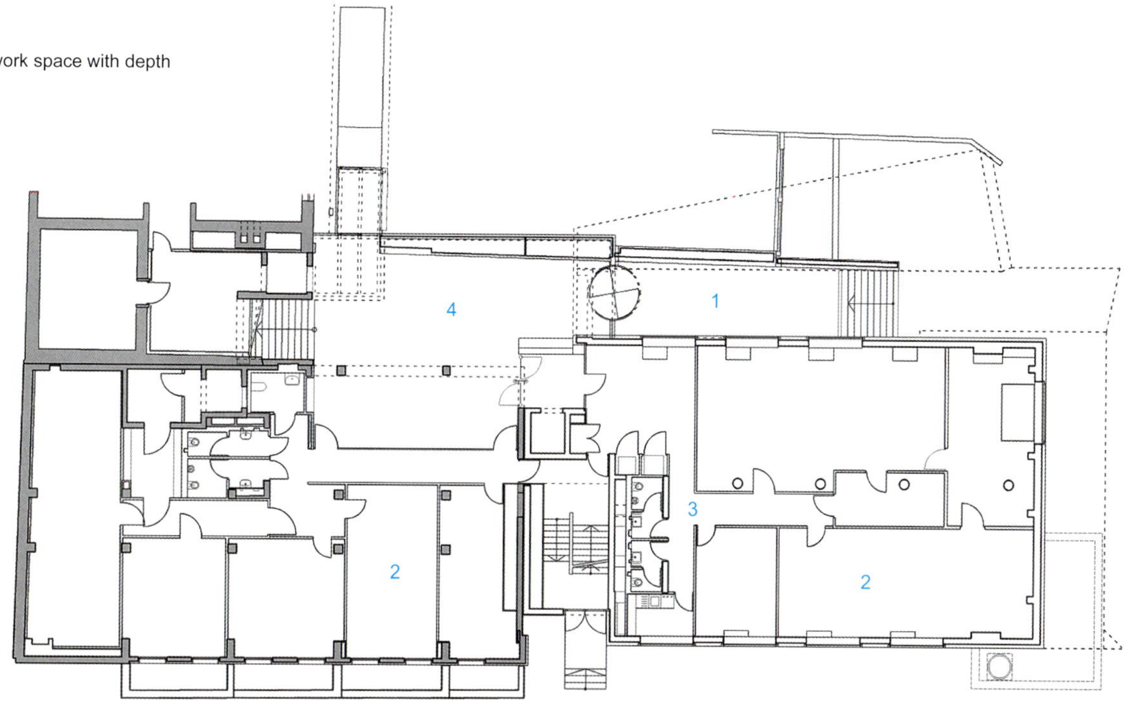

4
1
3
2
2

Ground Floor Plan (Left)
1. Main Entrance
2. Office Area
3. Toilet
4. Entrance Hall

2

Saxo Bank

Location: Copenhagen, Denmark
Completion Year: 2008
Designer: 3XN
Photographer: Adam Mørk

Saxo Bank is a young dynamic internet bank with focus on online-trade with currencies, shares and futures on the bank's self-developed platform, Saxo Trader. Saxo Bank was founded in 1992 in Denmark and counts around 850 staff members of 35 nationalities who serve customers from 115 different countries.

Saxo Bank's new headquarters in Copenhagen is designed by 3XN. Although the customers primarily encounter the bank in cyberspace, the physical premises of the head office is of great importance to the management of the bank who participate actively and are highly dedicated to the development of the building.

The building is of great iconographic significance, and there is a strong conviction that architecture and design affect each staff member's performance and awareness of the company. The architectural design is based on Saxo's cutting-edge profile and branding. The lines of the building design define a sharp balance between reliability and dynamic expressivity in dialogue with the local plan.

The building is shaped like two blocks with the end walls pointing towards the canal, joined together by façades that are withdrawn from the end walls. The façades are shaped like double curved glass that wave like a piece of textile. The interior of the building is open and transparent with a large sense of community. The open plans centre round a softly shaped atrium with a glass roof. In the atrium, the main stair case winds up to the top. However, the main room and largest attraction of the building is the so-called Trading Floor where share prices are monitored intensely and resemble scenes from American movies about stock exchanges. Furthermore, the building encompasses a large number of rooms for technical support, kitchenettes and recreational areas.

1. The façades are shaped like double curved glass that wave like a piece of textile
2. Night view of the exterior

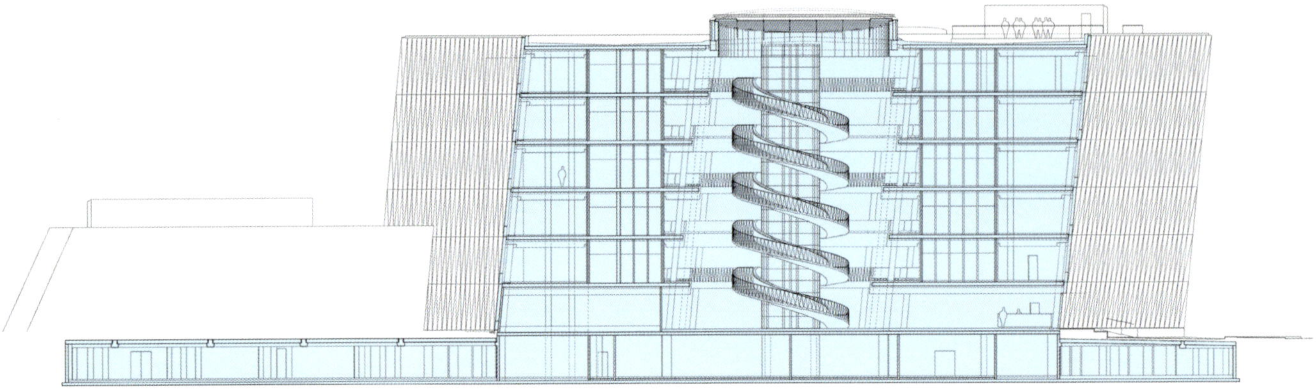

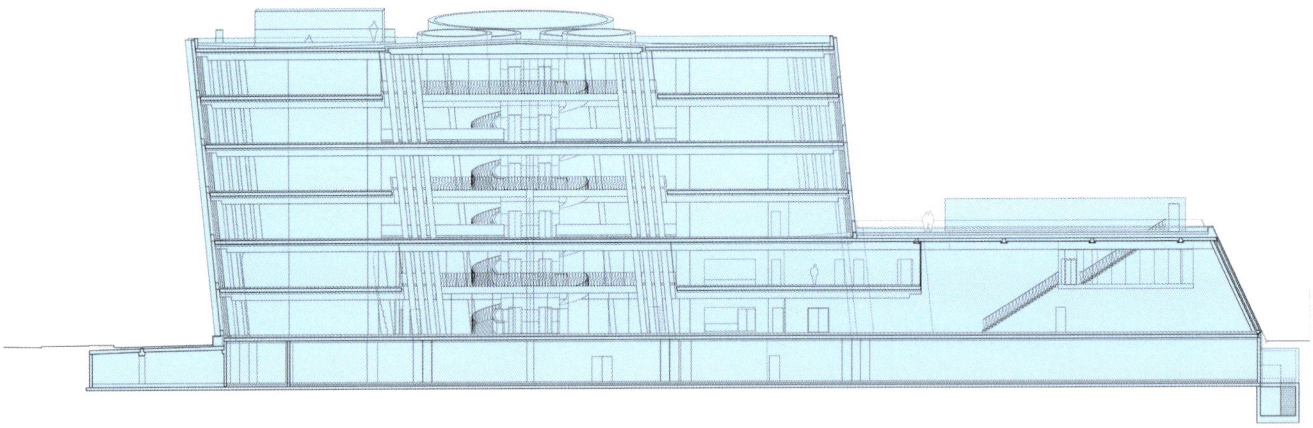

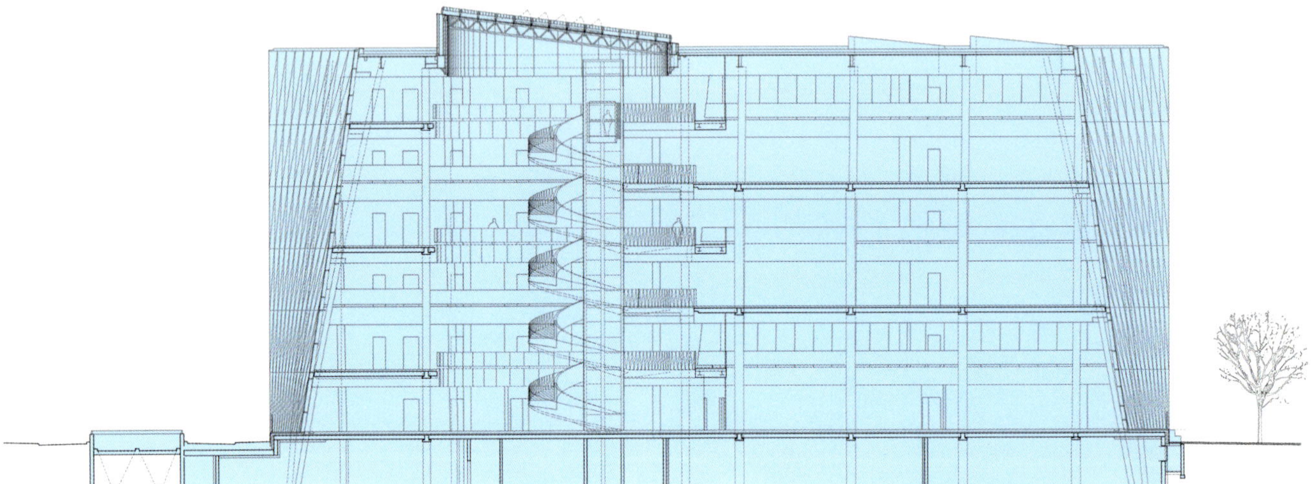

Sections

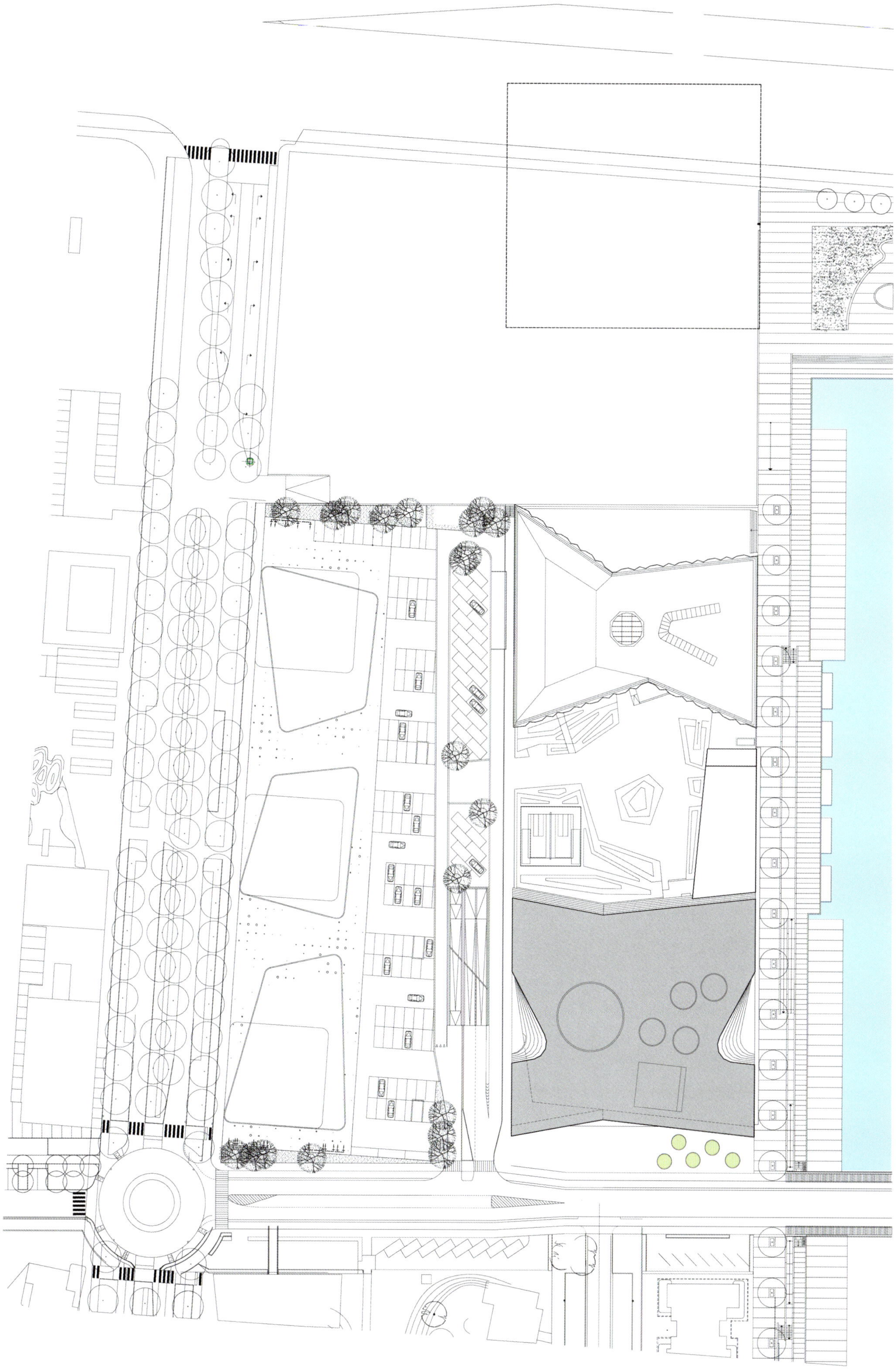

Site Plan

3

4

3. In the atrium, the main stair case winds up to the top
4. Rest area in the atrium

13
12
10
9
8
11
3
2
4
1
6
7
11
5

Ground Floor Plan (Right)
1. Entrance
2. Reception
3. Foyer
4. Waiting Room
5. VIP Area
6. Café
7. Play / Lounge
8. Auditorium
9. Canteen
10. Meeting Room
11. Server Room
12. Kitchen
13. Café / Canteen

5

5. The interior of the building is open and transparent
6. Trading hall
7. Restaurant
8. Rooms for technical support

6

7

8

Italease, Headquarters for a Bank

Location: Milan, Italy
Completion Year: 2009
Designer: Albera Monti & Associati
Photographer: Beppe Raso
Area: 20,000 m²

An obsolete data centre has been rejuvenated and refitted into high-tech offices. Construction was completed in less than 11 months; it included extensive demolitions, the addition of extra floors and new volumes, the complete redesign of internal circulation and workspace distribution, the implementation of up-to-date equipments, the creation of a 2-storey, 120-car, underground parking.

The project has evolved through the development of numerous design studies, particularly concerning the northernmost part of the building. The office complex (three partially connected buildings, nine storeys) altogether 20,000 square metres, 12,000 of which offices, now hosts 800 workstations, meeting rooms and support spaces, a cafeteria, terraces for outdoor uses.

The fit-out was designed to accommodate the needs of multi-tenant, Italease Bank, relocating its head office; however, the architects designed spaces in order to guarantee future maximum flexibility of use, including multi-tenant use. Minimalist fixtures, full-height glass-walls, soft hues, characterise the office spaces, while stronger tones are used to visually link workspaces to support areas.

The redevelopment of the surrounding area involves the transformation of a parking lot into a pedestrian square and garden. The new plaza is split in a "green" setting, with a lawn, green walls and a playground, and a "dry" setting, with pergolas and trellis covered with climbing plants.

1. Courtyard elevation
2. North Façade, main elevation towards the square

3. Main pedestrian entrance and reception
4. Work space
5. Meeting room

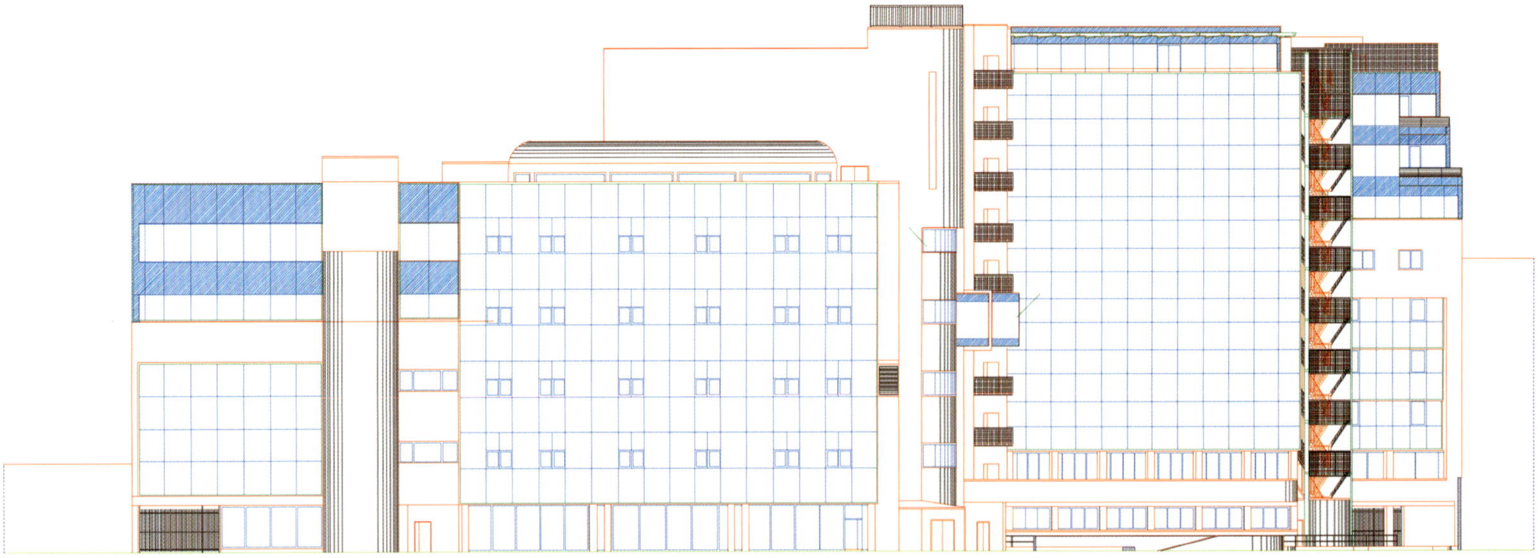

Elevation

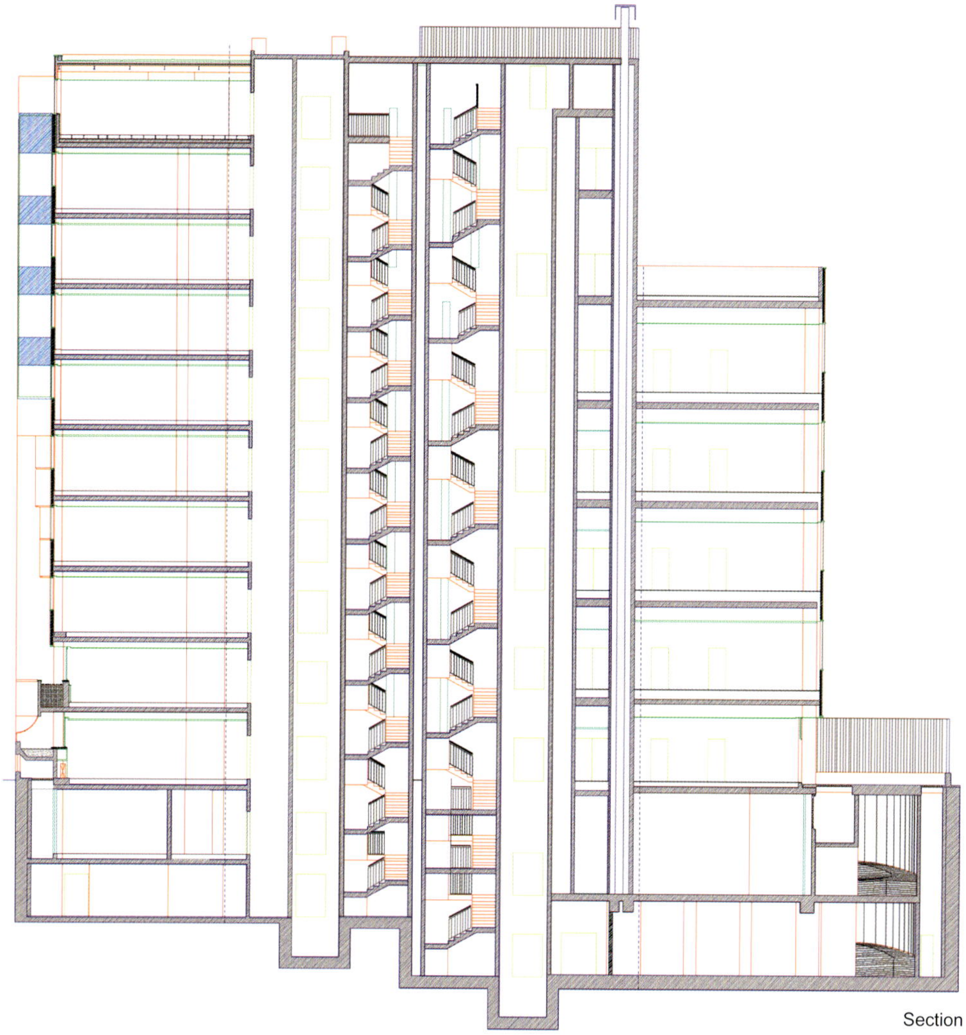

Section

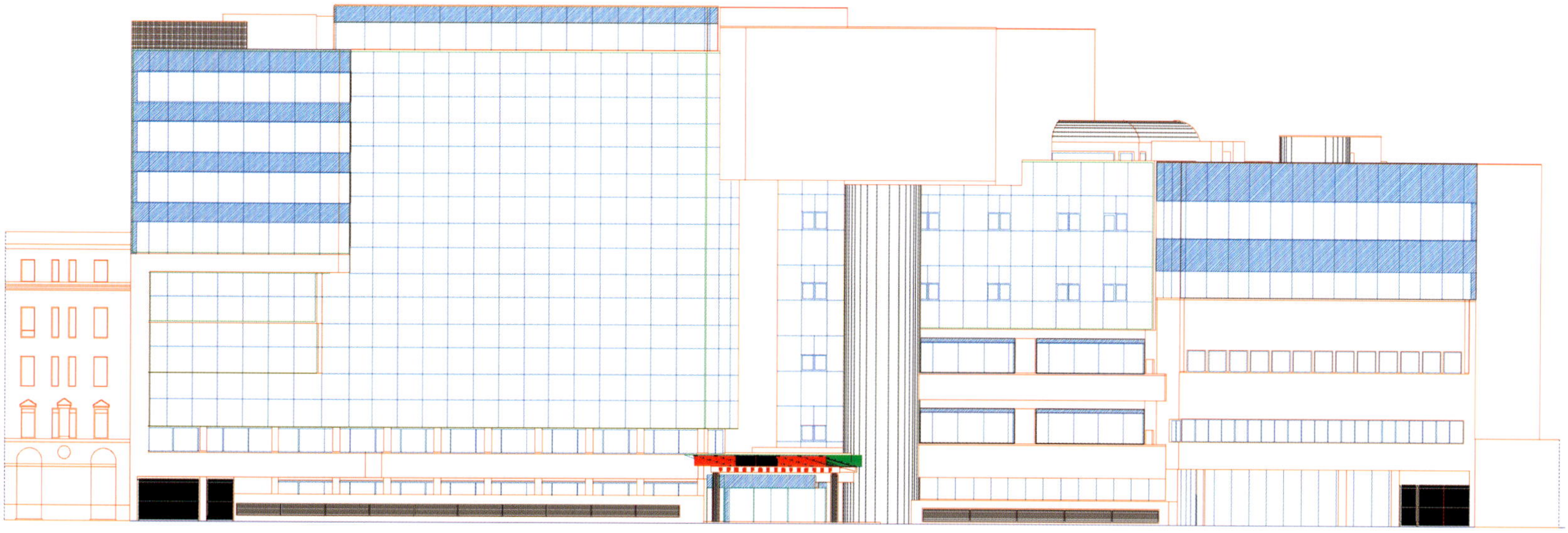

Elevation

Ground Floor Plan (Below)
1. Open Space Office
2. Break Area
3. Lifts Lobby
4. Toilet
5. Toilet Anteroom
6. Electrical Board Room
7. Corridor
8. Entrance Hall
9. Back Office
10. Filter

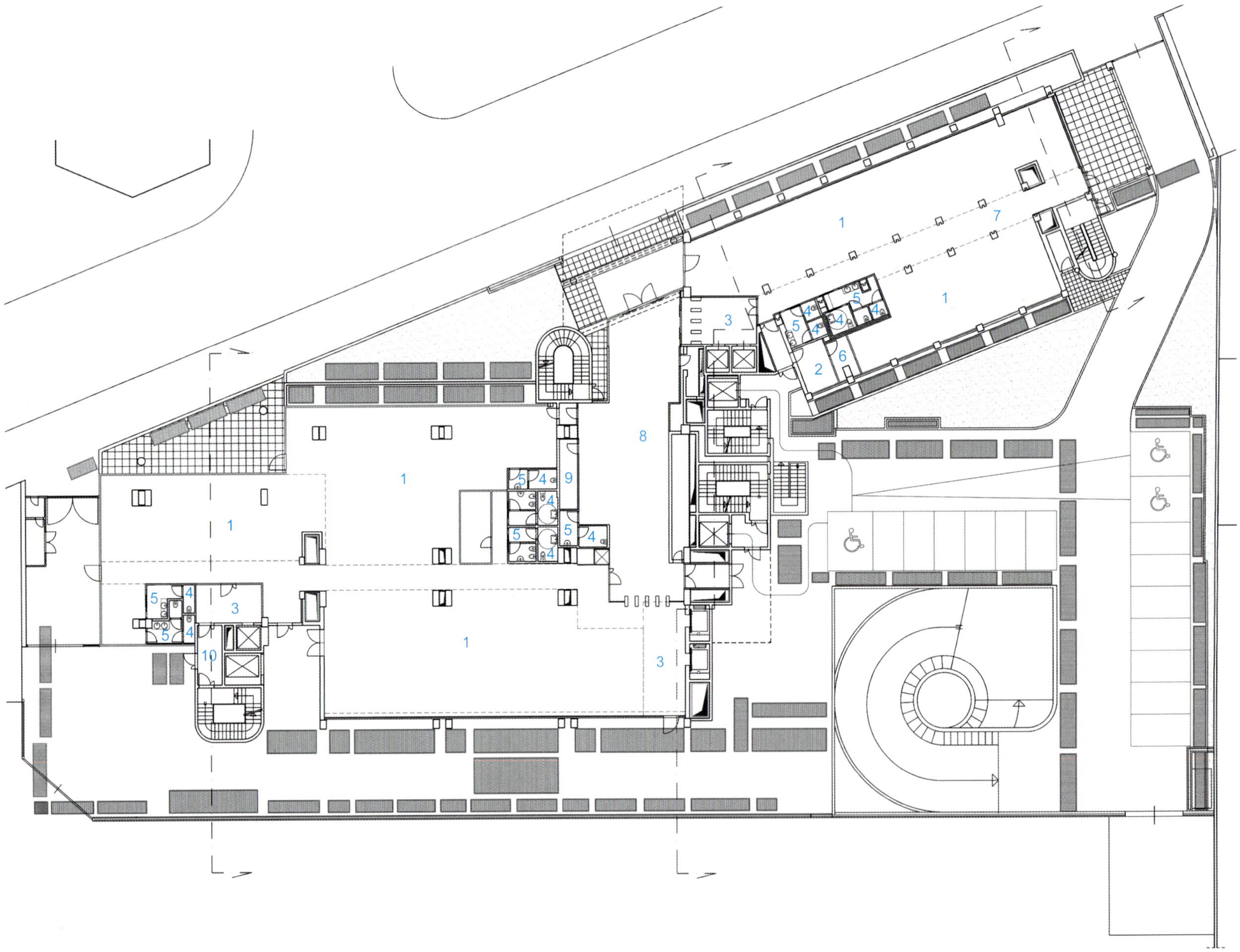

4

5

European Investment Bank

Location: Luxembourg
Completion Year: 2008
Designer: Ingenhoven Architects
Area: 72,500 m²

The new headquarters building for the European Investment Bank (EIB), with its compelling 13,000-square-metre glass roof, extends Sir Denys Lasdun's existing buildings on Luxembourg's Kirchberg plateau. Located between boulevard Konrad Adenauer and Val des Bons Malades, it provides 72,500 square metres of office space and other facilities for up to 750 employees.

The striking tubular glass roof spans the entire, 170-metre-long and 50-metre-wide structure. In combination with an extremely lightweight glass and steel superstructure, it offers a maximum of daylight and transparency. In addition, the building's zigzag plan encourages a non-hierarchical office layout that promotes interaction and communication. This unrivalled office environment is carried by an environmental programme that reflects a progressive approach towards sustainability in architecture.

Key to the new headquarters' ecological concept is the glass roof which curves around the floor plates to create the atriums in the V-shaped "gaps" of the building wings. The landscaped winter gardens on the valley side are unheated and act as climate buffers. In contrast, the atriums on the boulevard side serve as circulation spaces; hence temperatures have to be kept at a comfortable level. Both winter gardens and "warm" atriums are naturally ventilated through openable flaps in the shell to draw fresh air into the building and to reduce heat gain especially in the summer months.

The entire office space benefits from natural light and outside views. Mechanical systems such as lighting, sun shading, heating, cooling and ventilation can be controlled individually. Excessively wasteful behaviour is still being avoided as individual settings are reset to the most efficient levels several times a day by the central control unit. Staff members can open their windows to the atriums and winter gardens or to the outside at almost all times. As a result of all environmental measures, the EIB Group New Building has been granted an "excellent" ranking by UK's Building Research Establishment Environmental Assessment Method (BREEAM).

1. The whole building is cladded in glass, offering a maximum of daylight and transparency
2. The tubular glass roof spans 170-metre long
3. Distant view of the building

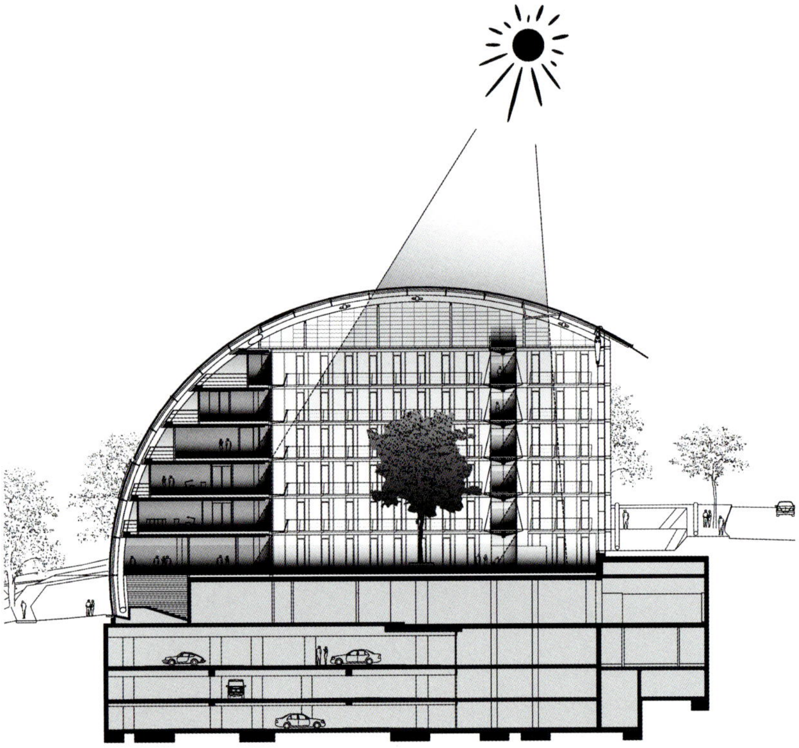

Section

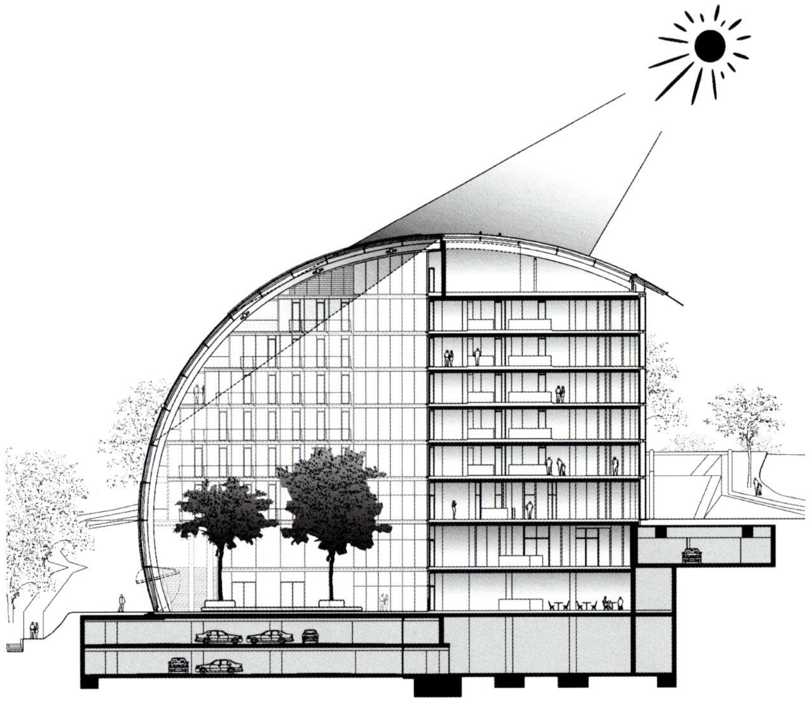

Section

1
2
3
4

4. Outdoor rest area and plantings

Ground Floor Plan (Facing Below)
1. Entrance Hall
2. Office Area
3. Meeting Points
4. Passage

5

5. Glass wall details
6. Atrium

6

7

7. The extremely lightweight glass and steel superstructure
8. The public space

NRW.BANK

NRW.BANK

2

NRW. Bank Muenster

Location: Muenster, Germany
Completion Year: 2009
Designer: Eisfeld Engel Architekten,
Sabine Eisfeld, Ulrich Engel
Photographer: Christian Richters
Area: 13,146 m²

The new building of the NRW. Bank - in interplay with the listed old building of the former Landesbank - shows an image of an open and future-oriented bank, without denying its roots.

The overall aim of the structural planning is the creation of a distinct and simple, mainly space-creating structure, evolving urban spaces and securing a high efficiency of the buildings. The layout of the new building runs parallel to the monument, referring to it in its height, proportion and materiality and emphasises the coordinated image, originated by the layers of history.

The new building is designed as compact volume with different surface structures and towers with its seven storeys above the one-storey basis of the newly created square. The six-storey lobby interacts with the exterior area by the fully glazed façade towards the square. The listed old building merges into an urban-spatial symbiosis together with base and new building.

The listed building of the former Landesbank is used as an office building and is connected at the ground floor with the new building of the NRW. Bank. The historic entrance situation to the Friedrichstrasse – as it was up to 1945 – was restored. The passage to the new building takes place via paths with natural daylight, which are connecting the foyer zones of the buildings.

The decision to place the new building as a solitaire behind the existing listed monument "Landesbank" creates a surprising new urban situation with a freely publicly accessible square. Well-proportioned atriums produce a high quality of natural light inside the office and the conference room. Though very compact, the building with its natural stone surfaces radiates lightness and elegance.

1. Façade of the new building
2. View of old and new buildings

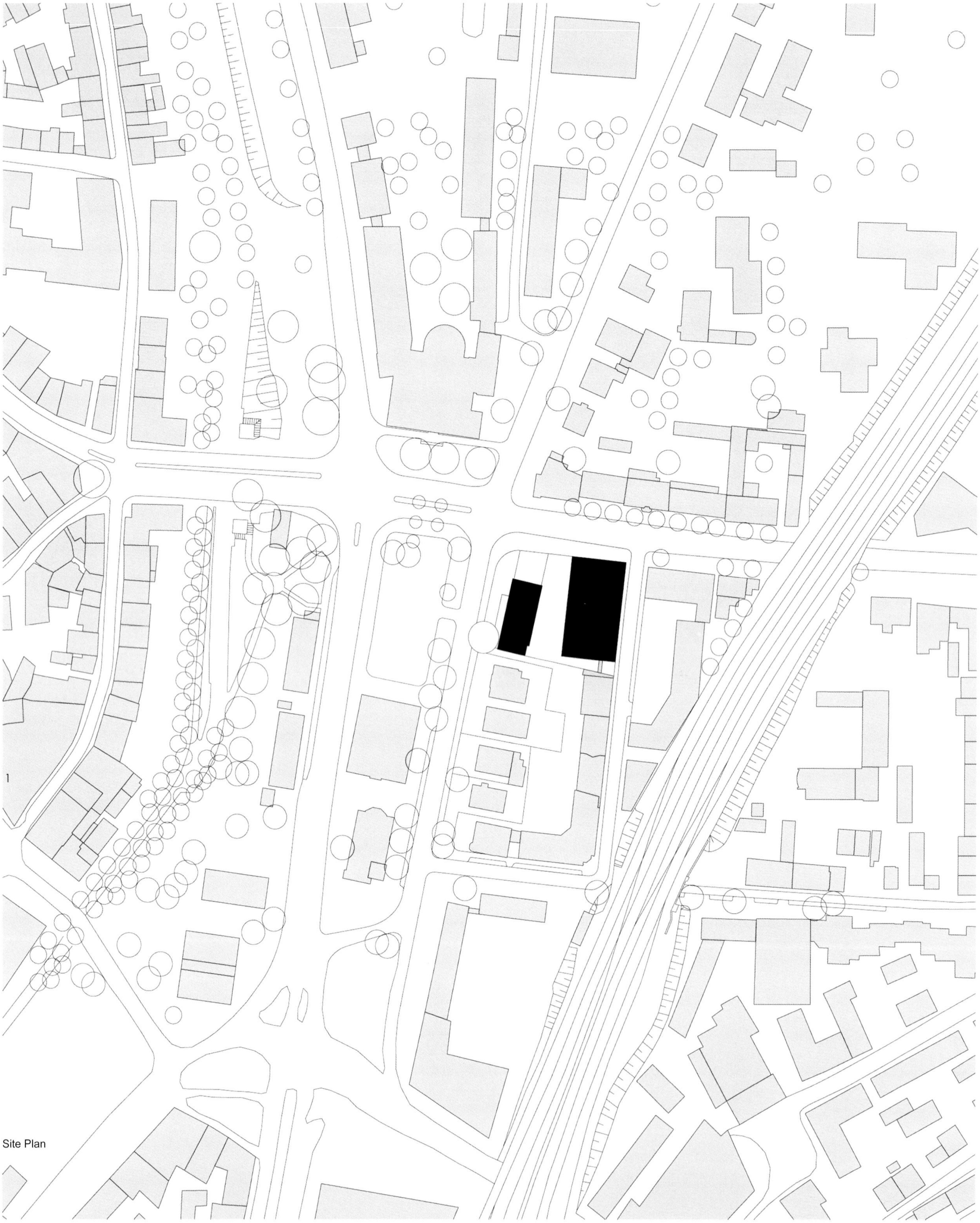
Site Plan

NRW. BANK

3

Concept

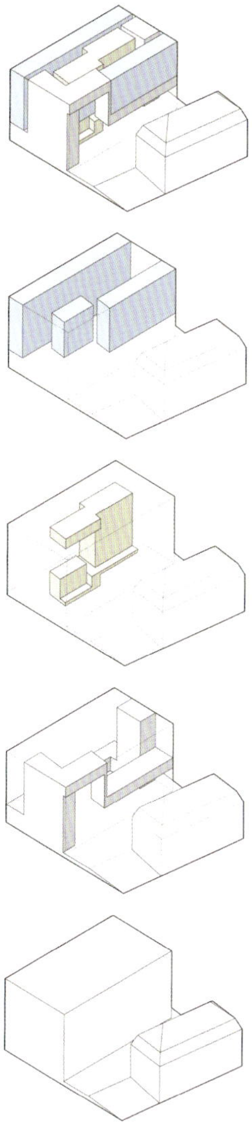

3. Night view of entrance
4. Stairway in listed building
5. Back façade details of new building
6. Passage towards listed building

Section

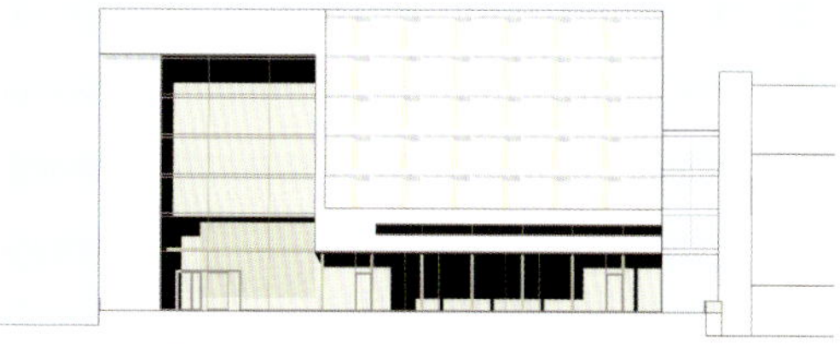

Section

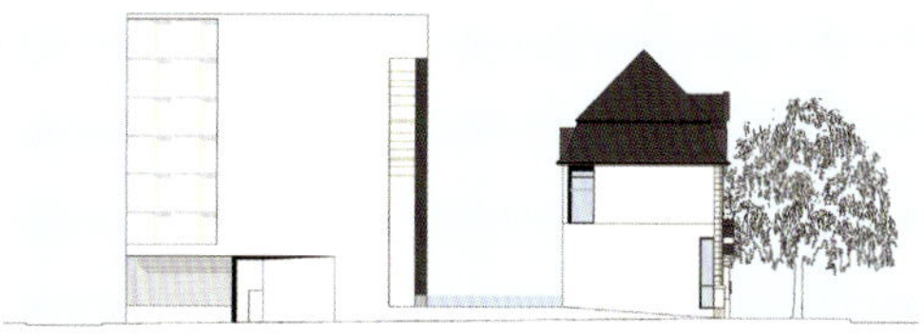

Cross Section

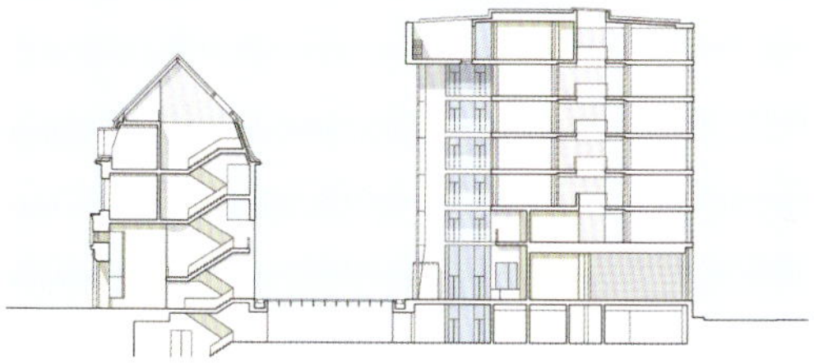

Longitudinal Section

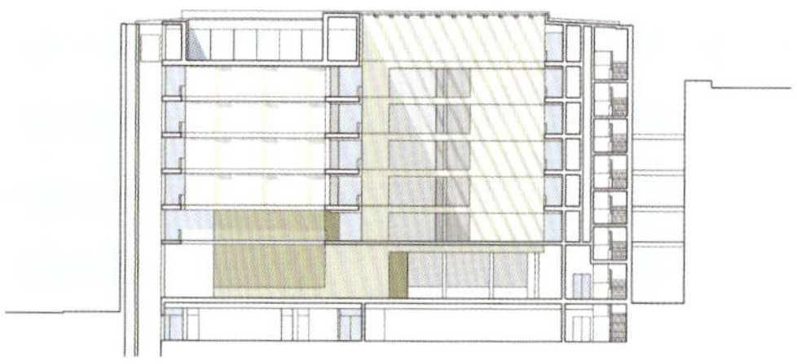

4

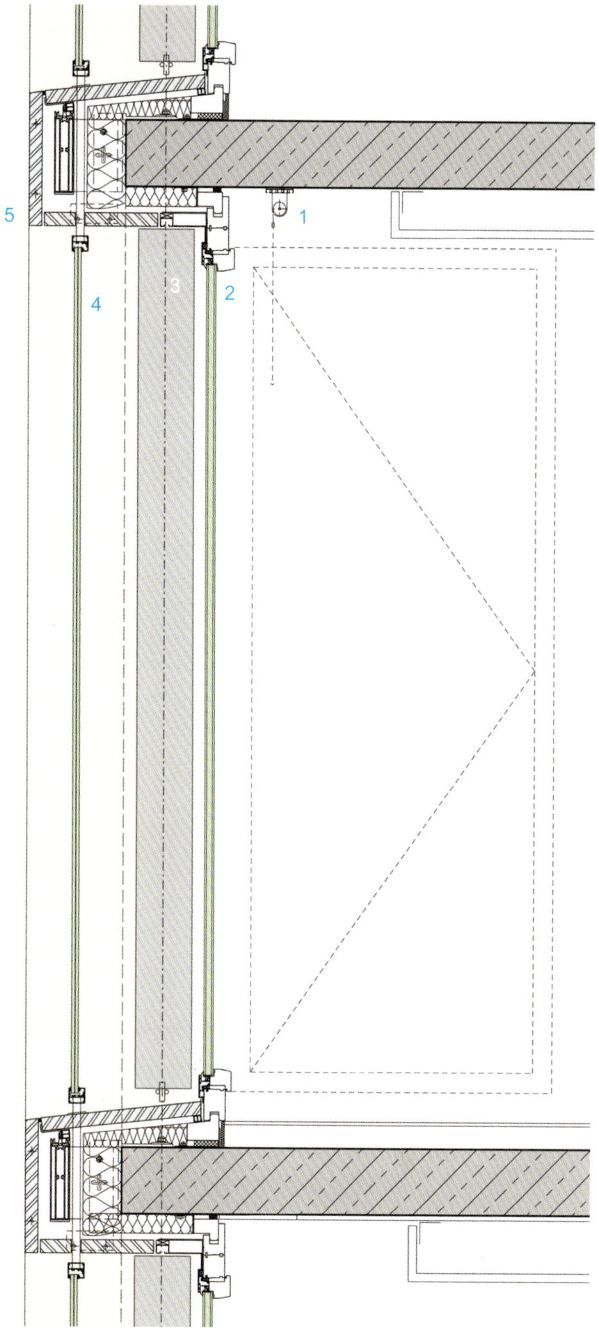

5
1
4
3
2

Section of the Office Façade (Above)

1. Glare Protection
2. Pivoting and Tilting Door, Wood/Aluminium Combination
3. Aluminium Vertical-lamel Curtain, Moveable
4. Glass Plate Fall Protection
5. Natural Stone Cladding

7

8

7. Restaurant
8. Atrium in the office zone of the new building

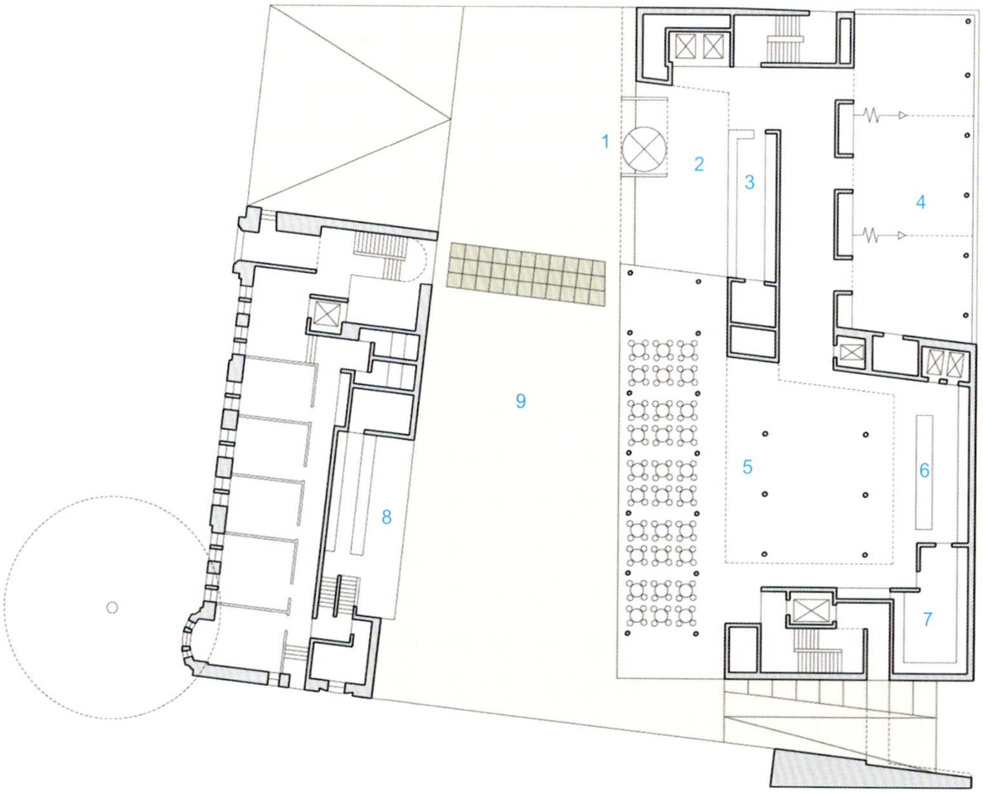
1
2
3
4
5
6
7
8
9

Ground Floor Plan (Right)
1. Main Entrance
2. Foyer
3. Reception
4. Conference Area
5. Restaurant
6. Food Output
7. Sink Area
8. Café
9. Plaza

VOLKSBANK
KARLSRUHE

1

2

Reconstruction of the Headquarters of the Volksbank Karlsruhe

Location: Karlsruhe, Germany
Completion Year: 2008
Designer: Herrmann+Bosch Architekten
Photographer: Roland Halbe,
Werner Huthmacher
Area: 8,600 m²

The personal title of the Volksbank Karlsruhe project "3xL" returns the special qualities of the building, which originates from three atrium sections. 3xL stands for light, air and quality of life.

Programmatic aims of this project were on the one hand to increase the quality of life at the office that have a positive effect on the working culture, working processes, motivation and productivity and on the other hand contributes to the corporate identity and branding.

To the north, the building unfolds into a quiet idyllic park. The offices are protected to the south against the pollution of the heavy traffic and against the strong solar irradiation by a "shield" that simultaneously forms a façade and roof. The "shield" directly catches the sunlight, which is then filtered through the "Open Spaces" that lie behind. These "Open Spaces" or vertical lobbies are rest areas and offices with stimulating, communication areas and integrating atmosphere.

The "Open Spaces" permeate the office levels vertically and produce a spatial network of all the levels. They loosen up the horizontal layout and structure of conventional offices, offer the possibility to experience space and create a clear sense of orientation in all areas of the building.

The resulting open plan structure allows for a working atmosphere with a greater individualisation of the respective work stations. The building should not only take the quality of life of current employees into account but rather include the importance of the quality of life of future generations.

The responsibility toward the environment and society are once again found in the energy concept of the reconstruction of the building: Approximately 86 tons of the environmentally harmful carbon dioxide are cut down per year, through the consequent use of regenerative energy sources of the earth and the sun.

1. Entrance
2. The building is protected by the dark blue south façade against noise and heat

Site Plan

Section

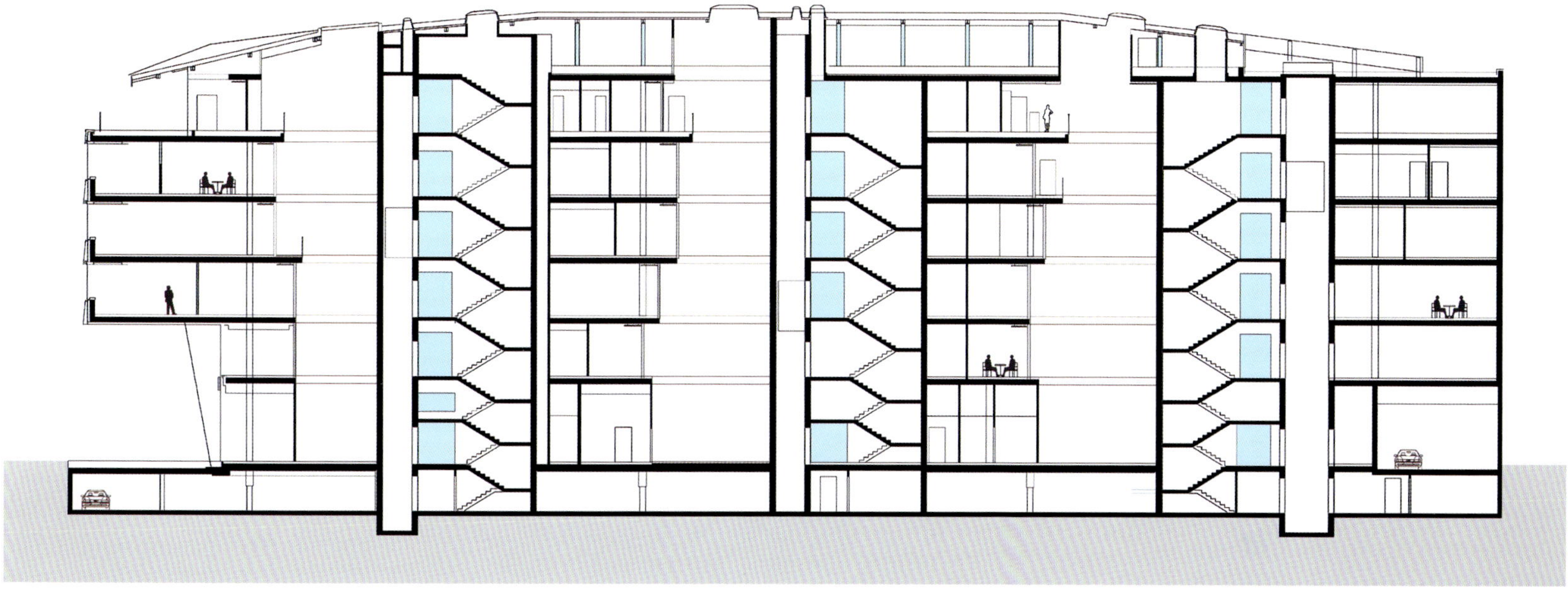

Section

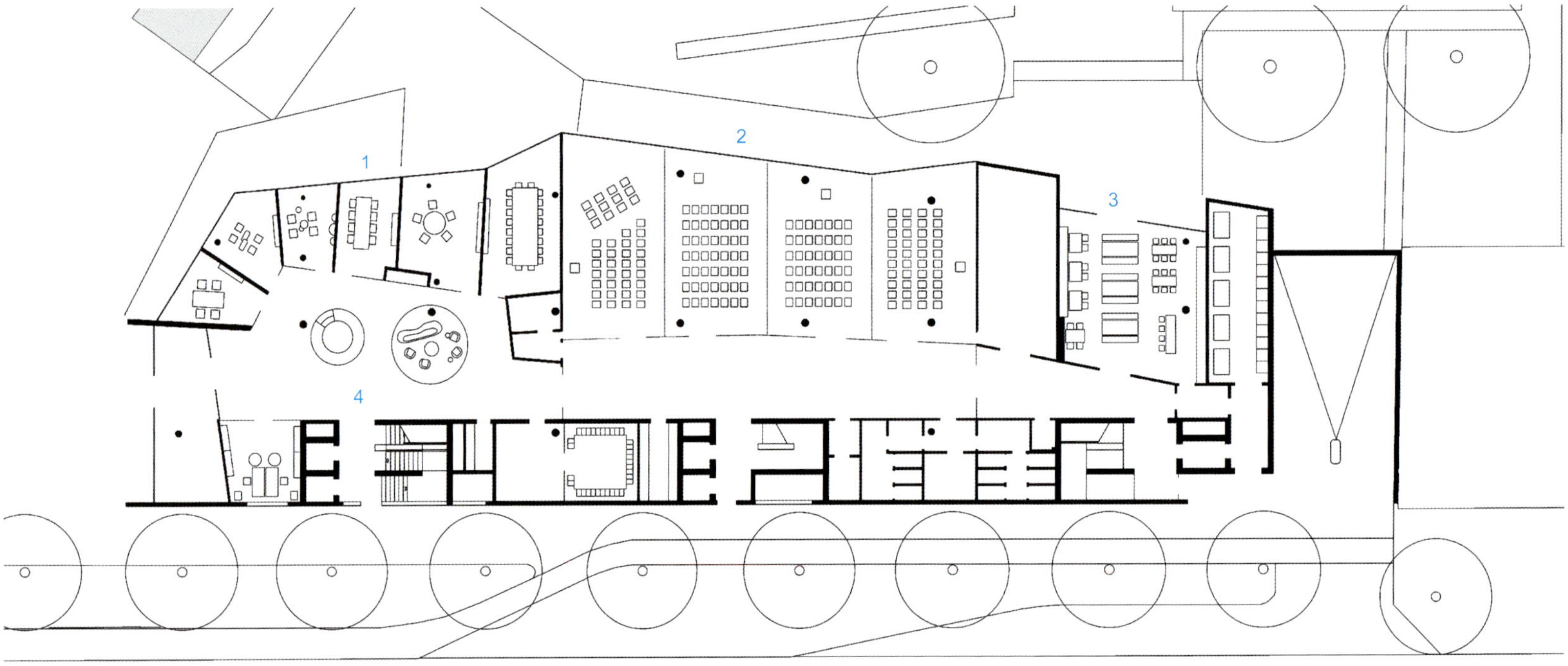

1
2
3
4

Ground Floor Plan
1. Meeting Room
2. Seminar Area
3. Cafeteria
4. Lobby / Reception

3. The furniture of the offices
4. The atrium offers plenty of opportunities to communicate

KOGEL
BW|Bank
BW|Bank
SCHÜTA - schenken und genießen
Tee
Zigarren
Tabak
SCHÜTA
natürlich aus
eigener Herstellung
in bester Qualität

1

BW Bank

2

Branch of BW-Bank Böblingen, Germany

Location: Böblingen, Germany
Completion Year: 2007
Architect: Kauffmann Theilig & Partner, Freie Architekten BDA, Ostfildern
Photographer: Roland Halbe (Stuttgart)
Client: LBBW Landesbank Baden-Württemberg, Stuttgart
Gross Floor Area: 1,500 m²

Because of the specific location in the historic centre and the its corner position the design of the new building of the Baden-Wüttembergische Bank was influenced by the heights and eaves of the surrounding buildings. So the house was inserted in a self-evident way: parts of the maximum volume were cutted out in the way that the resulting edges have relation to the height of other roofs and eaves around. The punshed-out surfaces appear as uniform transparent glass façades; in contrast the original surface of the volume appears as a massive natural stone façade. This conceptional idea can be followed from design to detail. The architecture of the building creates different images for the different views that were spatially related to a whole.

The entrance to the building is right at the most representative corner. On the ground floor there is the foyer with the automatic tellers and the customer's area with the service desk. On the four storeys above there are mainly offices, conference and consultation rooms completed with additional service rooms. In the basement there are technical and store rooms and the bank's vault. Every floor is reachable through a central staircase with the elevator and all rooms are arranged around this central development zone. Because of a separate access to the development zone every floor could be rented individually if required. The storey itself could be partitioned flexibly with lightweight construction walls. The support structure of the building is reinforced concrete. For the bracing and the main load transfer the central cores with the elevation zone and some parts of the external walls are used.

1. East façade
2. North elevation

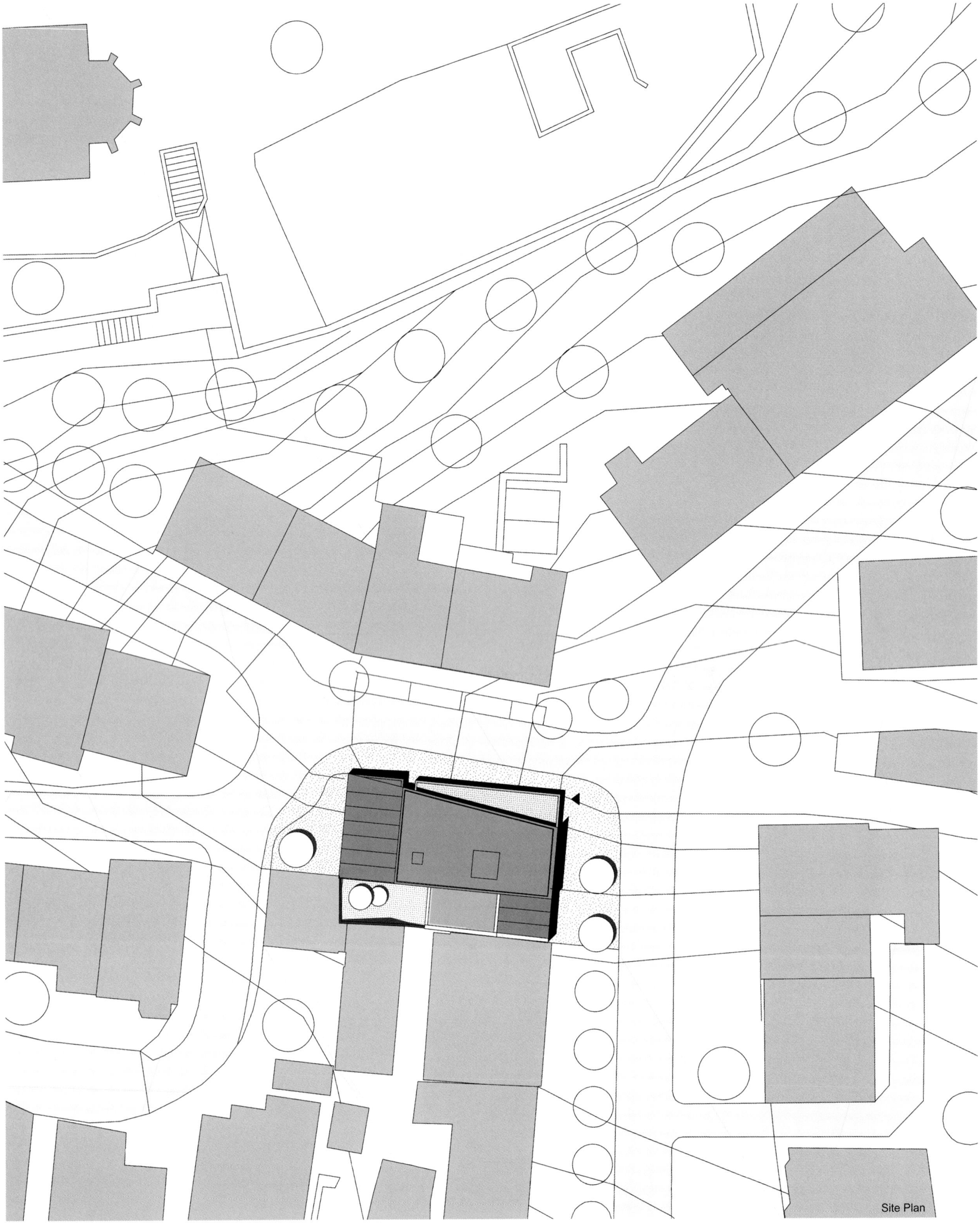

Site Plan

Cross Section

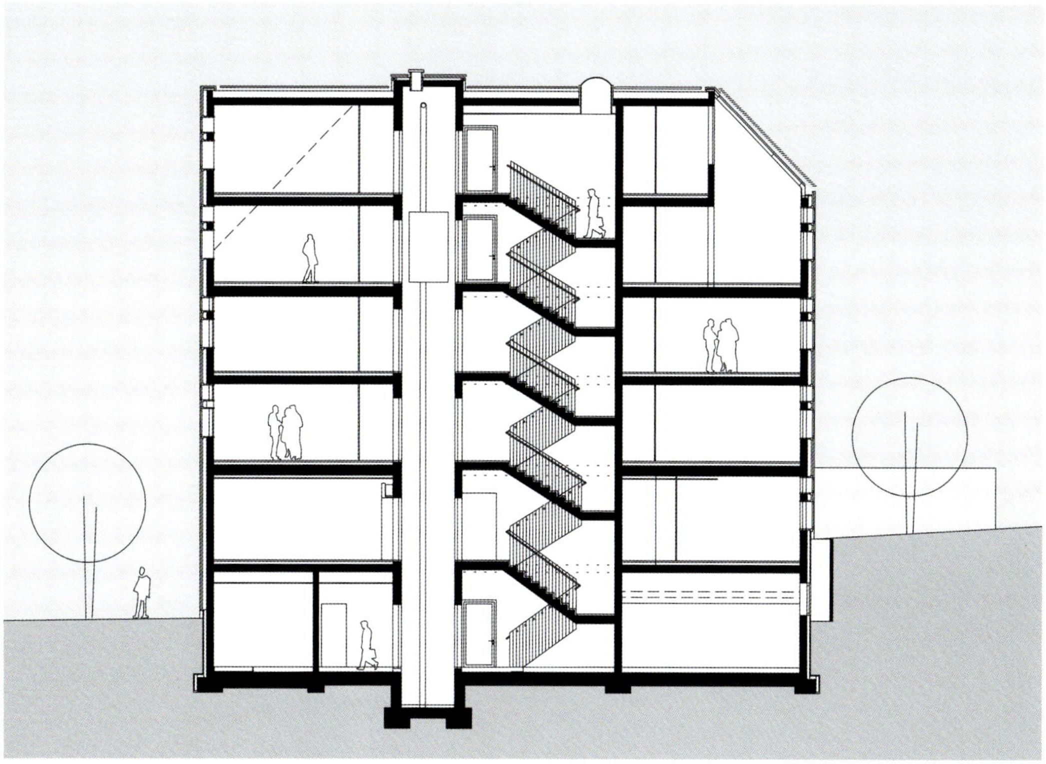

Longitudinal Section

References to the Surrounding Buildings

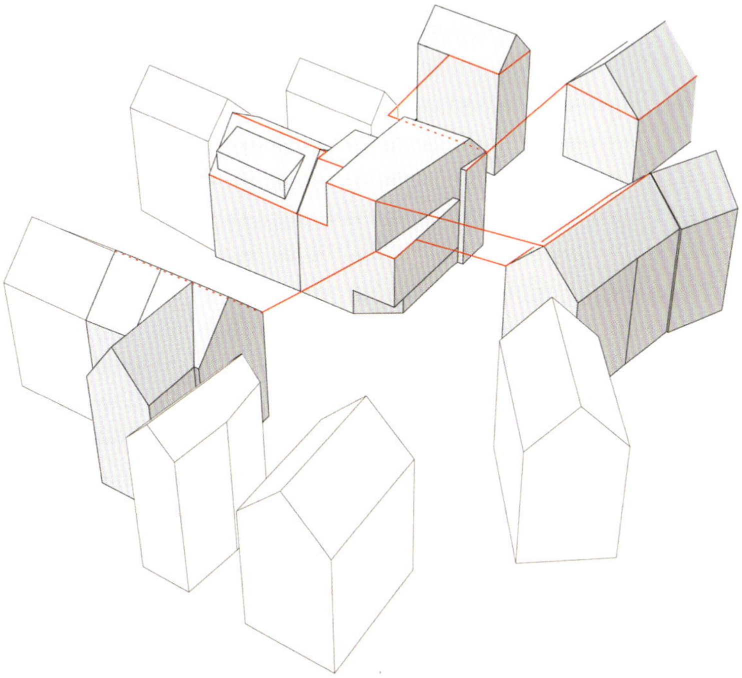

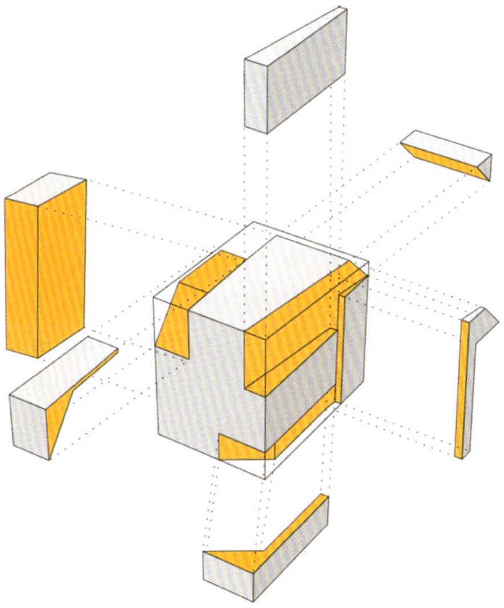

Insections in the Maximum Volume

3

4

3. Customer's area
4. Circulation core of the customer's area
5. Corridor at the courtyard
6. Kitchenette

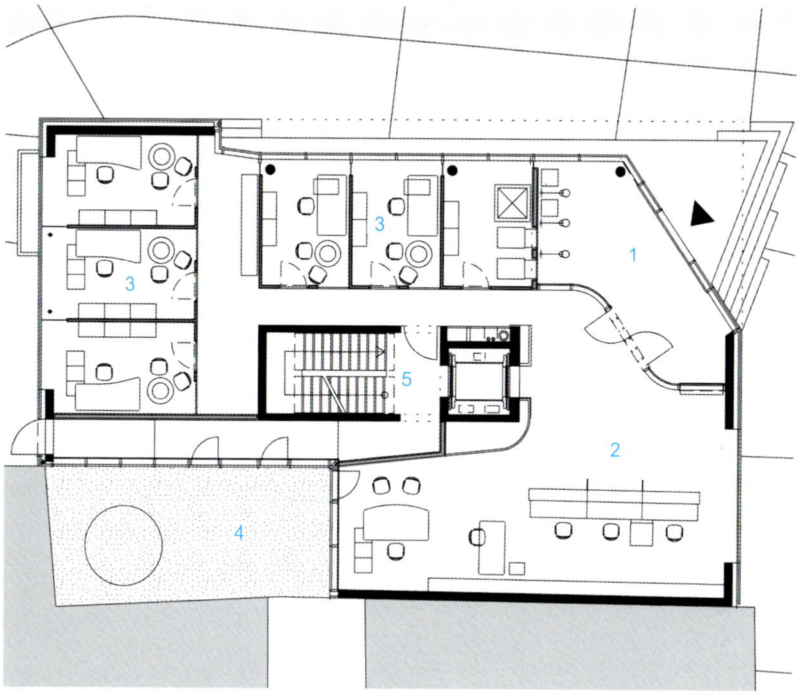
1
2
3
3
4
5

Ground Floor Plan (Above)
1. Foyer
2. Customer's Area
3. Advisory Service
4. Courtyard
5. Circulation Core

5

6

7

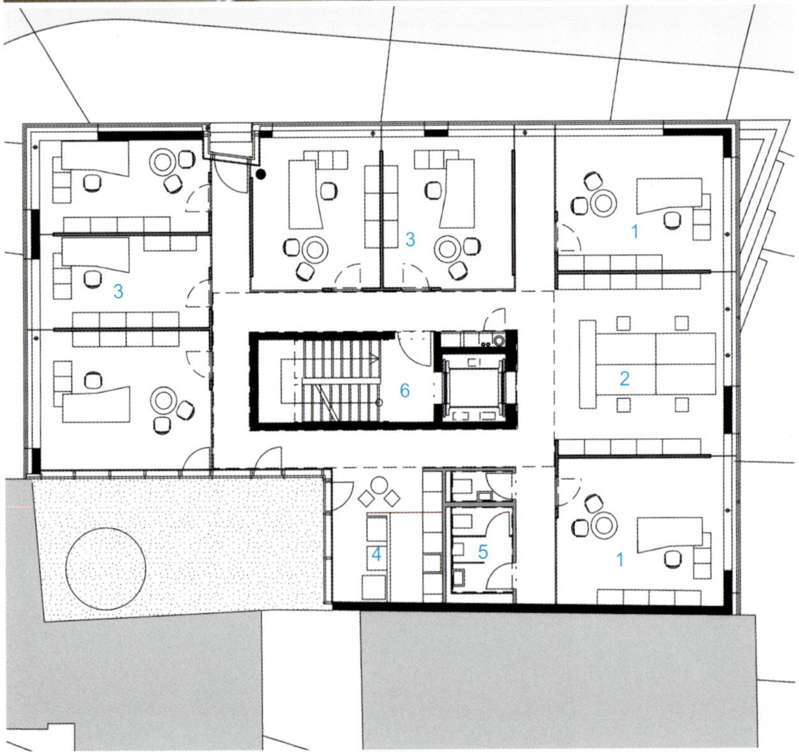
1
1
2
3
3
4
5
6

First Floor Plan (Left)
1. Office
2. Secretariat
3. Advisory Service
4. Kitchenette
5. Toilette
6. Circulation Core

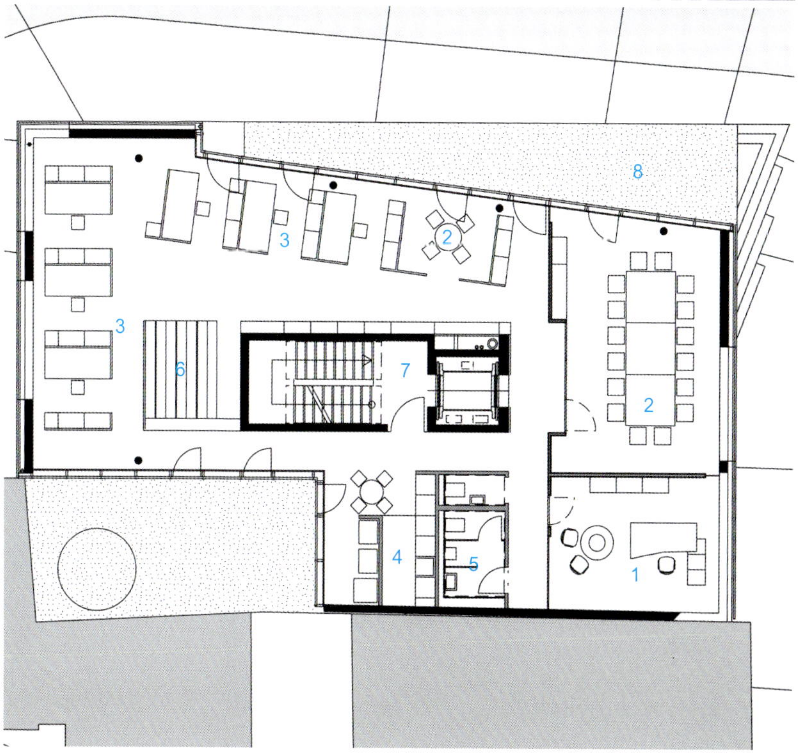
8
3
2
3
6
7
2
4
5
1

7. Office area with the perforated wall and the natural stone façade
8. Office area with the transparent glass façade
9. West elevation

Third Floor Plan (Right)
1. Office
2. Conference Room
3. Processing
4. Kitchenette
5. Toilet
6. Storage
7. Circulation Core
8. Terrace

巣鴨信用金庫志村支店

1

Sugamo Shinkin Bank - Shimura Branch

Location: Tokyo, Japan
Completion Year: 2011
Designer: emmanuelle moureaux architecture+design
Photographer: Nacasa & Partners Inc.
Area: 762 m²

Sugamo Shinkin Bank is a credit union that strives to provide first-rate hospitality to its customers in accordance with its motto, "we take pleasure in serving happy customers." Having completed the design for branch outlets of Sugamo Shinkin Bank located in Tokiwadai and Niiza, the designers were also commissioned to handle the architectural and interior design for its newly rebuilt branch in Shimura. For this project, the designers sought to create a refreshing atmosphere with a palpable sense of nature based on an open sky motif.

A rainbow-like stack of coloured layers, peeking out from the façade to welcome visitors. Reflected onto the white surface, these colours leave a faint trace over it, creating a warm, gentle feeling. At night, the coloured layers are faintly illuminated. The illumination varies according to the season and time of day, conjuring up myriad landscapes. Upon entering the building, three elliptical skylights bathe the interior in soft light. Visitors spontaneously look up to see a cut-out piece of the sky that invites them to gaze languidly at it. The open sky and sensation of openness prompt visitors to take deep breaths, refreshing their bodies from within.

The ceiling is adorned with dandelion puff motifs that seem to float and drift through the air. In Europe, there is a long and cherished custom of blowing on one of these fuzzy balls while secretly making a wish. Bits of fluffy down gently dance and frolic in the air, carried by the wind.

ATMs, teller windows, consultation booths and an open space laid out with chairs in 14 different colours are located on the ground floor. The first floor houses offices, meeting rooms and a cafeteria, while the second floor is reserved for the staff changing rooms. Three long glass airwells thread through the ground and the first levels of the building, flooding the interior with natural light as well as "blowing" air through it.

1. Façade view at night
2. Outside view, a rainbow-like stack of coloured layers

Ground Floor Plan (Right)
1. Office
2. Archive
3. Meeting Space
4. Open Space
5. ATM
6. Counter
7. Entrance

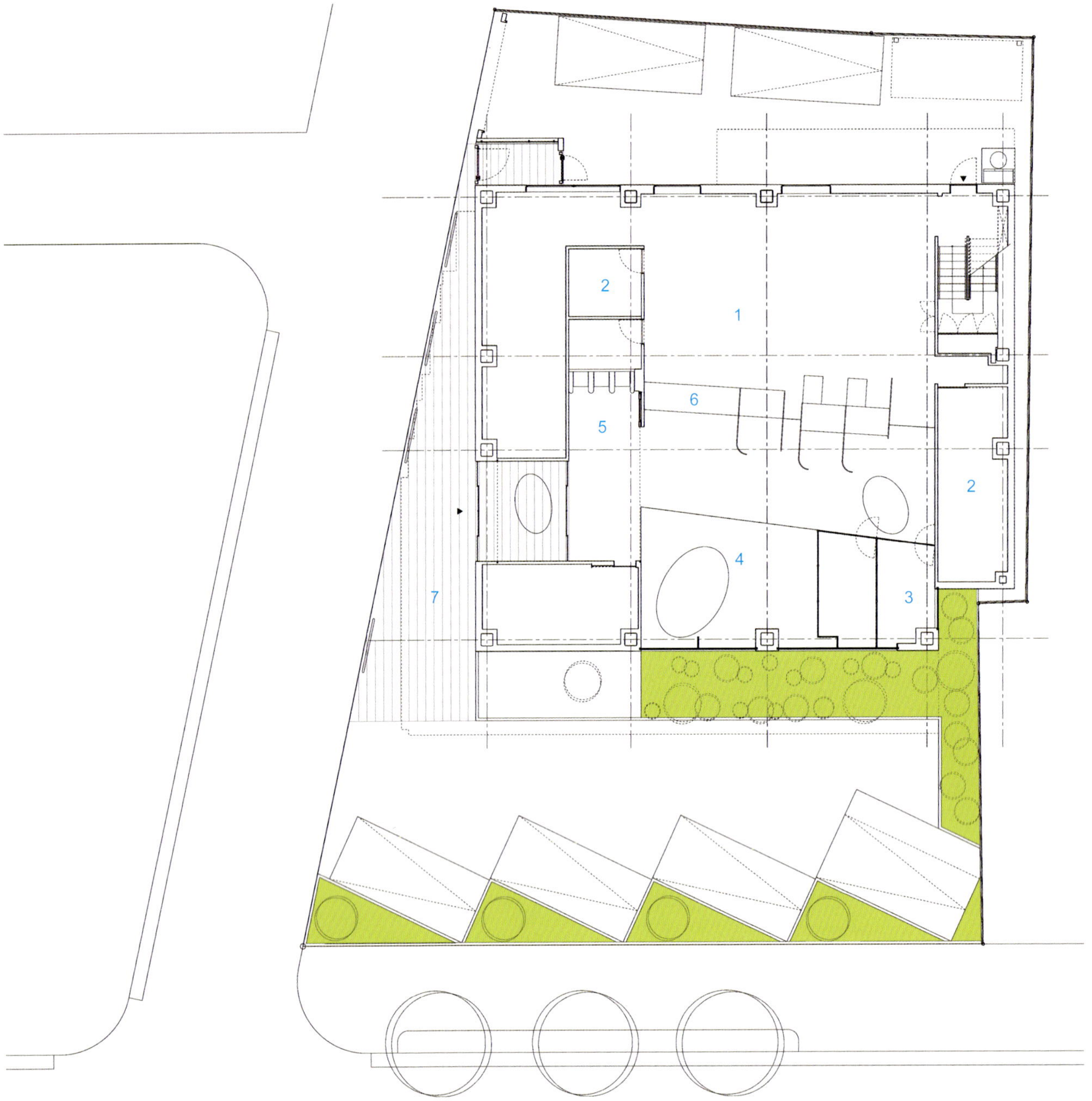
2
1
6
5
2
4
7
3

South Elevation

North Elevation

3

3. The ceiling is adorned with dandelion puff motifs
4. Open space laid out with chairs in 14 different colours
5. Meeting room
6-7. Three elliptical skylights bathe the interior in soft light
8. Light wells on the first floor

4

5

6

7

8

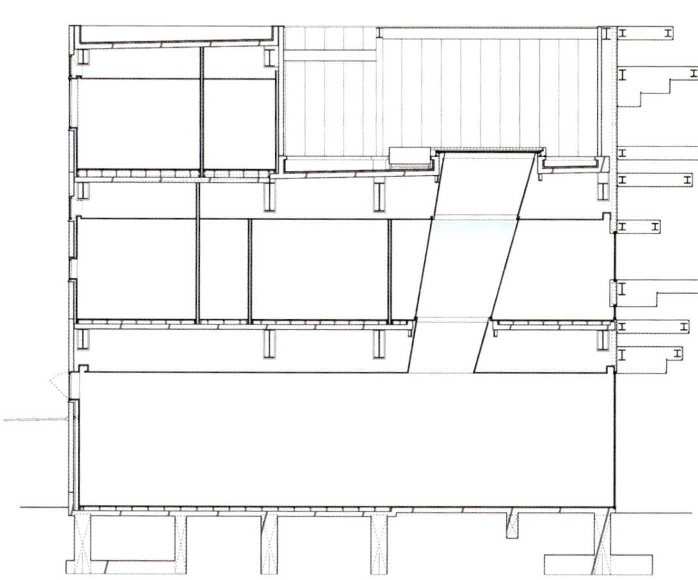

Section

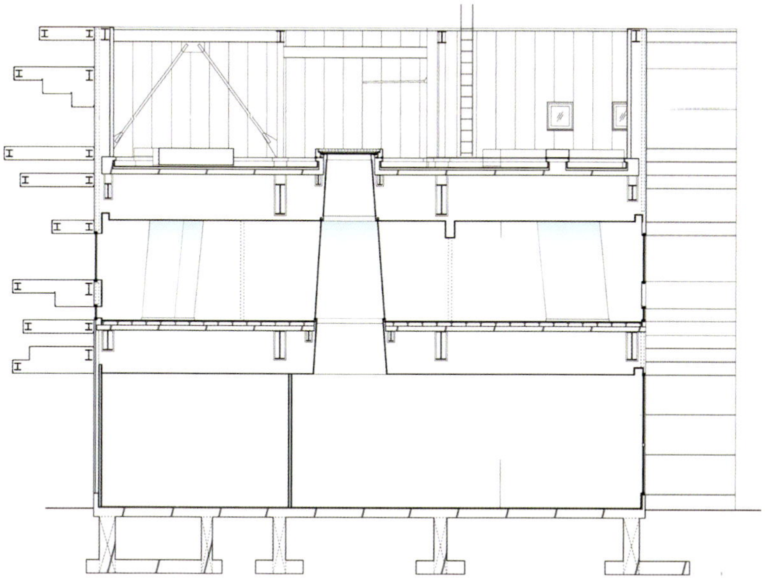

Section

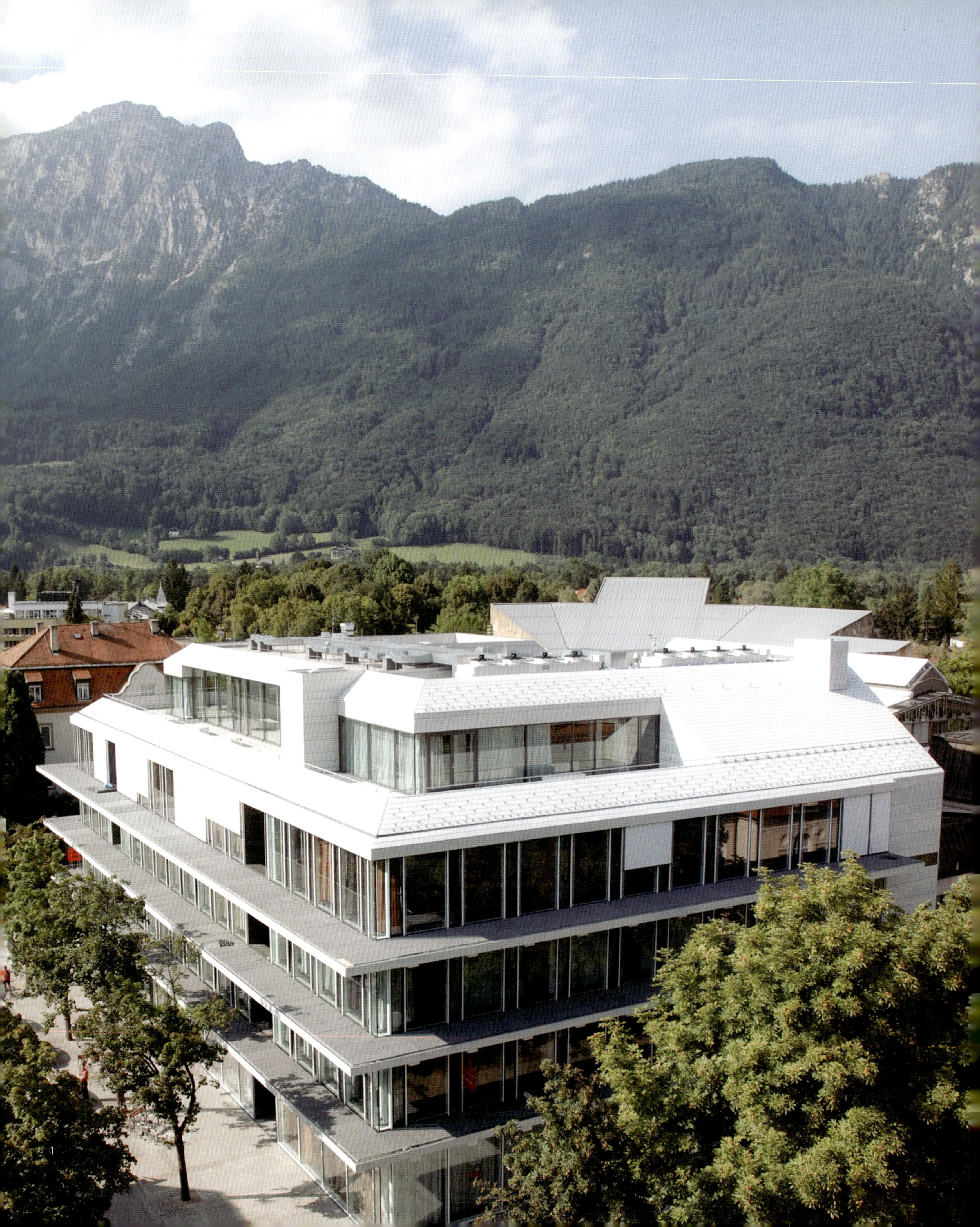

2

Sparkasse Berchtesgadener Land, Central Office and Branch in Bad Reichenhall

Location: Bad Reichenhall, Germany
Completion Year: 2008
Designer: Bolwin Wulf Architekten
Photographer: Rolf Sturm
Area: 7,947 m²

The central office and branch of the Sparkasse Berchtesgadener Land in Bad Reichenhall were comprehensively redesigned in terms of content and structure. Here the clients have decided to continue building on the existing site to provide resource-conscious continuity. Notwithstanding the corporate identity elements typical for the savings bank, the intent was to create a unique facility with a clear local commitment.

Therefore, the interventions in the 1970s substance are low, but with high effect: the originally suspended from the façade, insights and outlooks hindering sunshade was removed, commissure-heads exposed and covered with large horizontal surfaces. A simple sunshade was developed with maximum transparency and openness, a covered outdoor area for pedestrians, and not least a typically local element, which was already used on the cornices of the historic saline buildings. The building now has a white hipped roof, which coalesces with the surrounding mountains in winter.

Inside was for the time of origin typical function mix of banking, business premises, housing, and the associated complex connection given up. Two staircases at the entrance façade could be omitted and have made space for water trickle wall as high as the buildings. This can be seen not only as a typical local attraction, they also transport evaporation cool to the office levels.

The region around Bad Reichenhall owes its importance to salt (Hall = salt mine, salt). As a result, the overall design concept for the building is based on the natural colour spectrum of salt from light pink to dark purple. Throughout the facility, the colours are found in select shades and brightness levels of material and light.

1. The building has a white hipped roof, which coordinates with the green mountains
2. Side view of the building

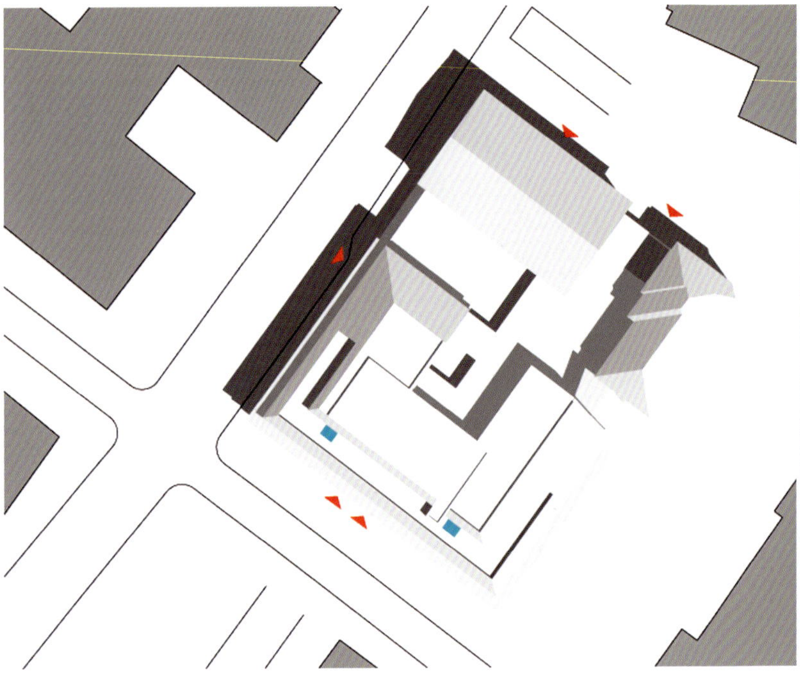

3
3. Patio

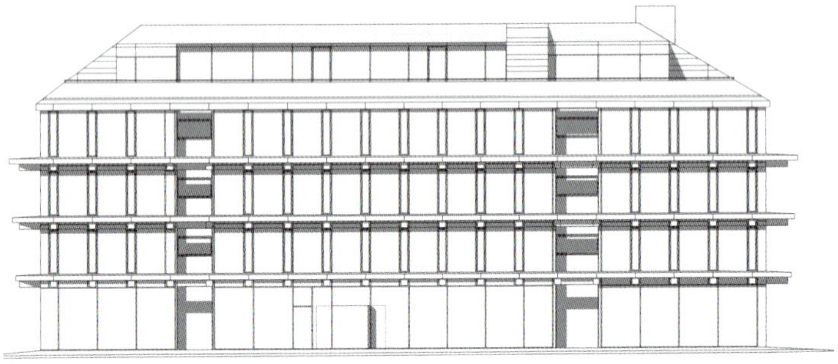
Southwest Elevation

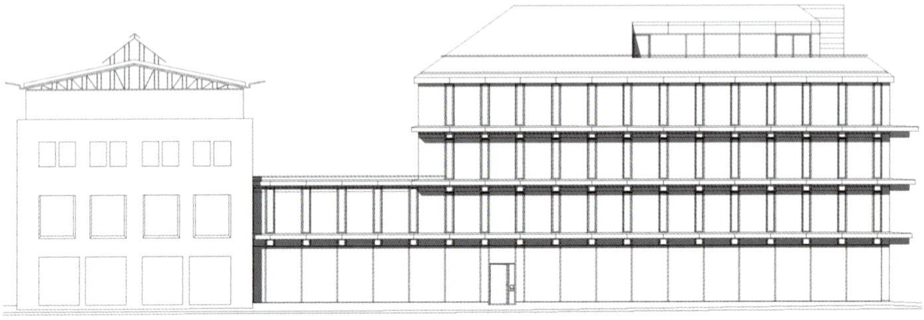
Northwest Elevation

Section

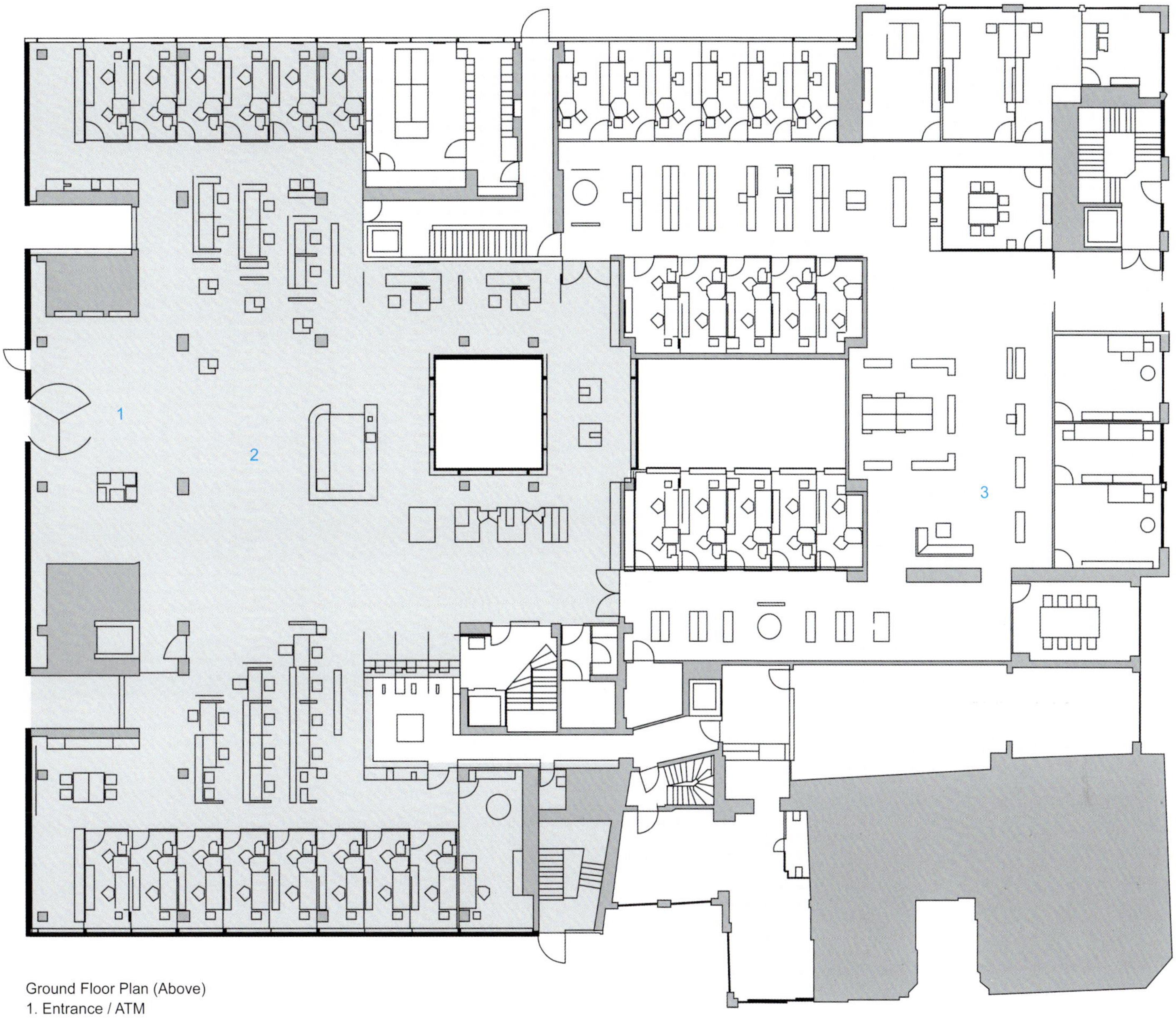
1
2
3

Ground Floor Plan (Above)
1. Entrance / ATM
2. Client Service Hall
3. Office / Meeting

info
immobilien
4

5

immobilien
immobi-
lien

557 693,91
RUPERT

4. Reception, interior space is decorated in pink
5. Working space
6. Meeting room

Middelfart
Sparekasse
Forsikring Fyn
1

Middlefart Savings Bank

Middelfart Savings Bank is a key institution in the town of Middelfart, located by the Lilleb waters on the Island of Funen, Denmark. Thus the Savings Bank wanted their new head office to provide a new public space for the local citizens as well as an architectural icon for the town and the savings bank.

The building is characterised by a dramatic roofscape accommodating multiple functions. 83 prism-like skylights compose the spectacular roof surface defining the geometry of the building – in reference to the maritime environment as well as the surrounding timber framed buildings. Thus, the new head office gently reflects and interacts with the dimensions, scales, roofs and cornice lines of the old town.

The roof is specially designed to frame a perfect view towards the water while at the same time shading from direct sunlight; thereby demonstrating a perfect synergy between design and function.

A bookshop, a café, a real estate agent and the cash desk are placed around a central plaza, resulting in the building forming an informal public meeting space at the ground floor level. The savings bank's work stations are located on three open terraces internally connected by broad staircases encouraging interaction and informal meetings or breaks. All plateaus are endowed with plenty of daylight and an unhindered view to the water.

The working environment is further improved by sustainable features such as natural ventilation and the latest technologies in energy efficient heating and cooling. Thermo active concrete elements facilitate energy savings of 30 percent to 50 percent.

Location: Middelfart, Denmark
Completion Year: 2010
Designer: 3XN
Photographer: Adam Mørk
Area: 5,000 m²

1. 83 prism-like skylights compose the spectacular roof surface

2
Bog&idé
Bog&idé

2. The unique exterior of the building echoes with the waterfront
3. View from the courtyard

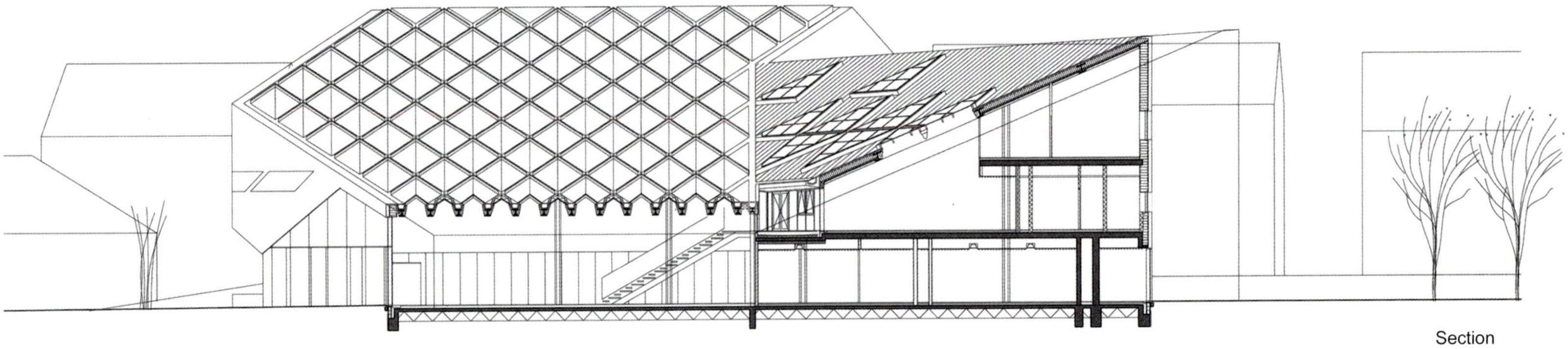

Section

Middelfart Sparekasse
3

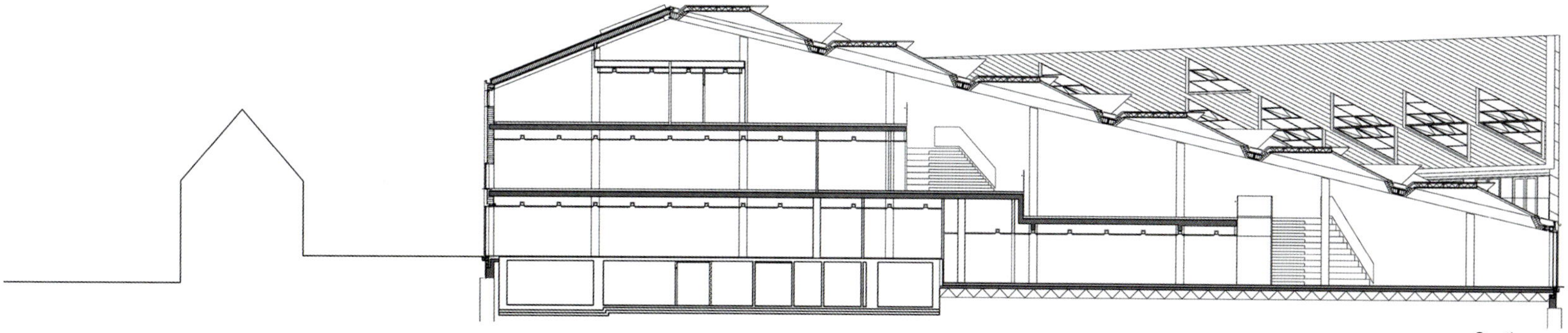

Section

4

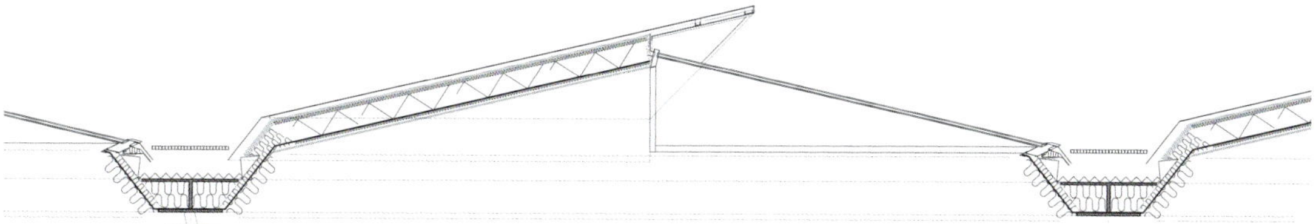

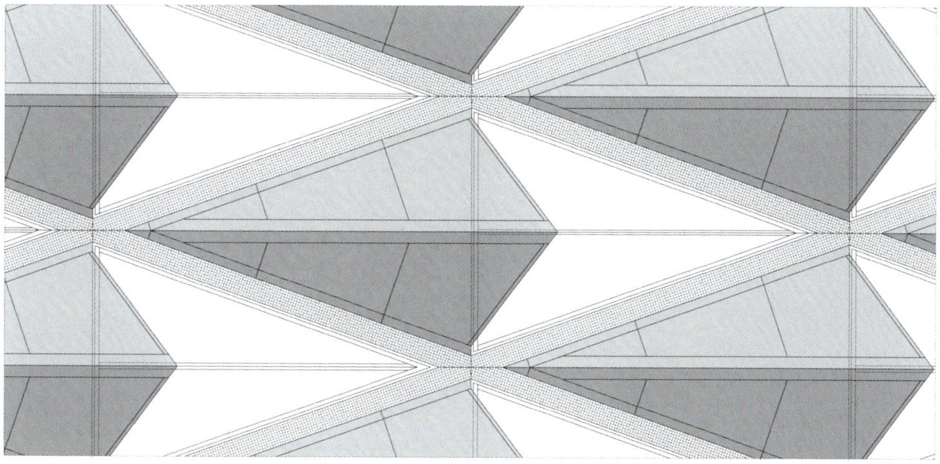

4. Towering roof
5-6. Roof details

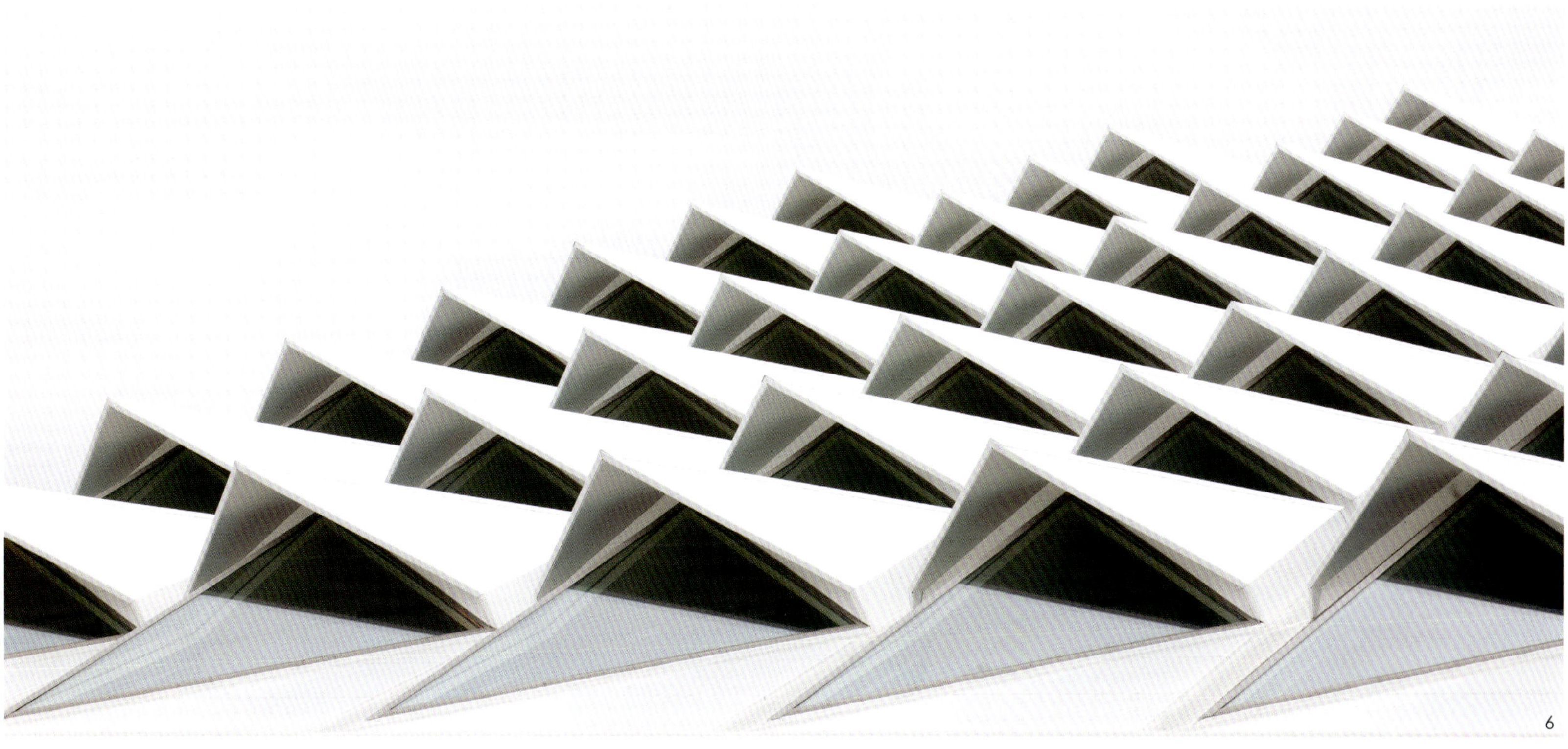

7

8

7-8. Entrance hall

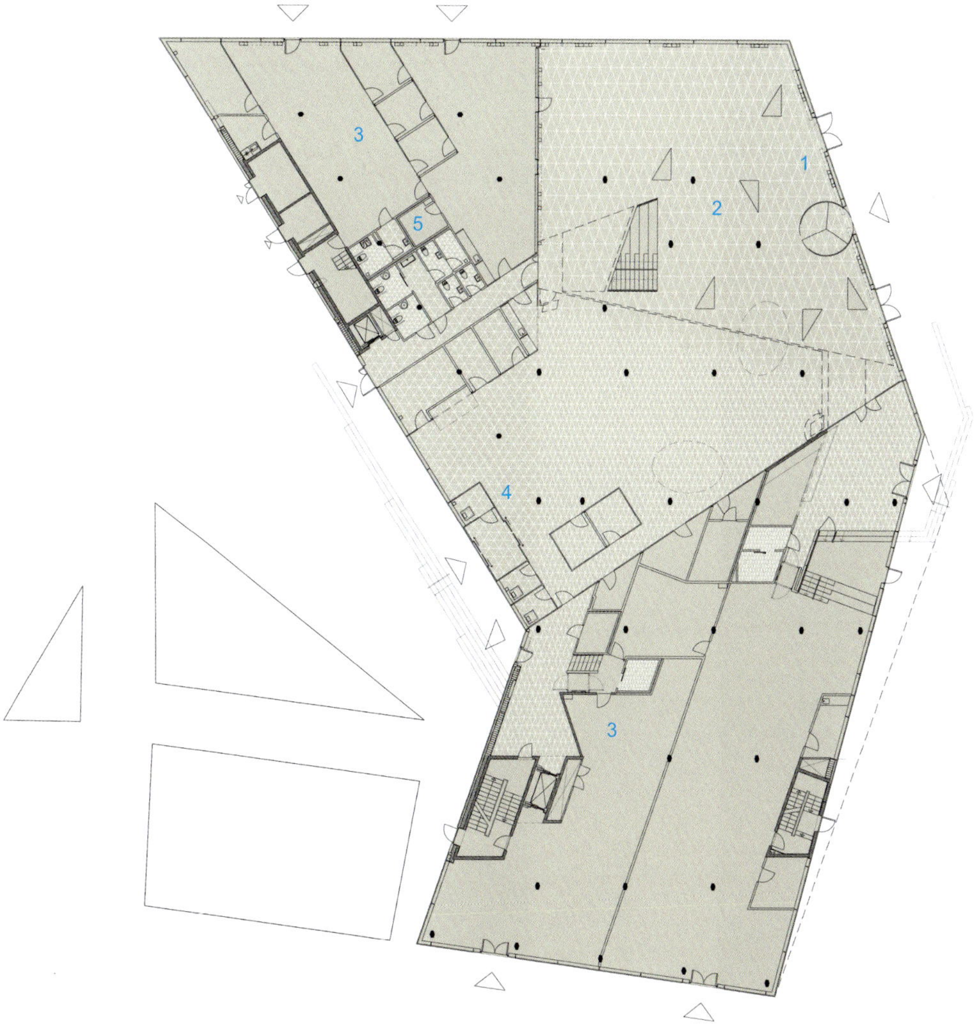
1
2
3
4
5
3

Ground Floor Plan
1. Entrance
2. Entrance Hall
3. Teller Area
4. Café
5. Toilet

BANCA DI CREDITO COOPERATIVO DI CASALGRASSO E SANT'ALBANO STURA

1

BANCA DI CREDITO COOPERATIVO DI CASALGRASSO E SANT'ALBANO STURA
2

New Branch of the Cooperative Credit Bank

Location: Fossano, Italy
Completion Year: 2007
Designer: Studio Kuadra
Photographer: Alberto Piovano
Area: 732 m²

A cascade of chains on the façade, dynamic space, mobile, changing, not what people would expect from a bank, especially in a province at the foot of the Maritime Alps. The branch of this Credit Agency, winner of a close competition, brings a breath of lightness and a levity that would be more common in a completely different sort of building; an exhibition centre or a performance venue, for example. This bank is stripped of that entire traditional image which characterises an institution of this type and instead presents a new unedited image of itself.

Surprising and innovative outside, intimate and welcoming inside. Although made up mainly of young people, the Kuadra studio of architects knows how to obtain the very best from the materials they use with rigour and finesse. Glass, metal and stainless steel are all combined in a clever alchemy that highlights consistency, form, quality and singularity, while never neglecting composition, which remains precise and clean. The best way to fulfill the needs of the future customers and employees are constantly taken into consideration during the process of the project.

Strips of light, transparent staircases and pathways at different levels mean that clients in this bank will not be limited to cueing at the teller's counter. They will have an opportunity to experience an architectural quality that Le Corbusier christened Architectural Promenade.

The architecture seems like an ode to clarity, transparency, to conceptual essence itself, while at the same time never losing sight of that direct functional relationship with the public, not just words from a bank worker's manual, but the real public; an old man, a parent, a child, all with differing needs. There is a wide, luminous open informal space given over to a children's play area, quite a novelty in a bank, besides the obligatory comfortable sofas at the entrance. Wherever one goes from the counters to the meeting rooms one is breathing in that atmosphere of ordinary domesticity that never descends into the banal or predictable.

1. A cascade of chains on the façade creates a dynamic space
2. Night view of front elevation

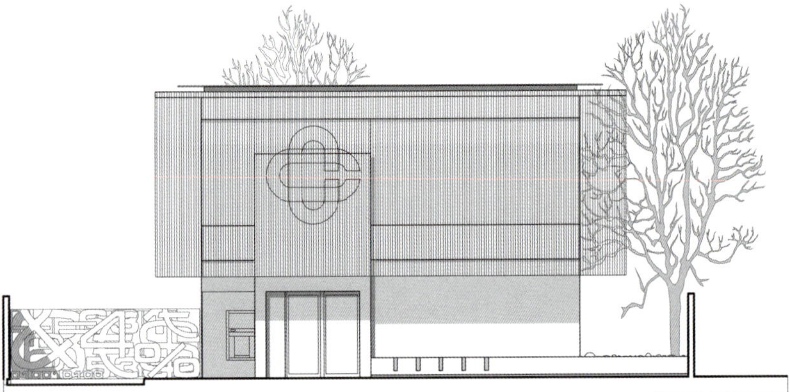

Front Elevation

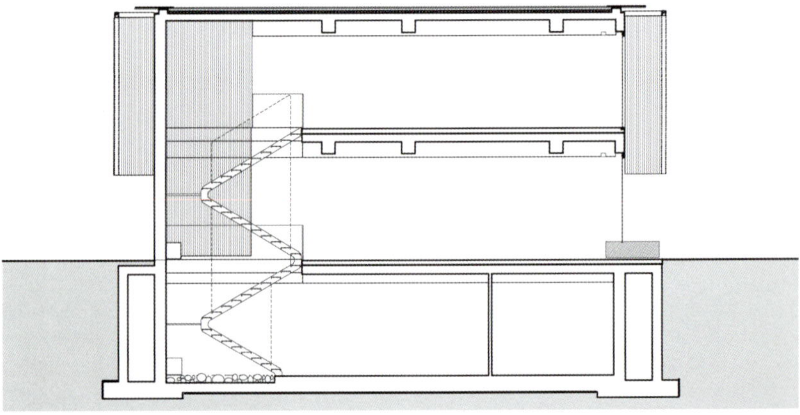

Section

BANCA DI CREDITO

4

5

3. Side elevation
4. Entrance details
5. Eaves details

6

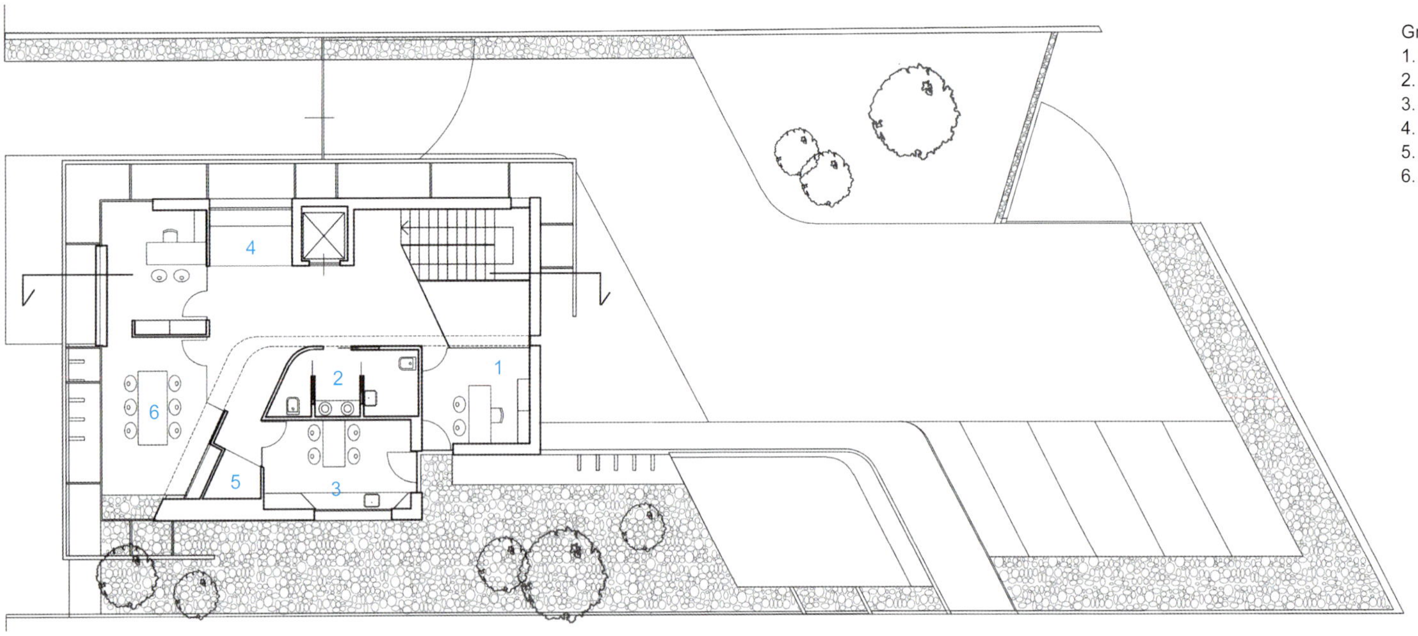

1
2
3
4
5
6

Ground Floor Plan (Left)
1. Office
2. Toilet
3. Kitchen
4. Waiting Area
5. Storage
6. Meeting Room

7

8

6. Reception, with glass and wood as materials
7. Meeting room
8. The glass wall forms a semi-open office space

9

10

11

12

13

14

9-14. Lights from different levels, transparent stairs and chains create a dynamic and changeable space
15. Staircase and chains produce a visual effect

15

MODESTO COMMERCE BANK
4204 DALE ROAD
SPEED LIMIT
35
1

2

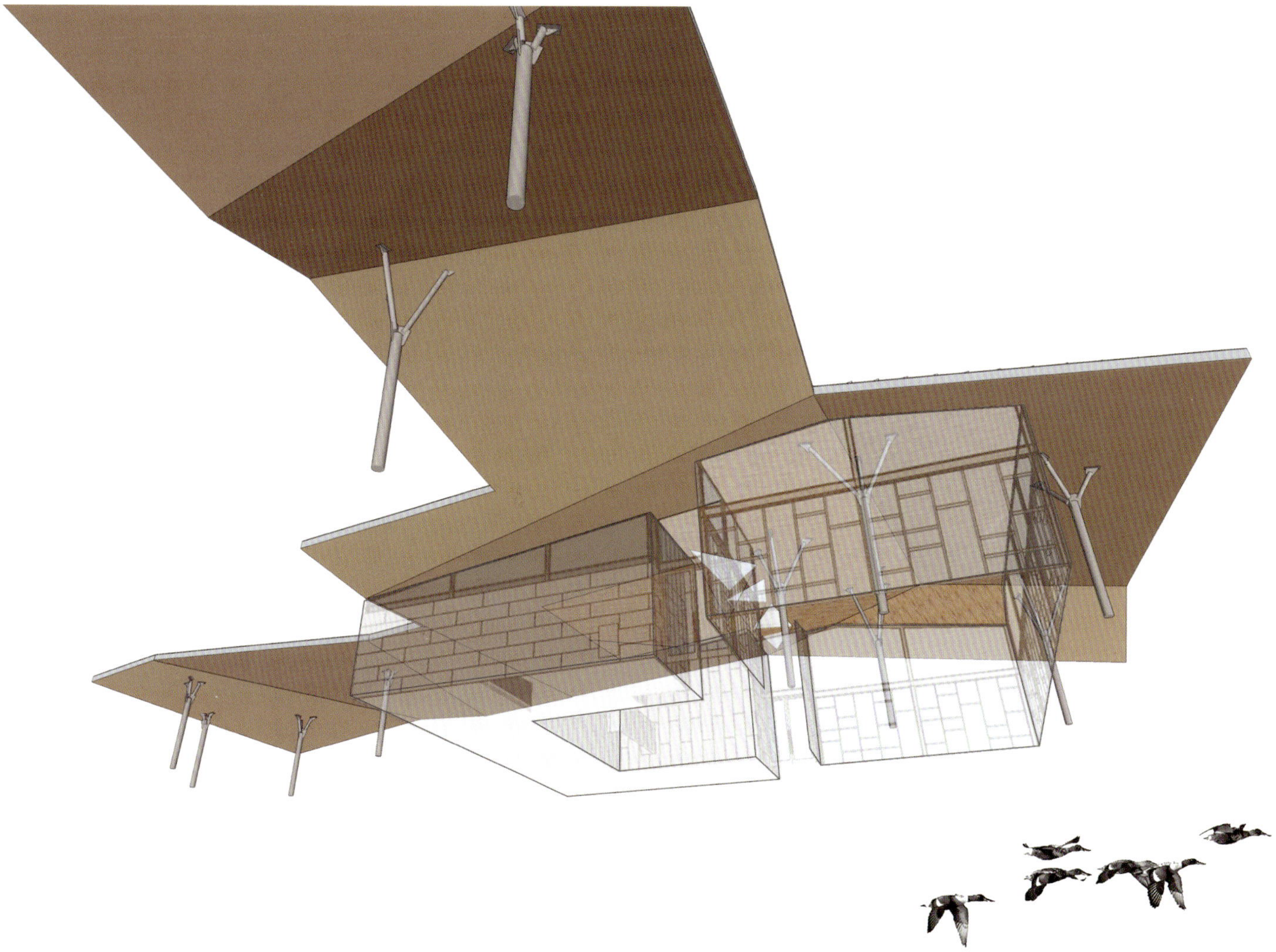

Bank of Stockton

Location: Modesto, USA
Completion Year: 2008
Designer: Mark Horton
Photographer: Ethan Kaplan
Area: 618m²

Located at the edge of an expanding new community, this branch of the Bank of Stockton provides a modern facility for a banking institution that is rooted in the history and landscape of California's Central Valley.

A pair of simple volumes join together to accommodate the various programmatic elements of the bank. The materials chosen for each volume conceptually reinforce the programme contained within. A transparent glass volume encloses the public banking area, while the private money-handling area and its accessory spaces are contained within an analogous opaque volume, clad with agglomerate tiles made from a recycled glass that also recalls Sierra granite. These two elements form a literal and figurative junction at the transaction counter, where the individual and the institutional come face-to-face. This dualistic scheme can be easily adopted to various conditions and utilised as a prototype for new branches as the bank expands throughout California.

In the tradition of Modernism, various building systems are integrated within the architecture itself: a photovoltaic laminate system is incorporated into the metal roofing; a raised access floor serves as a mechanical supply plenum; and prism-like skylights bring daylight into the central transaction area. The dominant building materials - structural steel, wood panels, glass tile - are honestly expressed and selected based on their recyclability, as well as their aesthetic.

A folded roof - both sculptural and functional - reaches beyond the perimeter of the bank building to shade the glass walls and shelter the covered parking and drive-through bays. This formal gesture, whose origin can be traced back to the surrounding landscape, is supported by a series of tree-like branched columns. Echoing the almond orchards that once prospered on the site, these columns, along with the roof, create an organic counterpoint to the orthogonal volumes of the bank enclosure.

1. The folded roof is both sculptural and functional
2. The public area and private area use different construction materials

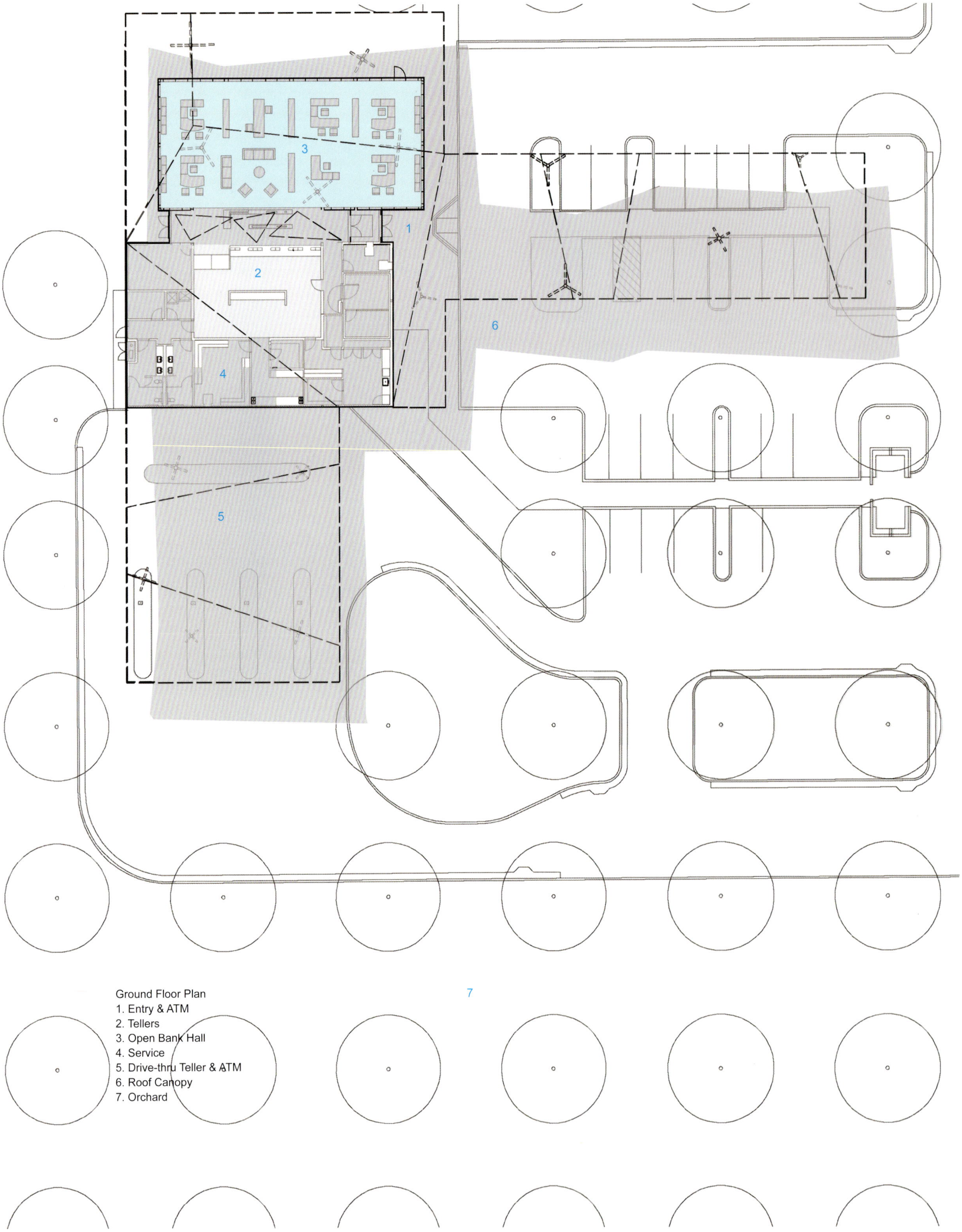
1
2
3
4
5
6
7

Ground Floor Plan
1. Entry & ATM
2. Tellers
3. Open Bank Hall
4. Service
5. Drive-thru Teller & ATM
6. Roof Canopy
7. Orchard

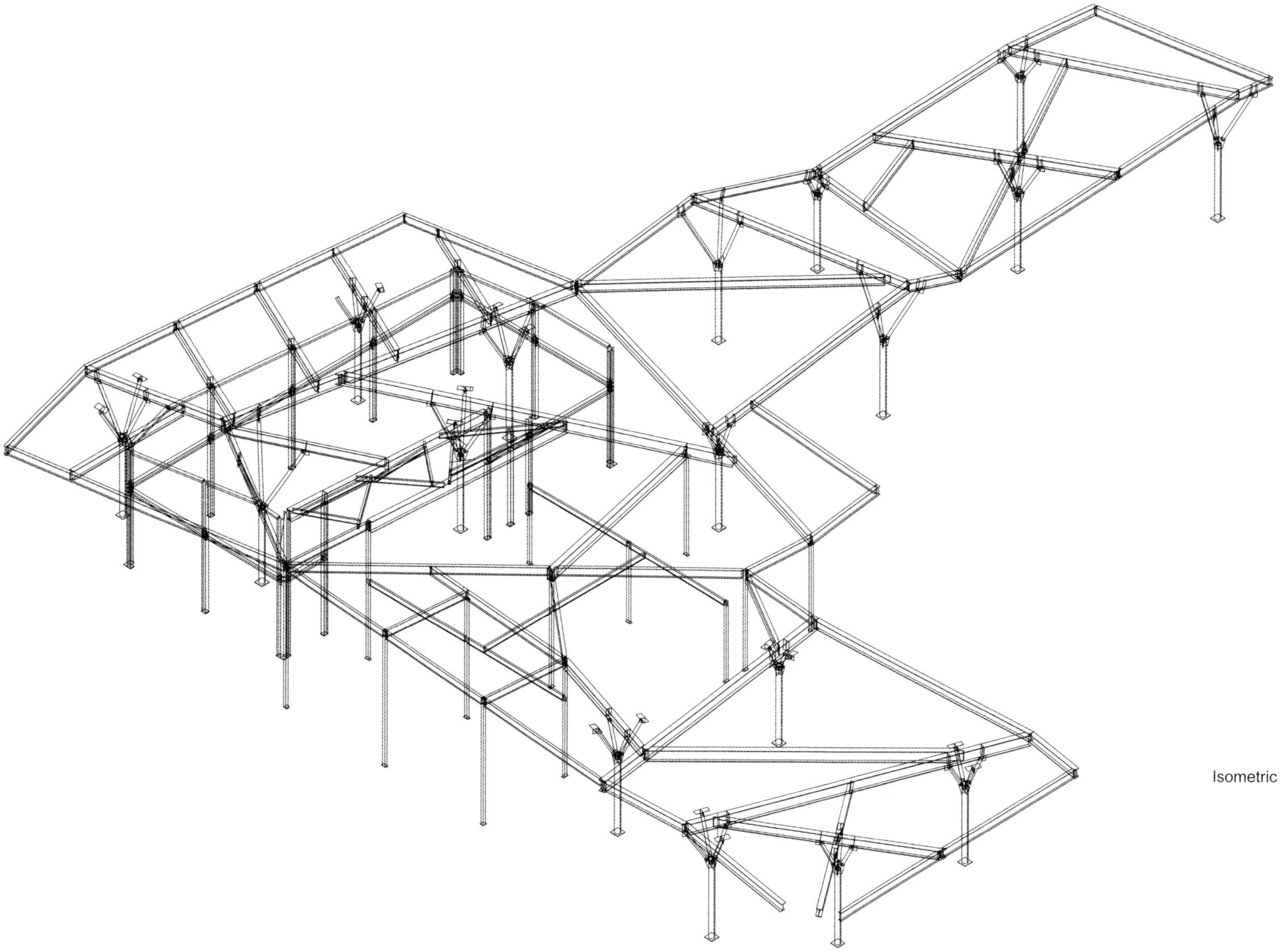

Isometric Drawing

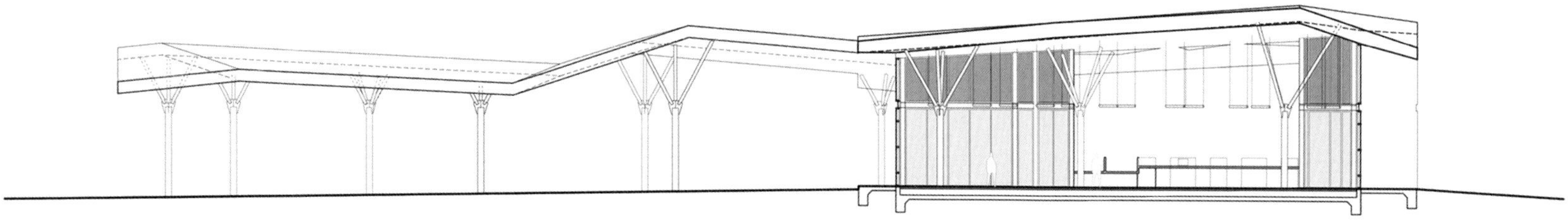

East Section

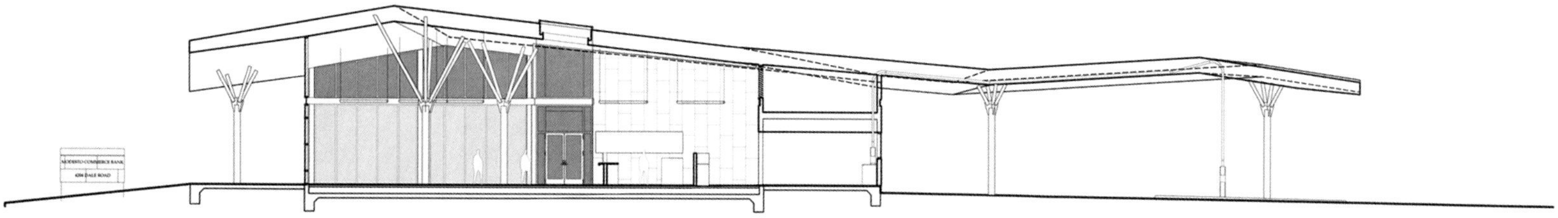

North Section

3

3. Triangular skylights provide daylight for the interior
4. The interior space is supported by a series of tree-like branched columns, both practical and aesthetic

Sparkasse
2

Sparkasse in Hettingen

Location: Heidelberg, Germany
Completion Year: 2007
Designer: Ecker Architekten
Photographer: Constantin Mayer
Area: 100 m²

A new glass banking pavilion for Hettingen signals an investment in the future of the community. This small bank was designed by Ecker Architekten. The main materials of the façade are glass and steel. This project plays well with security, transparency and shades. It looks very clean, simple and straight. With different colours in it, the atmosphere of the bank is not so formal for the clients; they could get the service in a friendly and relaxed space. Meanwhile it has also high-technology to support its function. The modern style of the bank brings a new look in the town.

The transparency of the façade invites bank clienteles while confidently demonstrating state-of-the-art security measures. The modern building contrasts markedly with the surrounding residential zone of traditional houses and gardens. Hand-polished aluminium curtain walls suspend glass panes of 3.7 metres in height. The flat roof edge conceals exterior sun-shades. The timeless, modern appearance extends through the building interiors. A free-standing cabinet wall conceals all of the technical functions of the bank, and gives character to the spaces for customer service and private transactions.

The building is supported by six cruciform columns; lighting, cooling and security monitoring devices are concealed in a plenum above a ceiling of fine aluminium louvres. With this new building, the bank has re-established its presence in this traditional town with a decidedly modern architecture.

1. Consultation area, interior decorations with different colours add a dynamic atmosphere
2. The façade using glass and steel as main materials

3

AUSZAHLUNG
Geldautomat
4

3. Client service area
4. ATM

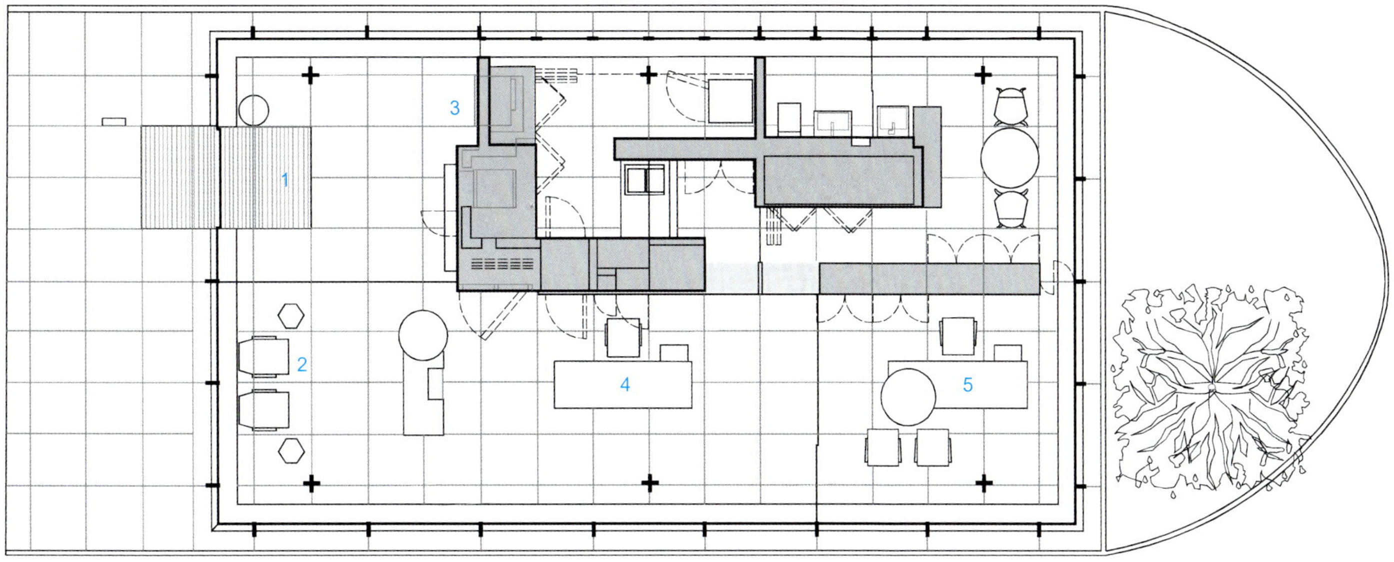
3
1
2
4
5

Ground Floor Plan (Above)
1. Entrance
2. Waiting Area
3. ATM
4. Customer Service
5. Consultation Bureau

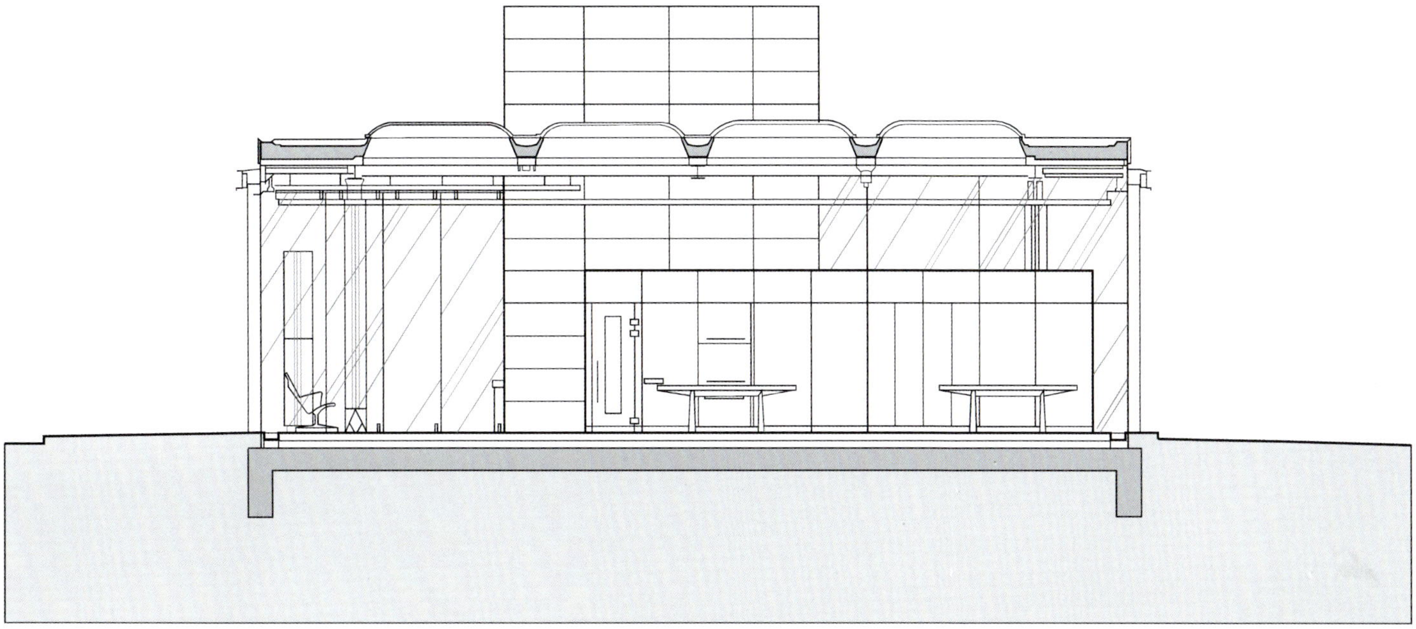

Section

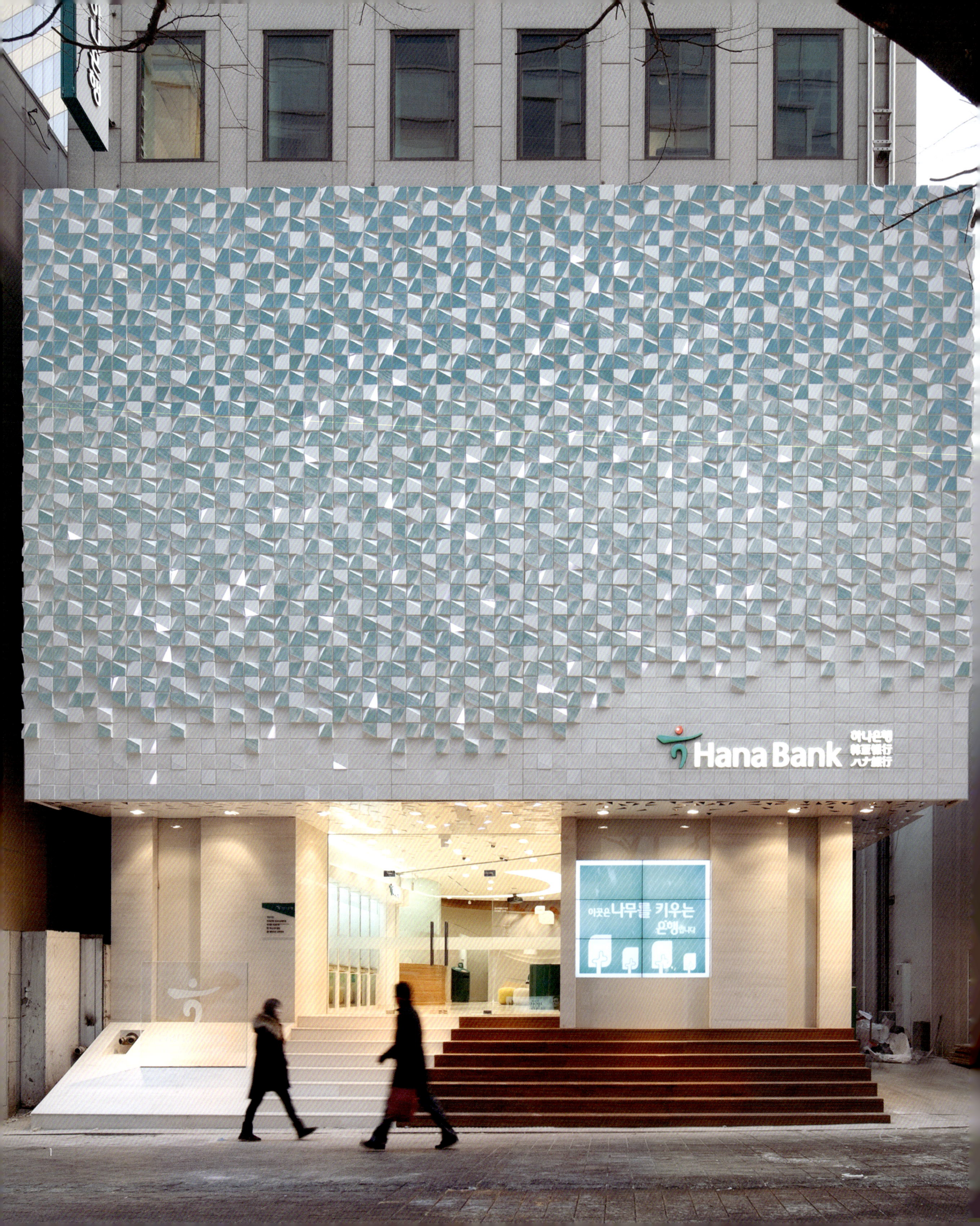
Hana Bank
하나은행
韓亞銀行
ハナ銀行
이곳은 나무를 키우는
은행입니다

4
5
번호표
하나은행
2

Hana Bank - Myeongdong Branch

Location: Seoul, Korea
Completion Year: 2010
Designer: Jay is Working. Co., Ltd.
Photographer: Sun Namgung

Changes in how work is handled at banks have led to changes in bank space, making a shift from a functionality-centred space to a sales and services-centred space. In addition, a bank's space now embodies corporate philosophies and is transforming into a public space to make social contributions.

General branches of Hana Bank adopted an innovative design to become a space focused on sales and services. For the bank's Myeongdong Branch, which is located at the centre of Seoul and where there is a high tourist population, the designers planned to create a flagship branch as an arena for communication. It would embody the bank's philosophical identity and deliver a message of contributing to society, in consideration of its location and symbolic significance. Hana Bank planned to build a flagship branch consisting of three floors based on the concept of a "bank that grows trees". Growing a tree can be likened to growing customers' assets so that they grow in size.

The ground floor is Hana Bank's brand PR hall. Here, a visitor can enjoy a digital experience where he grows a virtual "tree character" as part of environmental protection and donation activities. The ground floor also showcases a cultural space where customers can comfortably rest. Considering that there are many tourists in Myeongdong, a corner where visitors can quickly change money is available on the ground floor, together with an ATM zone. The first floor is where the bank's deposit and withdrawal-related work, as well as loan and foreign exchange-related work is handled. An individual counselling module system was developed to enable private and in-depth counselling. The second floor is a space for VIPs. Its design features the unique Hana Bank VIP pattern. This pattern was also used to create partitions, which serve to divide the space and also decorate the space. In addition, the "VIP identity image wall" was created.

1. Exterior of the entrance
2. Consultation area

3. First floor work area and client rest area
4. First floor conference room
5. First floor lounge

4

5

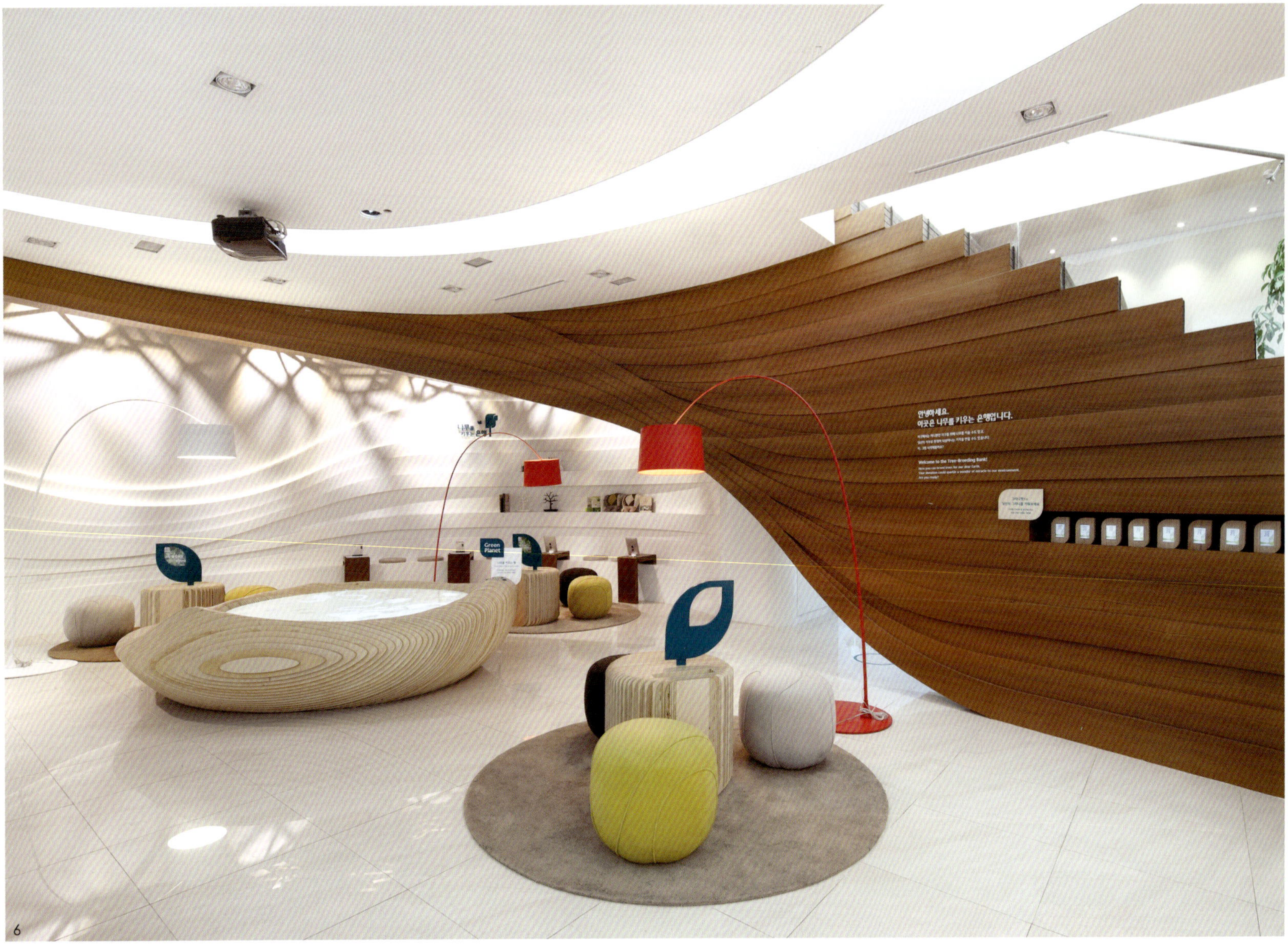
안녕하세요.
이곳은 나무를 키우는 은행입니다.
Welcome to the Tree-Breeding Bank!
Green Planet

6

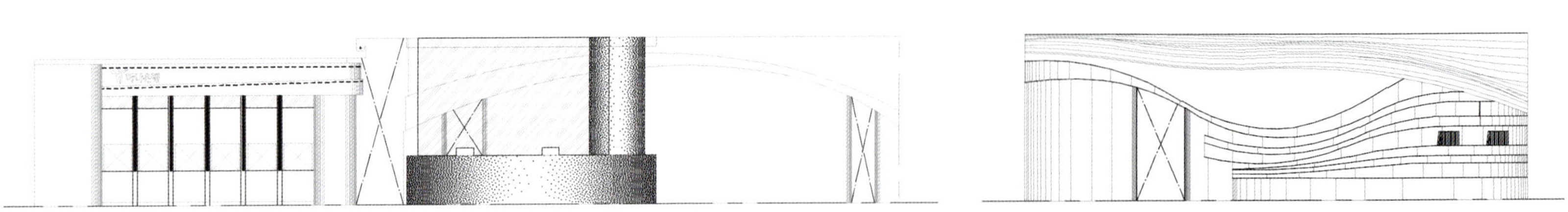

Elevations

Green
Donation
Green
Tree

7

6. Ground floor brand room and lounge, with trees as decoration theme
7. Ground floor detail cut of interactive media wall
8. Second floor VIP club
9. Second floor VIP service area, with VIP patterns on the wall
10. Second floor VIP meeting room

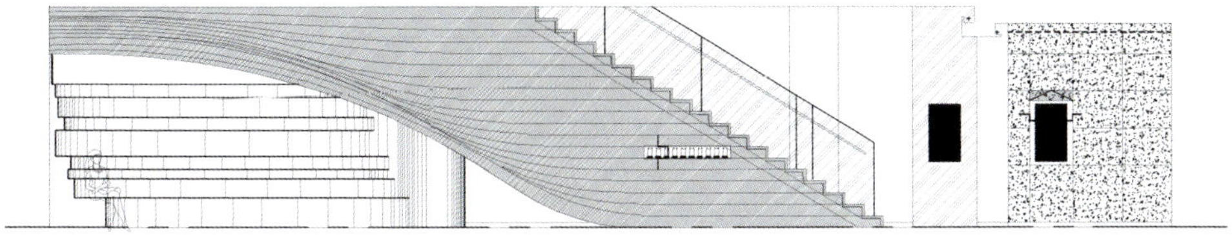

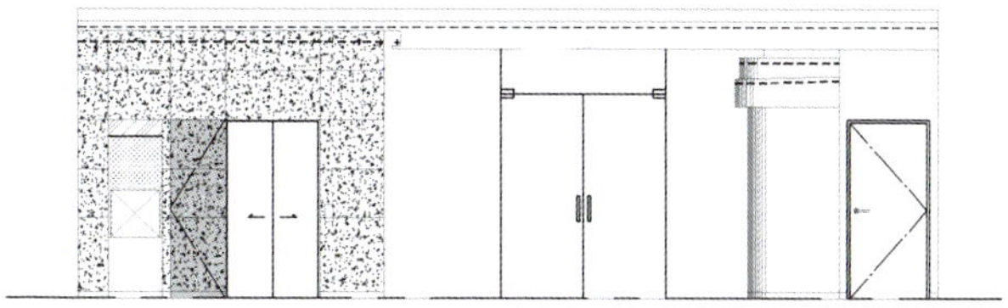

Elevations

8

Ground Floor Plan (Right)
1. Entrance
2. Currency Exchange
3. Media Pond
4. Lounge

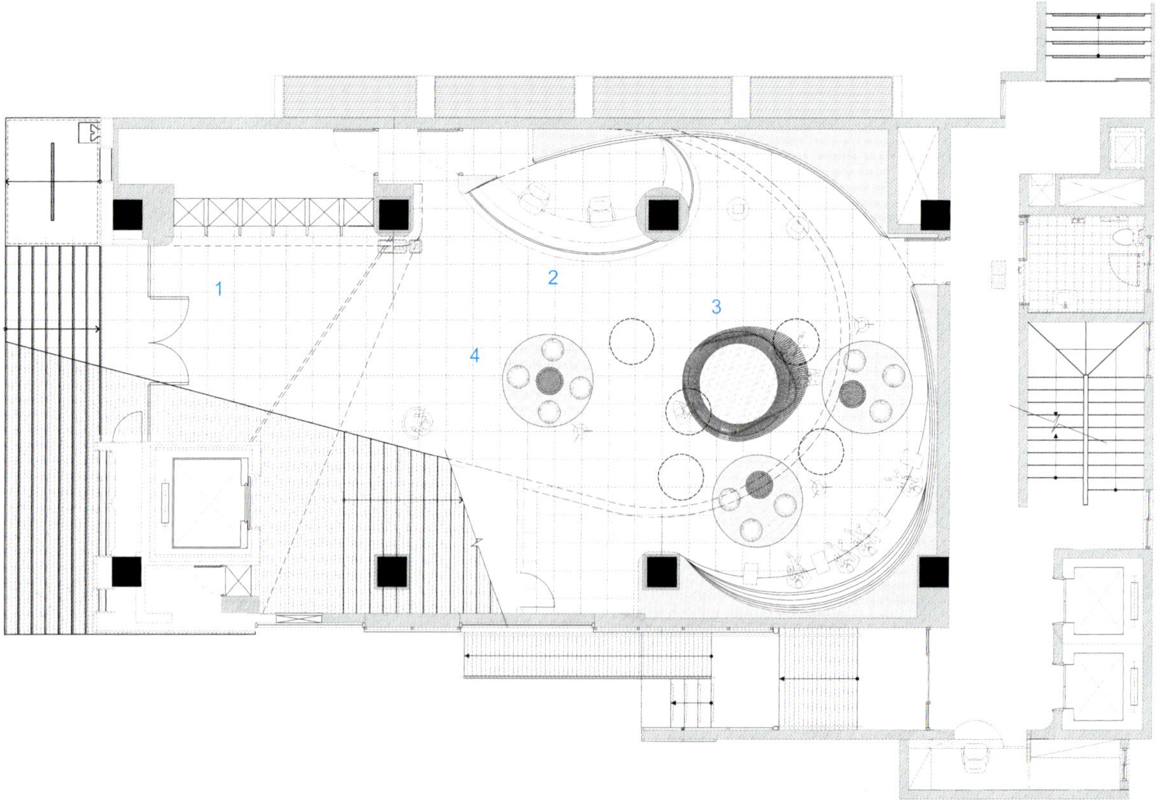
1
2
3
4

Hana VIP Club

9

1

Sugamo Shinkin Bank - Tokiwadai Branch

Location: Tokyo, Japan
Completion Year: 2010
Designer: emmanuelle moureaux architecture+design
Photographer: Nacasa & Partners Inc.
Area: 733 m²

Sugamo Shinkin Bank is a credit union that strives to provide first-rate hospitality to its customers in accordance with its motto: "we take pleasure in serving happy customers." Emmanuelle Moureaux Architecture + Design handled the architectural and interior design for the bank's newly relocated branch in Tokiwadai.

By basing the design around leaf motifs, the designers sought to create a refreshing space that would welcome customers with a natural, rejuvenative feeling. The façade of the building features silhouettes of trees and an assortment of both large and small windows in fourteen different colours arranged in a distinctive, rhythmical pattern that transforms the façade itself into signage.

ATMs and teller windows are located on the ground floor, along with three courtyards and an open space laid out with chairs in fourteen different colours. The first storey houses the loan section, reception rooms, offices and four courtyards, while the second floor is reserved for facilities for staff use, including changing rooms and a cafeteria. Thanks to the seven light-filled courtyards planted with trees and flowering plants, each of these spaces is loosely connected to all the others. A constellation of leaves in twenty-four different colours growing on the white branches of the walls and glass windows overlaps with the natural foliage of the real trees in the courtyards, creating the sensation of being in a magical forest.

1. The façade features large and small windows in fourteen different colours
2. Night view of the exterior

3

4

Ground Floor Plan
1. ATM
2. Office
3. Counter
4. Garden
5. Meeting Space
6. Open Space
7. Entrance Hall
8. Safe-deposit Box

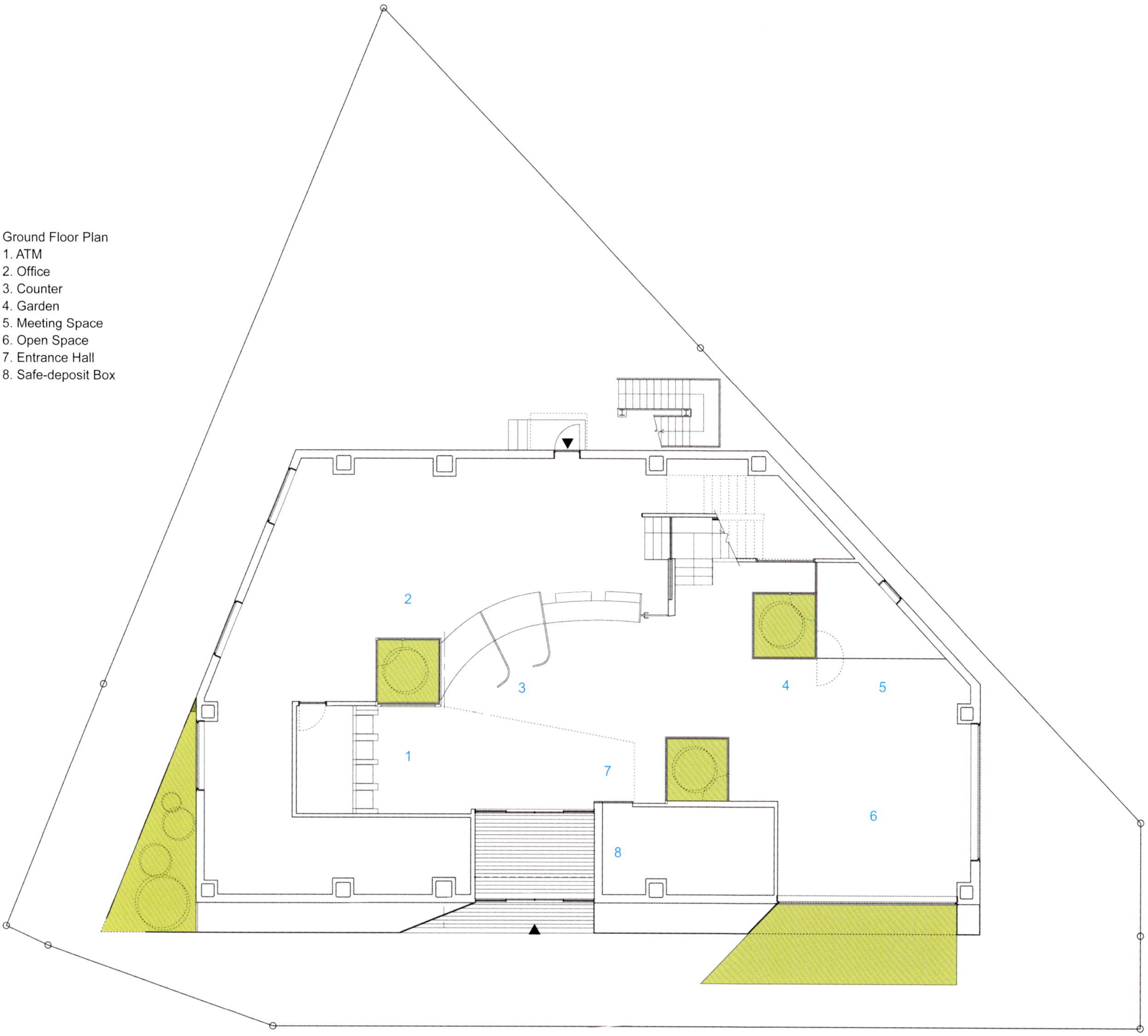

2
3
4
5
1
7
6
8

3. Entrance hall and ATM
4. Service counter, the leaves on the walls and tables create a fresh space
5. Meeting room
6. The first floor with green plants
7. Client waiting area, plants concept is everywhere in the interior design
8. Natural foliage of the real trees in the courtyards are combined with leaves on the window, creating the sensation of being in a magical forest

7

8

24 Hour Banking
VISA
NAPS
بنك بروة
BARWA BANK
Al Meera
TOYOTA

1

2

Barwa Bank

Location: Doha, Qatar
Completion Year: 2011
Designer: Crea International
Photographer: Jaber Al Azmeh
Area: 235 m²

The Barwa Bank branch design concept has been one of the most challenging projects that Crea International has ever developed: designing the most progressive Islamic bank of the future, showcasing either modernity and coolness strongly rooted with the tradition of the country was the brief assigned by the client. The objective was to propose an environment aimed to customers more and more familiar with most innovative technologies, a bank where people would feel comfortable and welcome.

Crea International team approached the project in a very logical and structured way: in the first place, they look into the history and traditions of the country to get familiar with the components Qatari people felt very belonging to their culture and were proud of. They also analysed throughout the mission of Barwa Bank and the values it stands for, and finally they looked at the banking models both in Western and Middle East countries to build a strong point of difference and a gap with the current models.

To ensure real distinctiveness versus such current banking models and to build the most innovative bank, Crea International designed a new service standard: only a central banking area hosting multifunctional comfortable workstations where the bank assistant can seat close or in front of the client looking together at touch screen table, where all banking functions can be performed with total transparency and almost paperless.

The final result is a delicate balance between tangibility, simplicity, intuitive space fruition of the service model together with the warm but still precious environment and design that characterises the banking space. The final result is feasible either from the quality of design and the kind of service experience which are perceived as a fully integrated experience driven by the unique Physical Brand Design projectual methodology.

1. ATM with delicate shape
2. Exterior

BARWA BANK
3

4

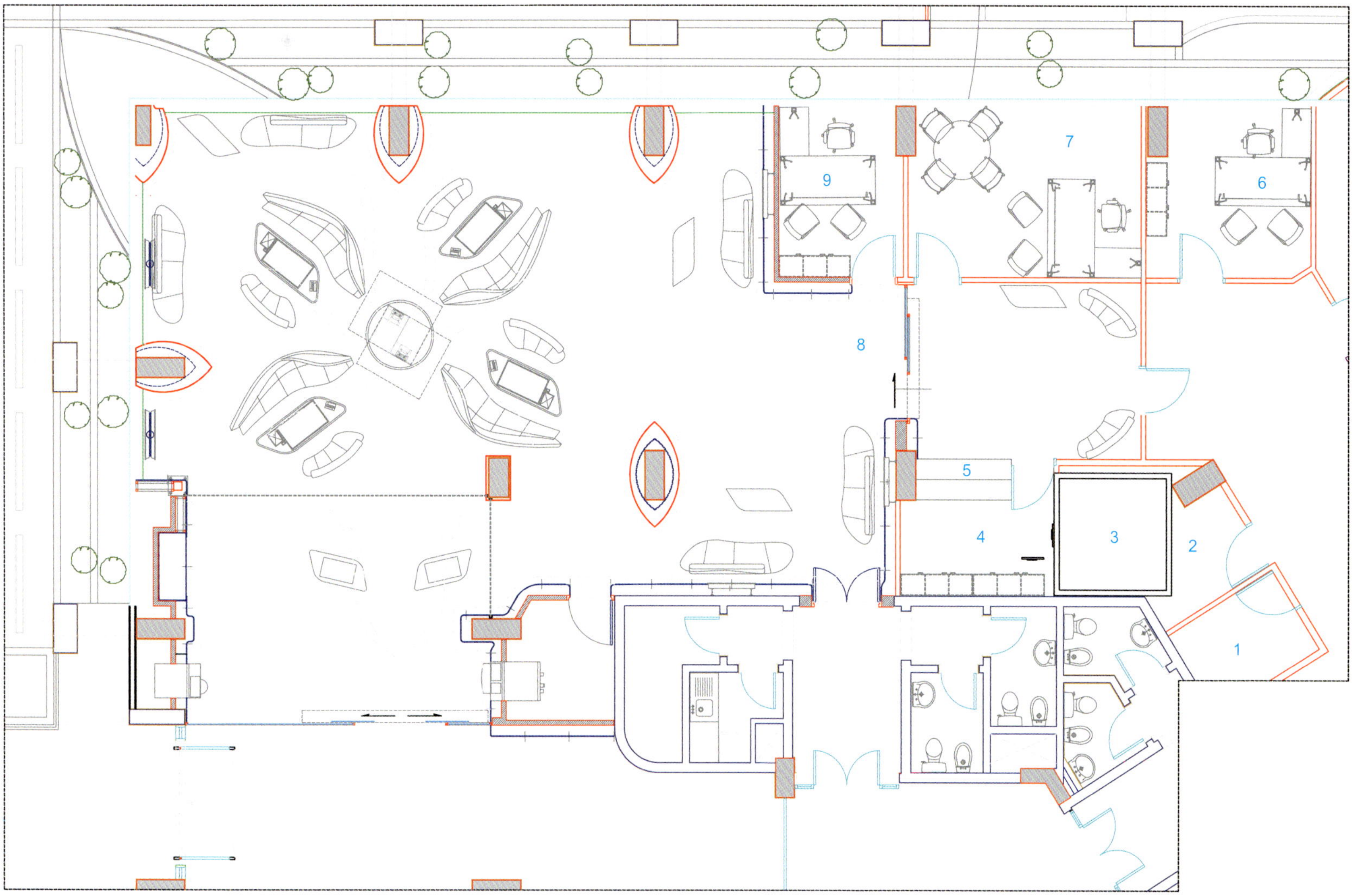
9
7
6
8
5
4
3
2
1

Ground Floor Plan (Above)
1. Check Printer Room
2. Server Room
3. Vault Room
4. Cash Room
5. Counter
6. AVP Finance Phase
7. Branch Manager Office
8. Sliding Door
9. Supervisor

3. Consultation area
4. Lounge, the colour of the seats and lighting create a warm service environment

BARWA BANK
5

5. Seats and beautiful lines on the ceiling create an elegant bank space
6. Muli-functional service desks, with which the staff can provide customers with full-scale services

RAIFFEISEN

2

Raiffeisen Bank

Location: Zurich, Switzerland
Completion Year: 2008
Designer: NAU Architecture
Photographer: Jan Bitter
Area: 300 m²

Raiffeisen's flagship branch on Zurich's Kreuzplatz dissolves traditional barriers between customers and employees, creating a new type of "open bank", a space of encounter. Advanced technologies make banking infrastructure largely invisible: employees access terminals concealed in furniture elements, while a robotic retrieval system grants 24-hour access to safety deposit boxes. This shifts the bank's role into becoming a light-filled, inviting environment - an open lounge where customers can learn about new products and services.

This lounge feels more like a high-end retail environment than a traditional bank interior. Conversations can start spontaneously around a touch screen equipped info-table and transition to meeting rooms for more private discussions. The info-table not only displays figures from world markets in realtime, but can be used to interactively discover the history of Hottingen, or just check the latest sports scores.

Elegantly flowing walls blend the different areas of the bank into one smooth continuum, spanning from the customer reception at the front, to employee workstations oriented to the courtyard. The plan carefully controls views to create different grades of privacy and to maximise daylight throughout. The walls themselves act as a membrane mediating between the open public spaces and intimately scaled conference rooms. Portraits of the quarter's most prominent past residents like Böklin, Semper or Sypri grace the walls, their abstracted images milled into Hi-macs using advanced digital production techniques. While intricately decorative, the design ground the bank in the area's cultural past, while looking clearly towards the future.

1. Exterior
2. Lobby and reception, with portraits of the local celebrities
3. Meeting room
4. Office space, the shape of the lighting fixtures will enliven the space

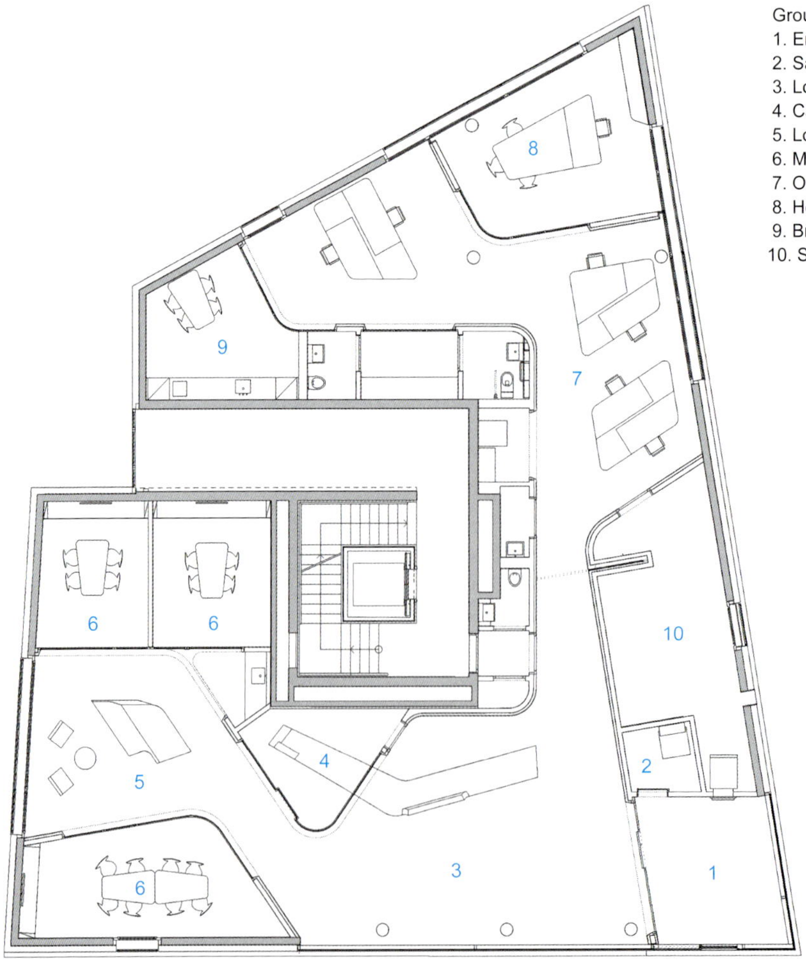

8
9
7
6
6
10
4
5
2
3
1
6

Ground Floor Plan (Left)

1. Entrance / ATM
2. Safety Deposit Access
3. Lobby / Reception
4. Cash Desk
5. Lounge / Info-table
6. Meeting Room
7. Offices
8. Head Office
9. Break Room
10. Secure Zone

BRINKS

National Bank of Greece

Location: Thessaloniki, Greece
Completion Year: 2008
Designer: Petra Consultants Architects Ltd
Photographer: Nikos Gkortsios
Area: 5,303 m²

This project is the regeneration of the preserved National Bank of Greece building, located in Thessaloniki. Due to old age and previous bad use, the main space as well as the skylight/dome had to be redesigned. This helped transforming the building into a modern bank equipped with high security systems and a functional interior.

The 1930s' building designed by architect Aristomenis Valvis was a historic landmark for the city of Thessaloniki in Greece. The building has five storeys with the central space featuring grand double arches that expand to the whole height of the building, supporting a dome with light metal profiles filled with very thin (and thus transparent) alabaster plates. Built featuring neoclassical elements as well as state-of-the-art engineering (for that time) such as piling systems and Zoellner slabs for lightening the construction, the building was in need of urgent restoration at the end of the 20th century.

The regeneration process began in 2000 with the gentrification of the old elements such as columns, staircases, floors and ceiling finishes with beautiful ornaments as well as new electromechanical installations in addition to redesigning of the whole second floor as well as the new office spaces.

With respect to the history of the building and working with sparse original drawings and representation of the initial structure, the new additions such as the meeting room, lifts false ceilings and the addition of the impressive transparent new roof protecting the 70-year-old dome, are of contemporary nature that blend in with the rest of the interior.

1. The interior design features Neo-classicism
2. Exterior

3

3. Rest area in the corridor
4. Meeting room

Front Elevation

4

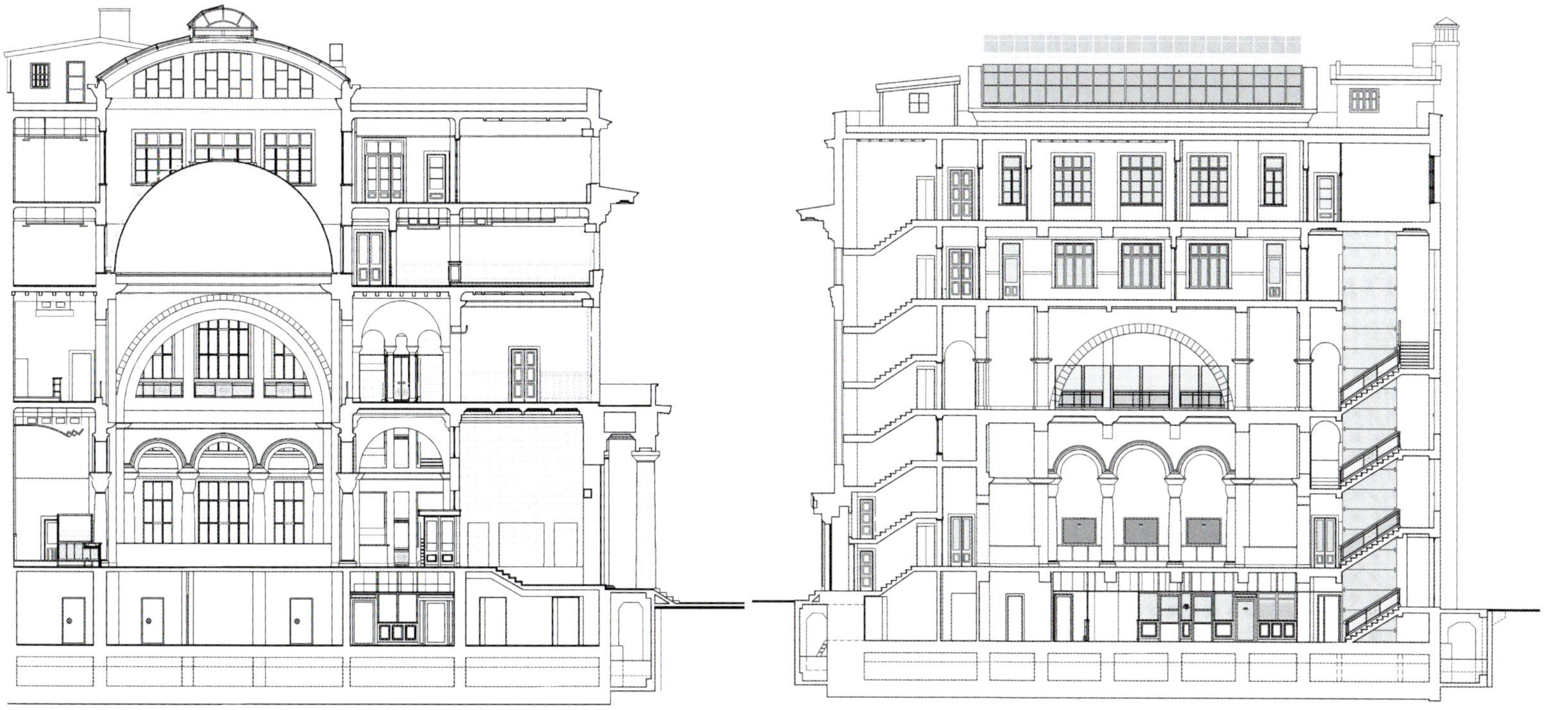

Sections

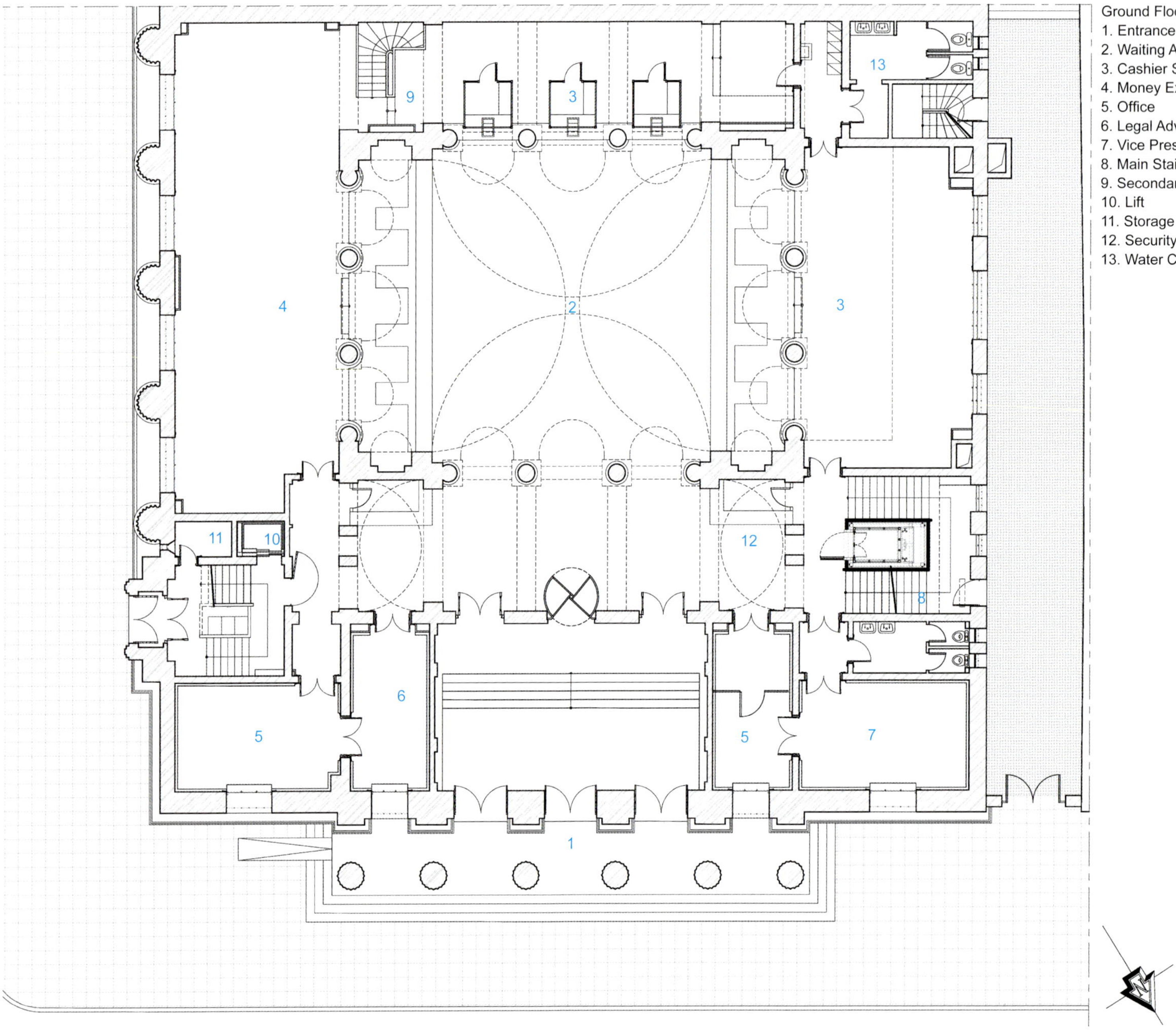

9
3
13
4
2
3
11
10
12
8
6
5
5
7
1

Ground Floor Plan
1. Entrance
2. Waiting Area
3. Cashier Space
4. Money Exchange Space
5. Office
6. Legal Advisors' Office
7. Vice President's Office
8. Main Staircase
9. Secondary Staircase
10. Lift
11. Storage
12. Security Booth
13. Water Closet

5. Advisory space
6. Office space

5

6

ATM
応接
室 1
1

2

Sugamo Shinkin Bank - Niiza Branch

Location: Saitama, Japan
Completion Year: 2009
Designer: emmanuelle moureaux architecture+design
Photographer: Hidehiko Nagaishi
Area: 421 m²

1. Lobby and ATMs
2. Squares of 24 colours form the bank's logo

This project sought to create a whole new look that refreshes the current image of this financial institution. For Sugamo Shinkin Bank's new 43rd branch, the designers redesigned not only the interior, but also Sugamo's brand image, including its façade, logo graphics, signage and brochures.

The key concept revolves around squares - besides incorporating square shapes, the building was conceived as a sort of public square where people gather. The colours of these squares play an important role: the logo on the façade of the building features as many as 24 colours visible from the main street, becoming a symbol for the area. These colours welcome customers as they enter the building, continuing on the inside and serving as natural dividers between the lobby, meeting spaces, ATMs and so on.

← 貸金庫
3

4

貸金庫

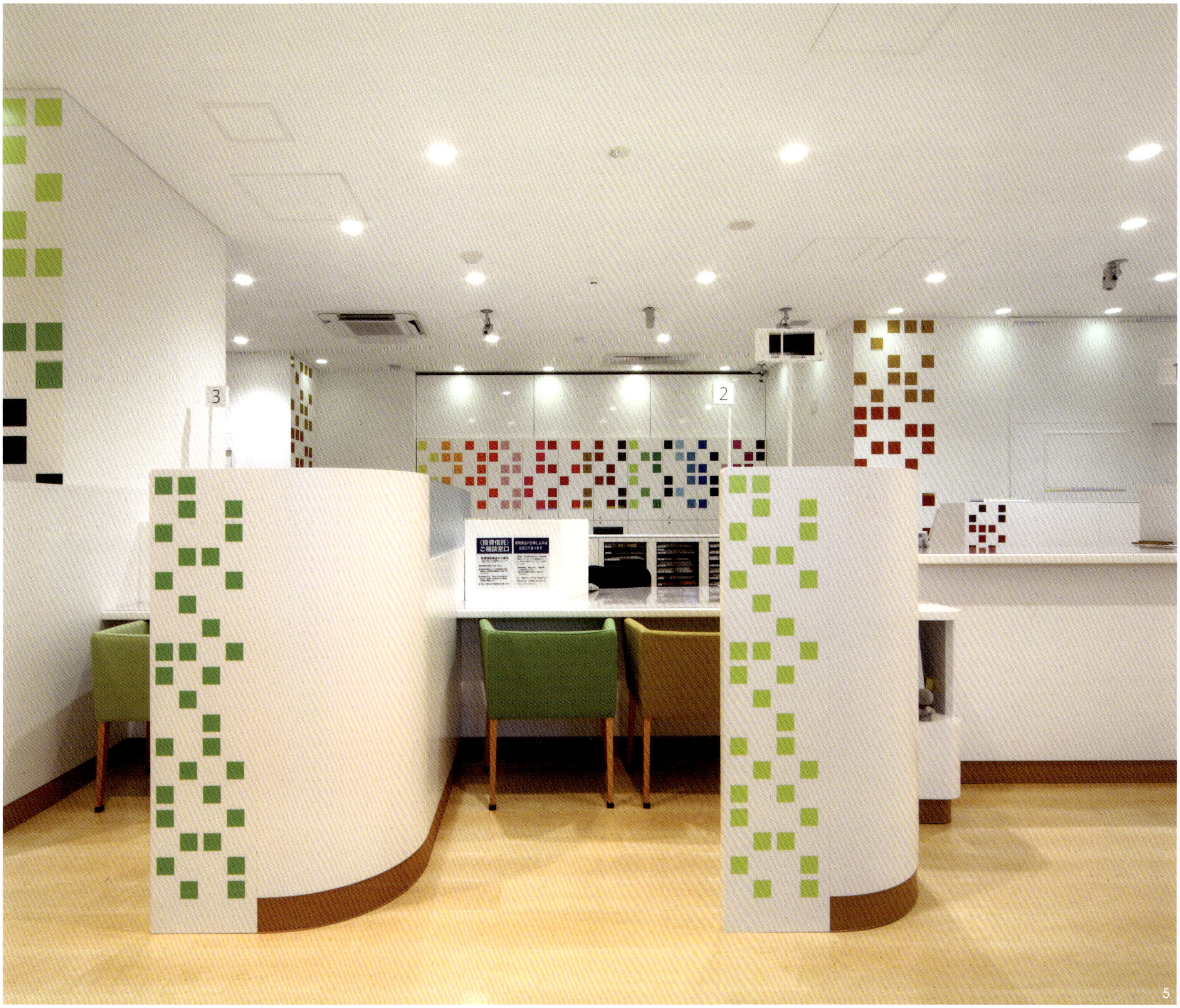
3
2
5

3. Service counter
4. Lounge, different areas feature squares of different colours
5. Counter zone

SOUND
COMMUNITY BANK
SOUND COMMUNITY BANK

1

2

SOUND COMMUNITY BANK
110

3

Sound Community Bank - Port Angeles

Location: Port Angeles, USA
Completion Year: 2010
Designer: Spore Architecture
Photographer: Aaron Kang-Crosby
Area: 325 m²

Port Angeles, Washington is a historic, coastal town with a rich past in the fishing and forest industries. The built surroundings reflect this lifestyle, and while there was appreciation and respect for the quaint, old-world charm of the downtown core, both the client and architects felt it was time to give this sleepy little community a needed boost toward the future.

The designers' first challenge was that they were re-using an existing foundation from the previously demolished building, which was a derelict, decaying fast food restaurant. The upshot, however, was not only cost saving but a footprint that offered a workable size and open layout needed to accommodate the new building programme. With "re-use and recycle" a mantra of Spore Architecture and Sound Community Bank, much of the restaurant demolition went somewhere besides the landfill. Homes were found for virtually everything: cooking equipments, furniture, doors & windows, lumber, even HVAC units.

Working closely with the bank's president and upper management, this project became an opportunity to update and redefine the company's image, giving them a signature branch with a fresh, modern experience. The client had fun, and the architects felt fortunate that they were able to look past many of the old-fashioned concepts of ultra-disciplined bank design. Throughout the process, there was encouragement to explore unconventional solutions, thereby, reshaping the customer experience into a comfortable, welcoming, and even at times, whimsical environment. The designers at Spore were also involved in the landscape design and concept of native plant selection, as well as working with Northwest artisans such as renowned steel artist Barry Harem.

1. Overall view of the exterior
2. The doors, windows and wood are recycled from the original building, saving the cost
3. Foyer and rest area

Is your Free Checking not so free anymore?

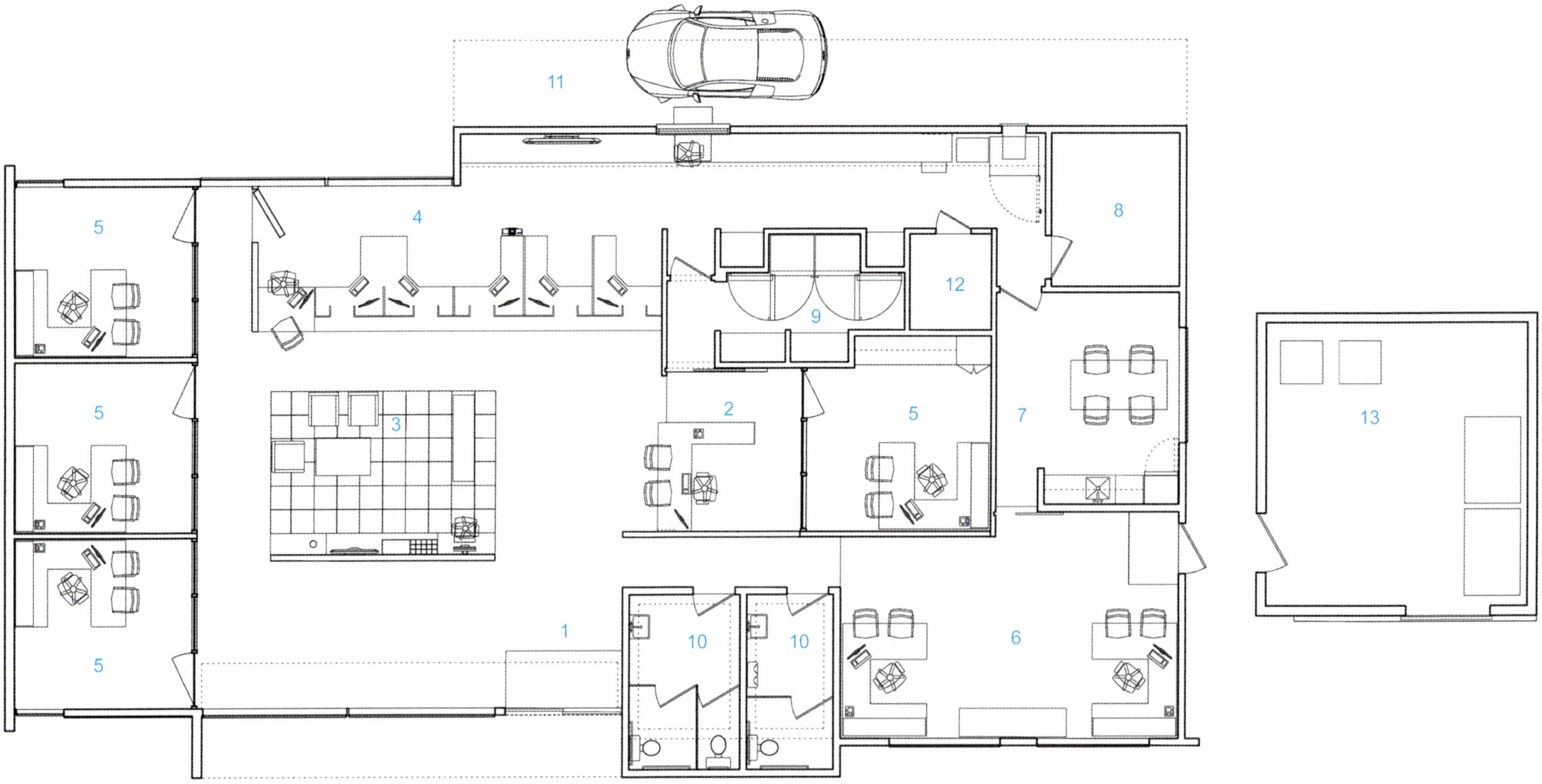
11
5
4
8
12
9
5
3
2
5
7
13
5
1
10
10
6

FDIC

4. General view of lounge and counter zone
5. Office space, the interior furniture also takes the principle of recycle

Ground Floor Plan (Facing Below)
1. Entry
2. Reception
3. Lobby
4. Teller Area
5. Office
6. Loan Office
7. Staff Room
8. Storage
9. Vaults
10. Restroom
11. Drive-thru
12. Service
13. Mechanical / Waste

5
6
4
3
하나은행
2

1

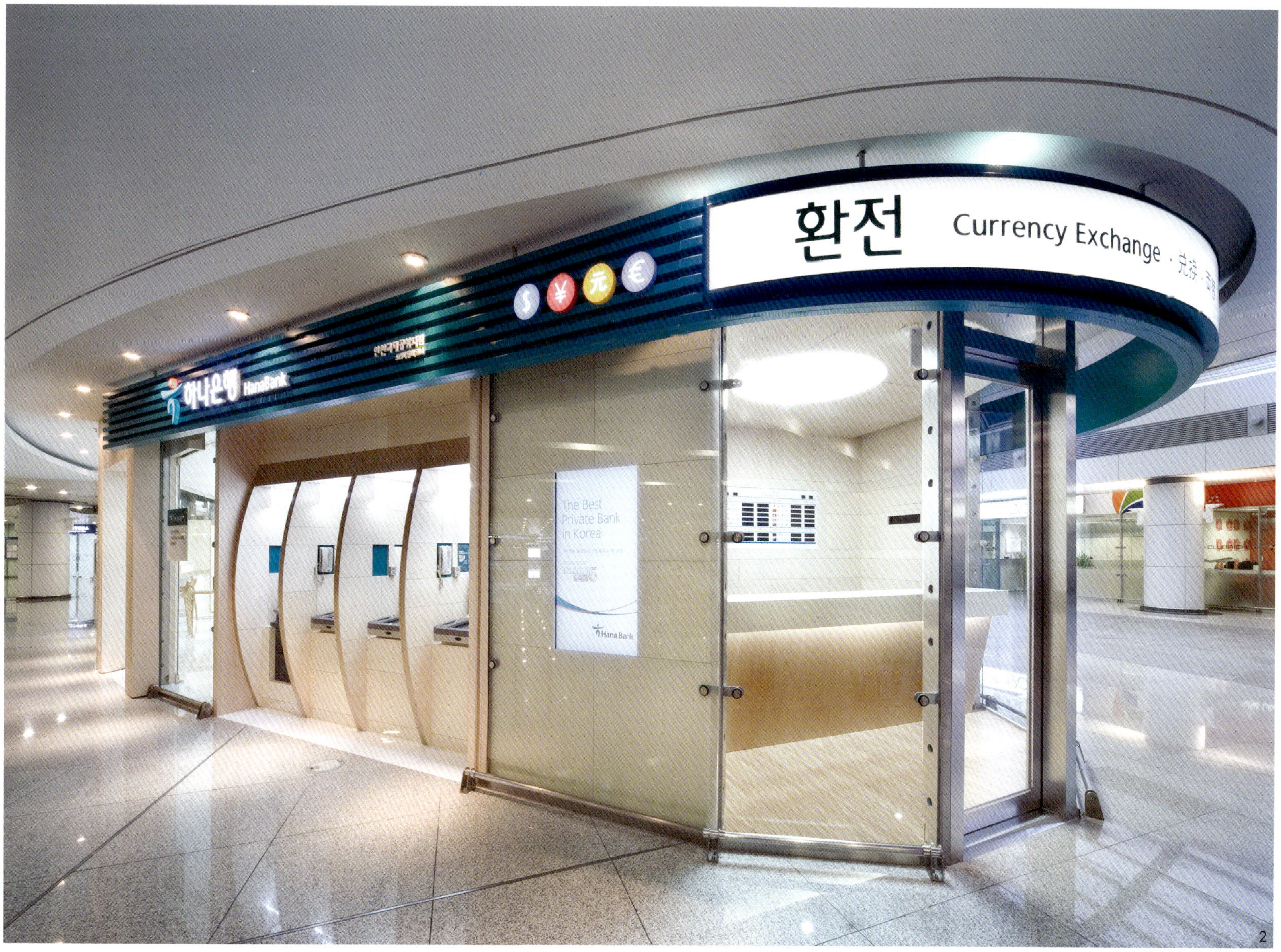
환전
Currency Exchange
하나은행
HanaBank
The Best
Private Bank
in Korea
Hana Bank

2

Hana Bank Incheon Airport Branch

Location: Incheon, Korea
Completion Year: 2009
Designer: Soon Gak Jang, Hye Jin Choi, Young Ji Suh (Jay is Working.Co., Ltd.)
Photographer: Sun Namgung

In-store branch design that used formative form of square box at Hana Bank in Home Plus was basic form; this project is more experimental and an applied plan of creative form. It can be said that this project keeps the basic design methodology - "the space in the space, divide the space by the space", and it is a flagship model which can confirm that transformation and mixture of them create another unified space image. This bank has the new theme, "Bank in the Airport". Bank in the airport that foreigners meet first is an important space that shows the first public image of the bank prior to basic service. It would be approached by foreigner's viewpoint rather than native's viewpoint, and would be the space that emphasises lounge function in the huge airport than immediate service. Existing method that entered by the lead of two dimensional signages has changed to raise absorption force and arouse active curiosity by opening the inside through the ceiling.

Entered the inside, combination of cylinder counsel module is arranged rhythmically, and made a group of design, and images of circle got settle with green plants that represent relaxation spaces. It is a symbol that shows eco-friendly design, "Space to Green" of Hana Bank, and offers intimacy and organic energy in the hard bank space.

The central circle form would raise the power of concentration in the counsel, and is conceived as playing an important role in communicating with the bank and the client. Also, the combination of them would form the flow in the whole spaces, showing the extension of sight and dynamic, not stopped space.

1. The central rounded table and chairs and opening on the ceiling promote the concentration of advisory
2. Exterior
3. Counter zone, the rounded partitions enforce the dynamism of the space

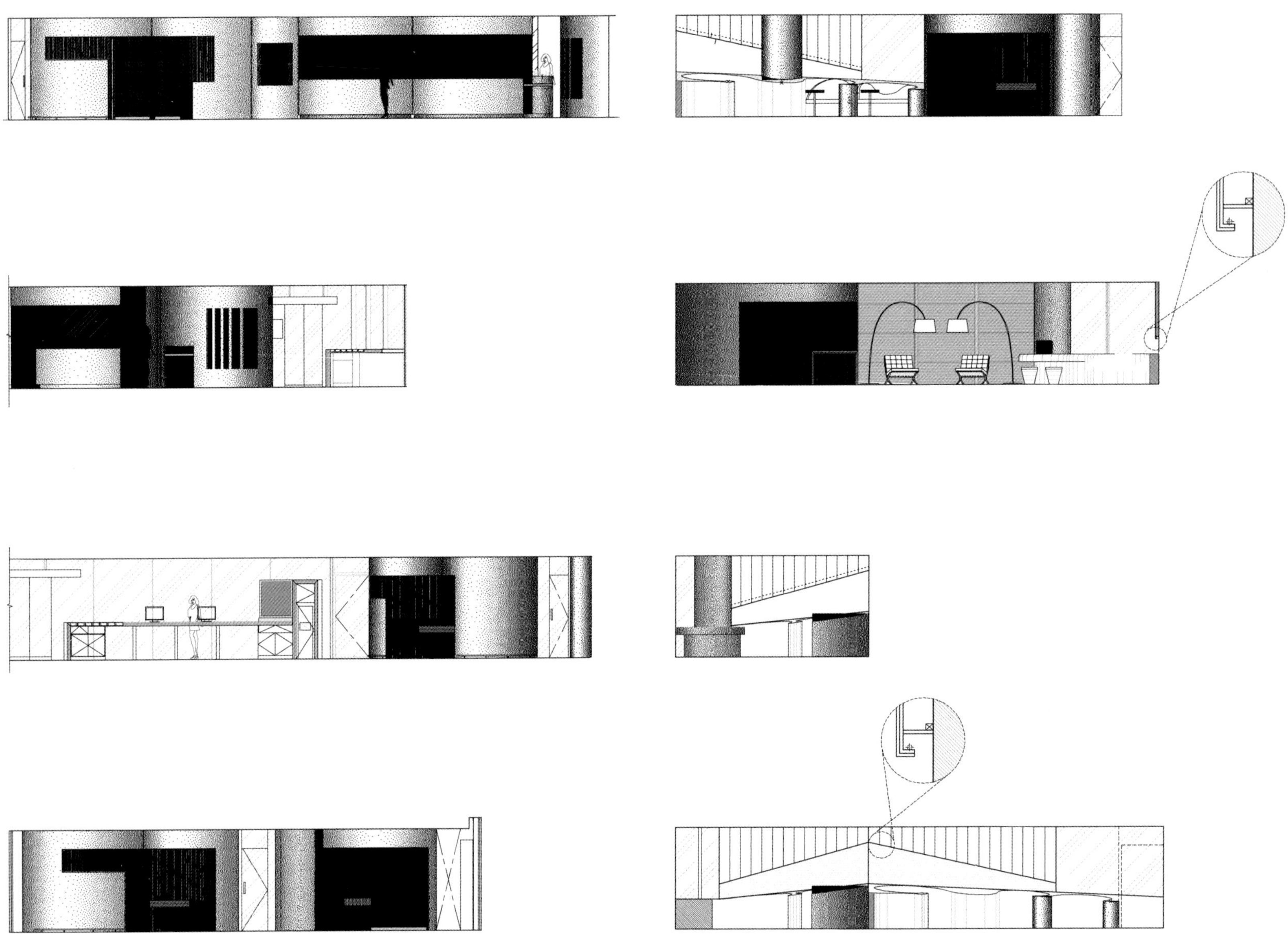

Ground Floor Plan (Facing Below)
1. Main Entrance
2. Exit
3. VIP Entrance
4. Main Hall & Waiting Area
5. Transaction Counter
6. VIP Private Lounge Booth

하나은행
2
1
3

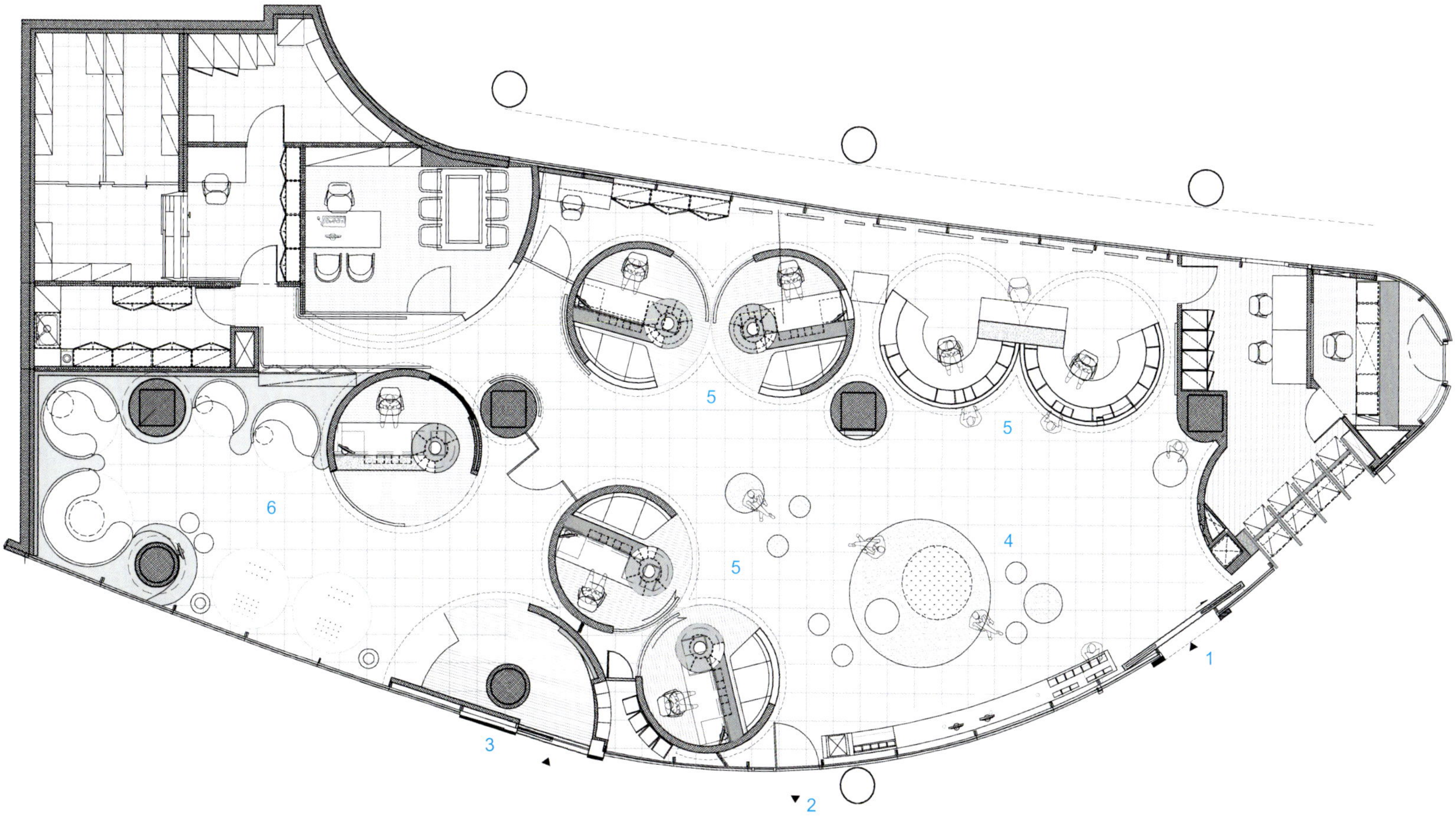
5
5
6
4
5
1
3
2

Hana
vip
Bank
4

5

5

6

7

4. VIP lounge
5. VIP private lounge, the rounded design creates privacy for the space
6. Rounded partitions in the advisory zone
7. Advisory zone details

2

Aktienbank Augsburg

Location: Augsburg, Germany
Completion Year: 2009
Designer: OTT Architekten
Photographer: Eckhart Matthäus
Area: 4,100 m²

The days of bullet-proof glass and security gates in banks are a thing of the past. Following the renovation of their building in Halderstraße, the Augsburger Aktionsbank now greets its customers with a refined openness and transparency. Through the redesign of the customer reception area into a visitor and consultation centre, the bank makes a concious step towards even more service and customer contact. The intention of the bank management was to create an individual and significant interior space, a point of particular importance in the implementation of the design concept.

With its dynamic curve, the central wall leads the customers from the main entrance of the bank past the service and reception desk into the heart of the circular customer service centre with visitor lounge area. Integrated into the curved wall are eight soundproofed glass consultation cubes for confidential conversations with bank customers. Behind these cubes, the newly designed broker centre in the back office areas can be found.

A new mezzanine level inside the two-storey service centre contains additional office space and break areas. Accessible for employees by a delicate glass bridge, the mezzanine provides a stunning view of the service centre below. A previously unused flat roof above was transformed into a generous bamboo garden with a wooden deck.

The demands of workmanship of the highest quality in conjunction with detailed and experimental solutions presented the planners and tradesmen with far from everyday challenges, as did the carrying out of the renovations alongside the continued operations of the bank.

1. A curved wall leads the clients from the main entrance into the customer service centre
2. Perspective of visitor lounge

3

3. Eight soundproofed glass cubes for confidential conversations with customers are arranged around the customer service centre
4. Consultation space inside a glass cube
5. Mezzanine space
6. Transparent office space in the mezzanine

Section showing mezzanine, visitor lounge and consultation areas

4

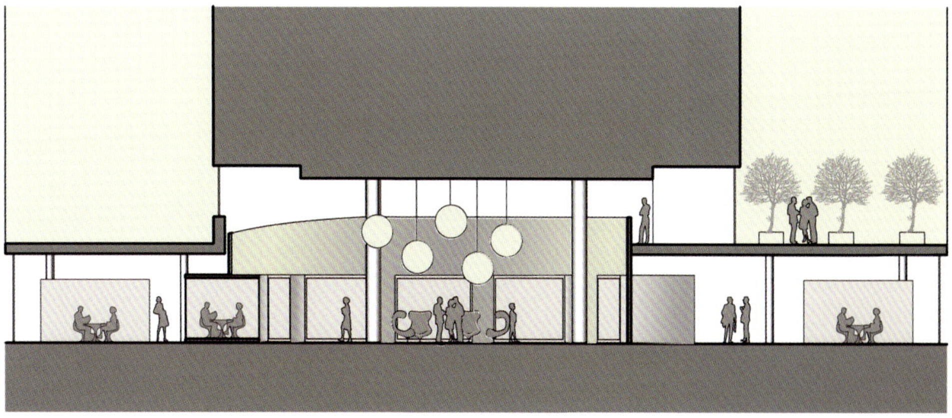

Section through visitor lounge and consultation area, with bamboo roof garden

5

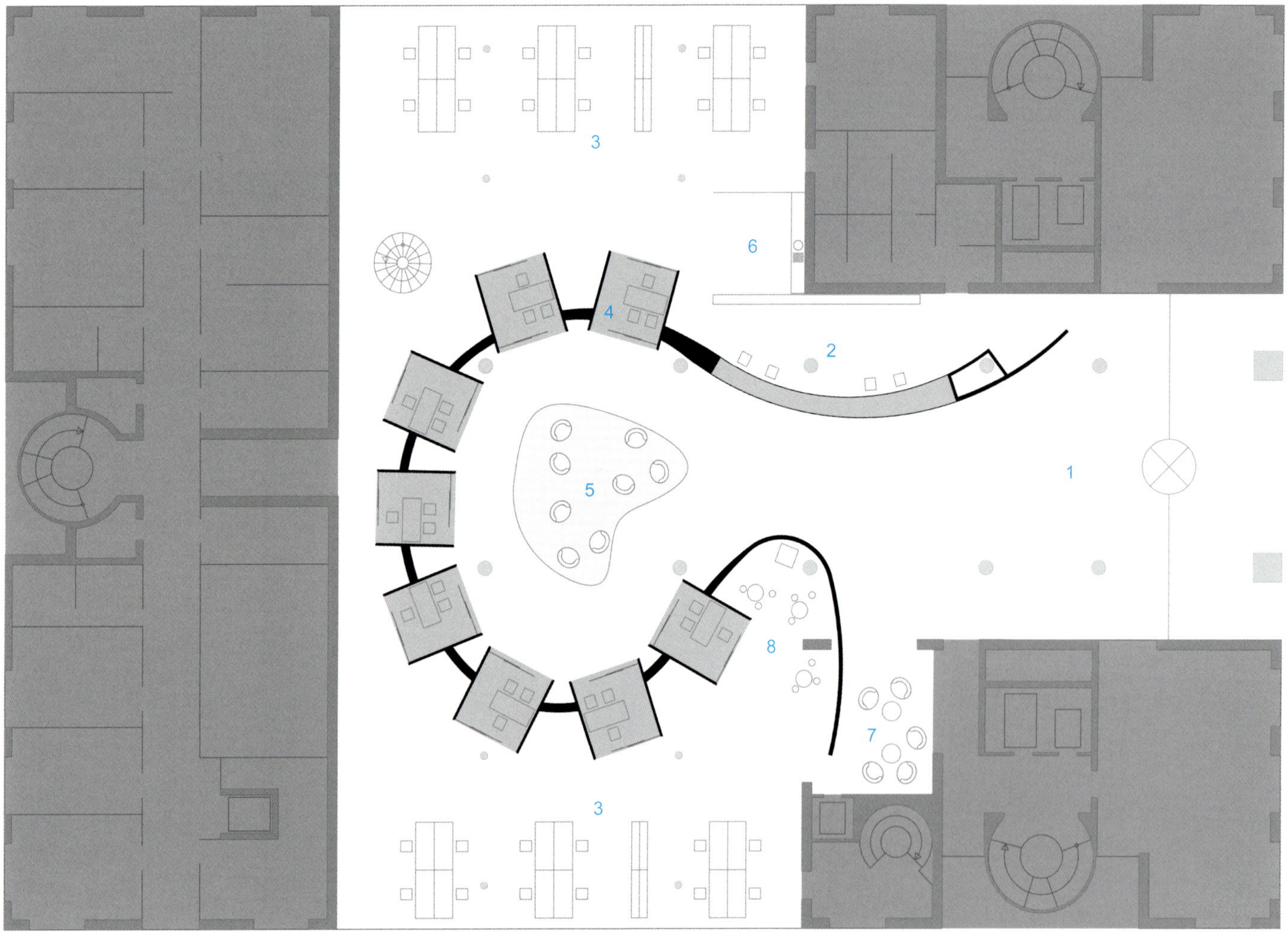
3
6
4
2
5
1
8
7
3

Ground Floor Plan (Left)
1. Entrance
2. Reception
3. Broker Centre
4. Consulting Cubes
5. Visitor Lounge
6. Tea Kitchen
7. VIP Lounge
8. Kids Area

6

64
44
33

2

One Shelley Street

Location: Sydney, Australia
Completion Year: 2009
Designer: Clive Wilkinson Architects
Photographer: Shannon McGrath
Area: 30,658 m²

One Shelley Street is an effort to reframe the requirements and performance of the 21st century office. On behalf of the Macquarie Group and working with Woods Bagot as executive architect, Clive Wilkinson Architects implemented a radical, large-scale workplace design that leverages mobility, transparency, multiple tailor-made work settings, destination work plazas, follow-me technology, and carbon neutral systems. The result is part space station, part cathedral, and part vertical Greek village.

Numerous work zones surround the atrium, designed to house 100 employees each in adaptable neighbourhoods. An arterial staircase links the zones forming a "Meeting Tree", emblematic of the interconnectedness of Macquarie's client relationships. The Main Street on level 1 offers communal spaces that are highly conducive to corporate and philanthropic events and includes a café and dining areas. Within the office floors "Plazas" were modelled after collaboration typologies – the dining room, garden, Tree House, playroom, and coffee house, where cross-pollination among business groups is encouraged through spontaneous encounters.

One Shelley Street has been designed to the highest levels of green star or LEED efficiency, using revolutionary technologies like harbour water cooling, chilled beams and zone controlled lighting. Overall energy consumption has been reduced by 50%. The interior staircase, linking the various neighbourhoods, has reduced the use of the elevators by 50%. There has been a 78% reduction in paper storage needs and a 53% reduction in printing paper. Mail is scanned and distributed electronically, decreasing the need for storage. Employees have lockers in which to store personal addenda, and are deterred from creating paper waste, so there's not a trash can in sight. Macquarie is providing an unmatched quality of life for its employees - benefiting clients, investors, shareholders and the environment.

Although activity-based work environments are not yet the norm, the acceptance level among Macquarie employees has soared beyond initial anticipation. Nearly 55% change their workspaces each day, and 77% are in favour of the freedom to do so. There has been an abandonment of stale business practices that are traditionally incubators of complacency. One Shelley Street is positioned to be a trail-blazer for the new global sustainable office building.

1. Atrium pods
2. "Tree House" office space on the fifth floor

3. Library, with semi-transparent glass to create a semi-open space
4. Business lounge, simple partitions create spaces of different sizes
5. Leisure plaza on the third floor, specially designed overhangs both create segmentations and fun
6. Library office, a separate space in the form of a stack of books
7. Café on the sixth floor

Ground Floor Plan (Facing Below)
1. Lift
2. Escalators
3. Business Lounge
4. Catering Kitchen
5. "Engine Room" (Mail Room)
6. One Desk (Concierge/IT Desk)
7. MCR
8. Multi-Purpose Room
9. Employee Entrance
10. Video Conference Room
11. ABW Work Neighbourhood
12. The Street
13. Café
14. Kitchen
15. FCR
16. "The Square"
17. Lift Lobby
18. Reception
19. Training Rooms
20. Client Transaction Area

4

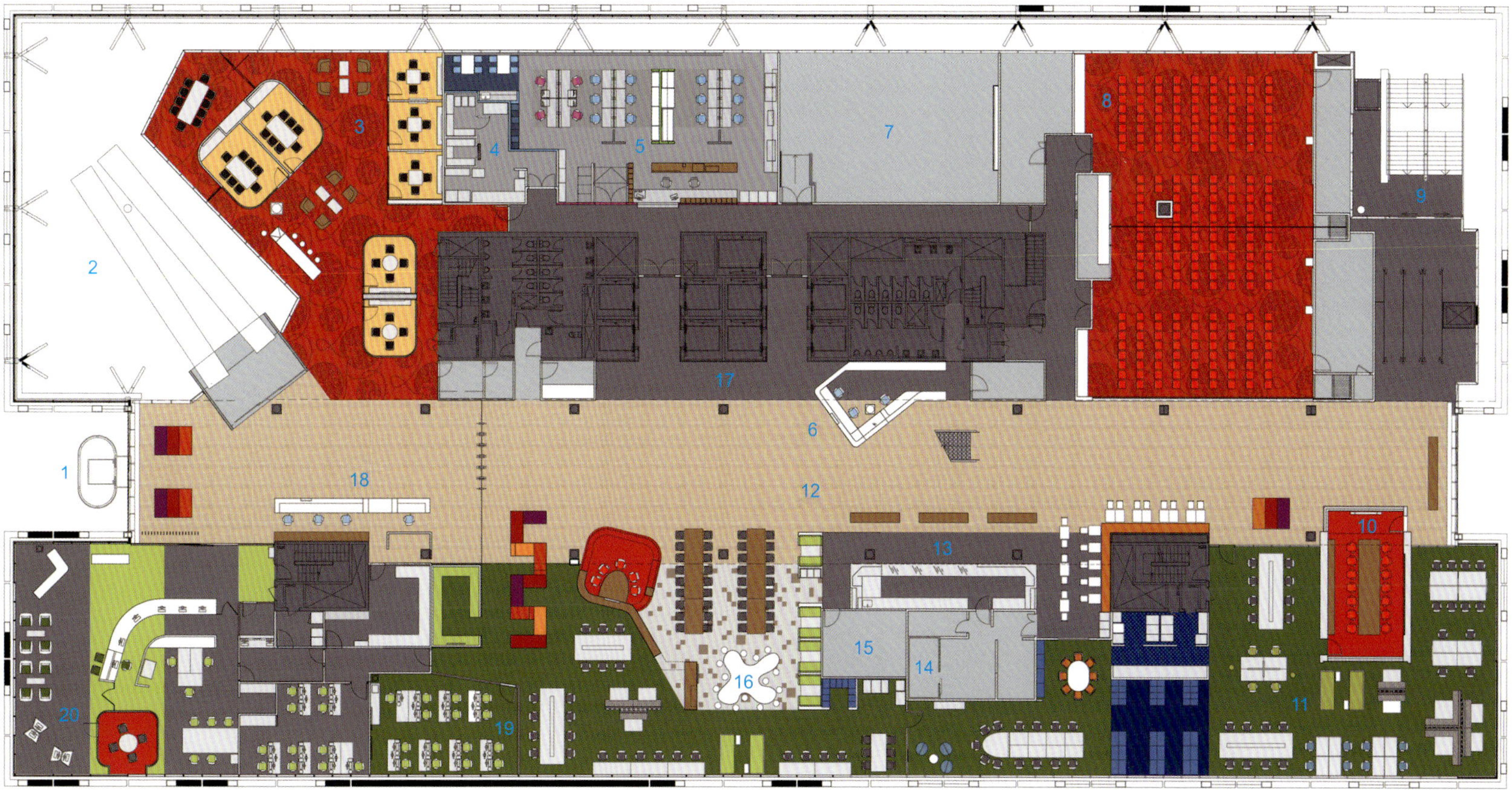
1
2
3
4
5
6
7
8
9
10
11
12
13
14
15
16
17
18
19
20

5

6

7

Fai da te !
Fai da te !
1

CheBanca!

2

CheBanca!

Location: Milan, Italy
Completion Year: 2008
Designer: Crea International
Photographer: Beppe Raso
Area: 150 m²

Crea International has designed the new and surprising retail format for the Mediobanca Group, CheBanca! a multichannel distribution model based on website, customer service and new generation light branches. The design of the new branches emphasises the consultancy, self-transaction and self-education activities, bringing the consumer at the centre of the process.

The yellow colour that permeates the environment reminds of the sunshine light; the aniline treated wood suggests a straight forward approach, and the methacrylic material printed with the honeycomb texture casts a friendly atmosphere.According to Massimo Fabbro, Managing Partner of Crea International, "While conceiving and designing CheBanca! we put together the oxymoron between innovation and reassurance thanks to a formal alchemy completely original for the banking format. An alchemy made up of space organisation and a completely unique furniture shape together with very reassuring and warmth codes on the other side."

Key innovations in this project are various: first of all the layout overturn with the presence of the central base point and the perimeter connection booths. An open and fluid space whose heart is the platform from which the store staff moves from to provide service to consumer. At the entrance the consumer is directed to the multitasking connection booths where any banking operation can be performed either in self-mode or through the support of the store staff, upon call.

1. Modular elements
2. Strong visibility from outside
3. Innovation in terms of model of service of layout
4. Touch screen information panel
5. Back office

The second important point is the environmental branding specifically focused on strong visual elements such as the portal, the windows. The interactive walls that transfer the product offer and the info about the cultural activities of the local community and two relax areas, coffee bar and kids garden.

Assistenza
Cassa
INTERESSI IN ANTICIPO!
CheBanca!
3

Ground Floor Plan (Below)
1. Entrance
2. Back Office
3. Waiting Area
4. Relax Area
5. Teller Area

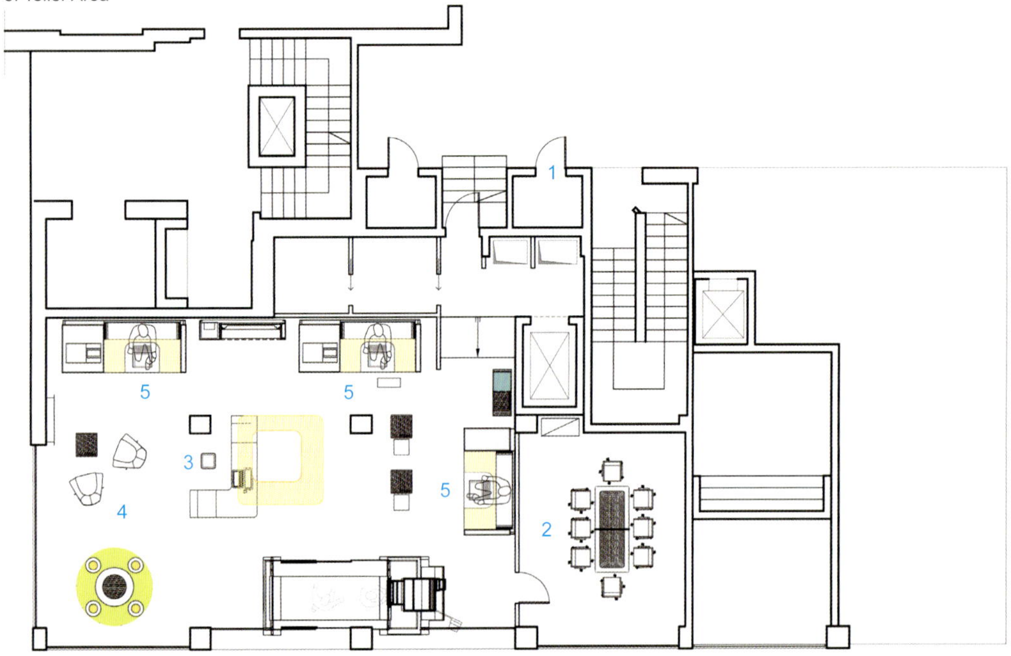
1
2
3
4
5
5
5

4

INTERESSI IN ANTICIPO!
CheBanca!
5

2 “Opera” BNP Paribas

Location: Paris, France
Completion Year: 2010
Designer: Fabrice Ausset, Zoevox
Photographer: Veronique Mati
Area: 1,000 m²

The architect Fabrice Ausset (Zoevox) signs the first BNP Paribas concept store, located in the historical building of 2, Place de l’Opéra in Paris. A user-friendly place set around a vast lounge dedicated to “active waiting” or leisure time. The 2 Opera defies the usual aesthetic codes of the banking world.

At 2 Opera, a creative scenography leads the client to discover the various services offered by Paribas in a playful and interactive way. He can gather information on the stock-exchange on his own or with the help of an advisor. Private rooms are dedicated to more formal appointments. An additional temporary exhibition area as well as another exclusively dedicated to children completes this new offering entirely devoted to an innovative client experience, in a surrounding destined to encompass true French elegance.

On both sides of the entrance hall, the particularly unusual vegetal design of the ATMs set the spirit of the self service area (cash withdrawals, change, cash deposits, etc.) In the lock chamber towards the welcome area, two screens inserted into the walls and placed behind mirrors broadcast information in a most poetic way. The welcome desk of 2 Opera is a long central table around which advisors are at the disposal of clients and prospects for guidance and directions. On the left-hand side is the exhibition area bordered by red walls, and on the right-hand side lies the monumental staircase leading to the management offices.

On the lounge's right-hand outskirts lay different succeeding areas: the playground zone, the banking shop, the info-business space and the non-banking shop.

In the playground zone, children can play, draw, or watch a cartoon network. This space is furnished with a Zoevox table and a round sofa by Paola Lenti, and bound by a wavy wall covered with slate paint that can be drawn on.

In the banking shop, BNP products are exposed on colour touch screens integrated into nine totems. Each bright-coloured folded metal sheet totem matches a topic - consuming/daily banking/international clients/savings/protect your close ones/real estate projects/youth area/retirement projects/couple life-family life. The graphic design of this project is signed by Roselab. The area enables the client to develop a self-sufficient and pro-active approach.

1. Waiting area
2. Receptiom

3. Glass door details
4. Children's space

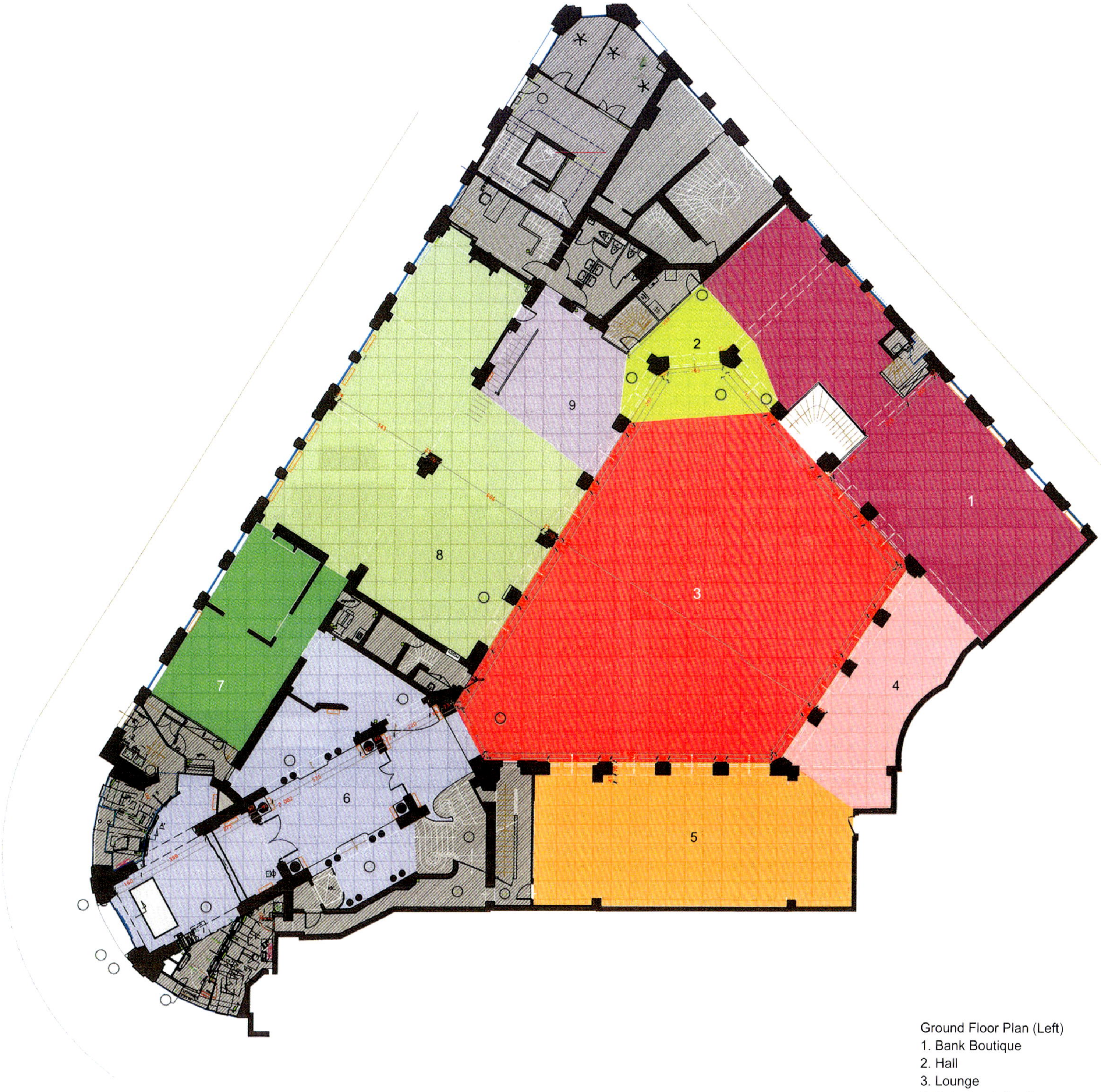

1
2
3
4
5
6
7
8
9

Ground Floor Plan (Left)
1. Bank Boutique
2. Hall
3. Lounge
4. Extra-bank Boutique
5. Special Space
6. Entrance Space
7. Meeting Space
8. Partitioned Salon
9. Entertainment Space

5

6

7

5. The unique honeycomb design of the ceiling broke the rigidness of traditional bank design
6. Conference space
7. The unique planting design in the spacious lounge

Deutsche Bank

Deutsche Bank
2

Deutsche Bank Bangkok

Location: Bangkok, Thailand
Completion Year: 2009
Designer: Orbit Design Co., Ltd.
Photographer: Basil Childers
Area: 4,200 m²

The Deutsche Bank, one of the leading financial institutions in the world, aspired an office interior design that reflected this distinguished status yet also boasting very significant local influences that show their commitment and respect to Thai culture. Therefore, their office at the exclusive Athenee Towers is a beautiful resemblance of Thai elements with a modern touch. The colour palette of the interiors takes direct reference from the colours of Thai temple and palace roofs, dating back from the Sukhothai period. The colours yellow, orange and green are assigned to the three floors of the Deutsche Bank office, and are picked up on the wall finishes throughout the working space areas. All solid and glazed walls also incorporate a graphic pattern representation of the Thai "Chedi" stupas.

1. Counter area and waiting area, the colours of interior design originate from temples and palaces
2. Reception
3. Lounge, the unique-shaped lamp adds elegance for the space
4. Meeting room
5. Café
6. Kitchen

3

4

5

6

1

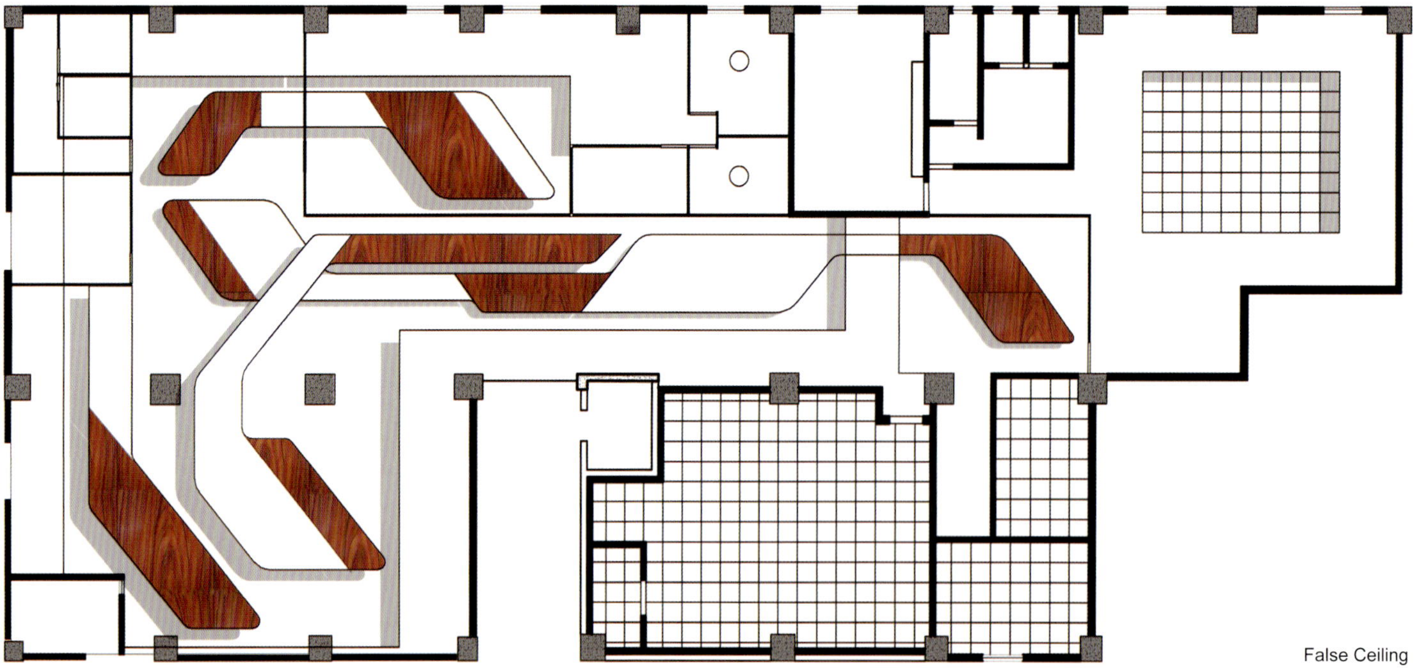

False Ceiling

2

Axis Bank, Branch at Lokhandwala

Location: Andheri, India
Completion Year: 2009
Designer: Planet 3 Studios Architecture Pvt. Ltd.
Photographer: Planet 3 Studios Architecture Pvt. Ltd.
Area: 702 m²

Lokhandwala is located in such a suburb of Mumbai where the residents aspire for the glitz, glamour of living without giving up the immediacy of local community, connections and convenience. Retail banking is evolving rapidly to keep up with shifting customer preferences. The days of nationalised banks that exuded customer un-friendliness are dated. Customers demand better services and facilities and they are aware of the fact that they can take that business elsewhere.

In a competitive environment, the more forward-looking banks are embracing change. In private banking, Axis Bank leads the charge. For this bank, as the client understands, the design of each of its retail banking outlets has to be unique to respond to the local context. This coupled with the organisation's requirement to maintain certain degree of design consistency over various locations and the need to reiterate the core brand identity demanded a carefully constructed response.

This project is about introducing new age banking. Working with a contemporary design sensibility, the designers created all individual interior elements that worked together to deliver the intended message. The entrance to the branch is wide and grand. Fast lines on the ceiling and the walls lead the eye to explore the interior that opens up as a surprise. The distinction between walls and the ceiling is blurred with planes that run continuously across both, turning, folding and descending at will. Individual bands direct visitors to the priority banking cabin, manager's cabin, the teller counter and such. The design language is carried on to the furniture and accessories. A writing ledge derives its design from the brand logo.

The choice of materials and colours is restricted to a palette that best complements the branding. The success of the project was in demonstrating that standard cost and time bound build of retail banking can also accommodate innovation and sensitivity. The design interventions are not lost on the customers, who appreciate the effort. For the client, the customer centric core values of the organisation are eloquently communicated through the physical construct.

1. Lobby, with guiding lines on the ceiling
2. Counter area
3. Office area
4. Back office

Priority
BANKING
LOUNGE

3

1
2
3
4
5
6
7
8
9
10
11
11

4

Ground Floor Plan (Facing Below)
1. Kids Room
2. Pantry
3. Back Office
4. 8-foot-wide Passage
5. Existing Electrical Room
6. Server
7. Electrical
8. Store
9. Locker Room
10. Lift
11. Cabin

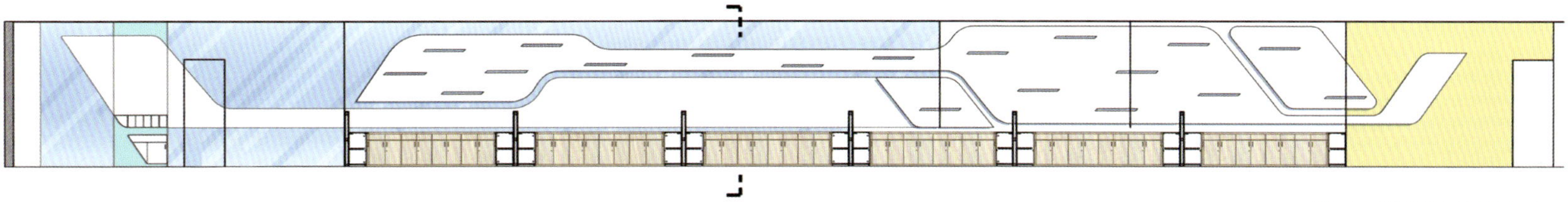

Glass Partition Front Elevation

2

Bank in Donoratico

Location: Livorno, Italy
Completion Year: 2007
Designer: Elda Bellone, Roseda Gentile,
Alessandro Mariani/Massimo Mariani Architetto
Photographer: Alessandro Ciampi
Area: 1,000 m²

The project concerns the redesign of a building in Donoratico (Livorno) located next to the head office of the bank "Banca di Credito Cooperativo di Castagneto Carducci" (also designed by architect Massimo Mariani in 2002). The building is on two levels. From the functional point of view the ground floor houses the areas most strictly connected with the banking business like the big hall with counter and advisory services for customers. The branch management offices as well as the loan management and administrative offices are encapsulated inside a long slice of coloured bureaus on the right of the entrance. A lot of other banking offices, safe deposits and services areas are in the basement.

Inside the hall, above the round waiting seat, there is a plasterboard ceiling randomly performed. Like a big drop, it comes out from the elongated corridor giving light to directional bureaus, service offices and common spaces. A single graphic sign features all public spaces, which are accessible to customers. All the furnishings and wooden walls are designed with vertical stripes in red, blue, yellow and green. In this way areas that in banks have traditionally been somewhat staid and "bleak" have been reinvented to give them an amusing and more optimistic look.

1. Counters, the rounded plaster ceiling provides lighting for the space
2. Rest area in the lobby, wooden walls are designed with vertical stripes in red, blue, yellow and green, getting rid of the staid image of traditional banks

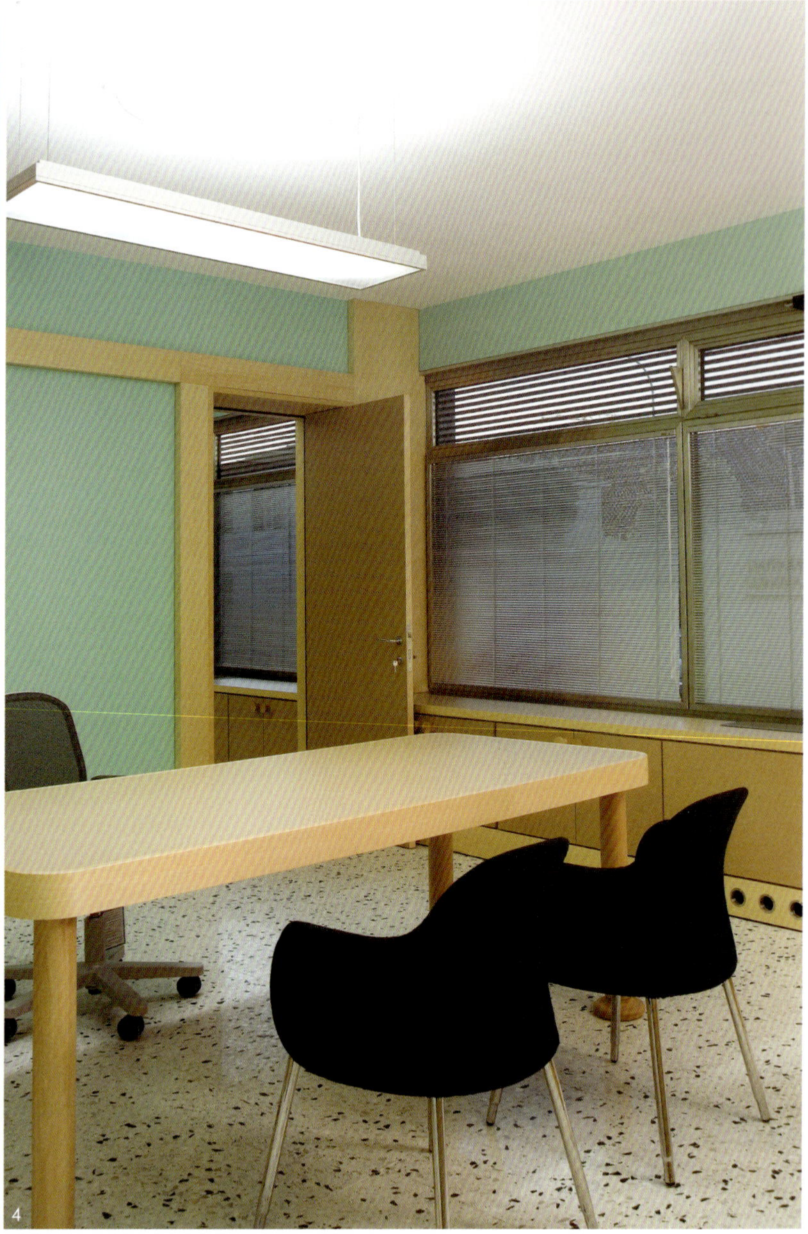

3. Passage
4. Office

Sections

Ground Floor Plan (Below)

1. Entrance
2. Waiting Area
3. Counters
4. Head Office
5. Contract Office
6. Secretary's Office
7. Office
8. Technical Room
9. Self Area

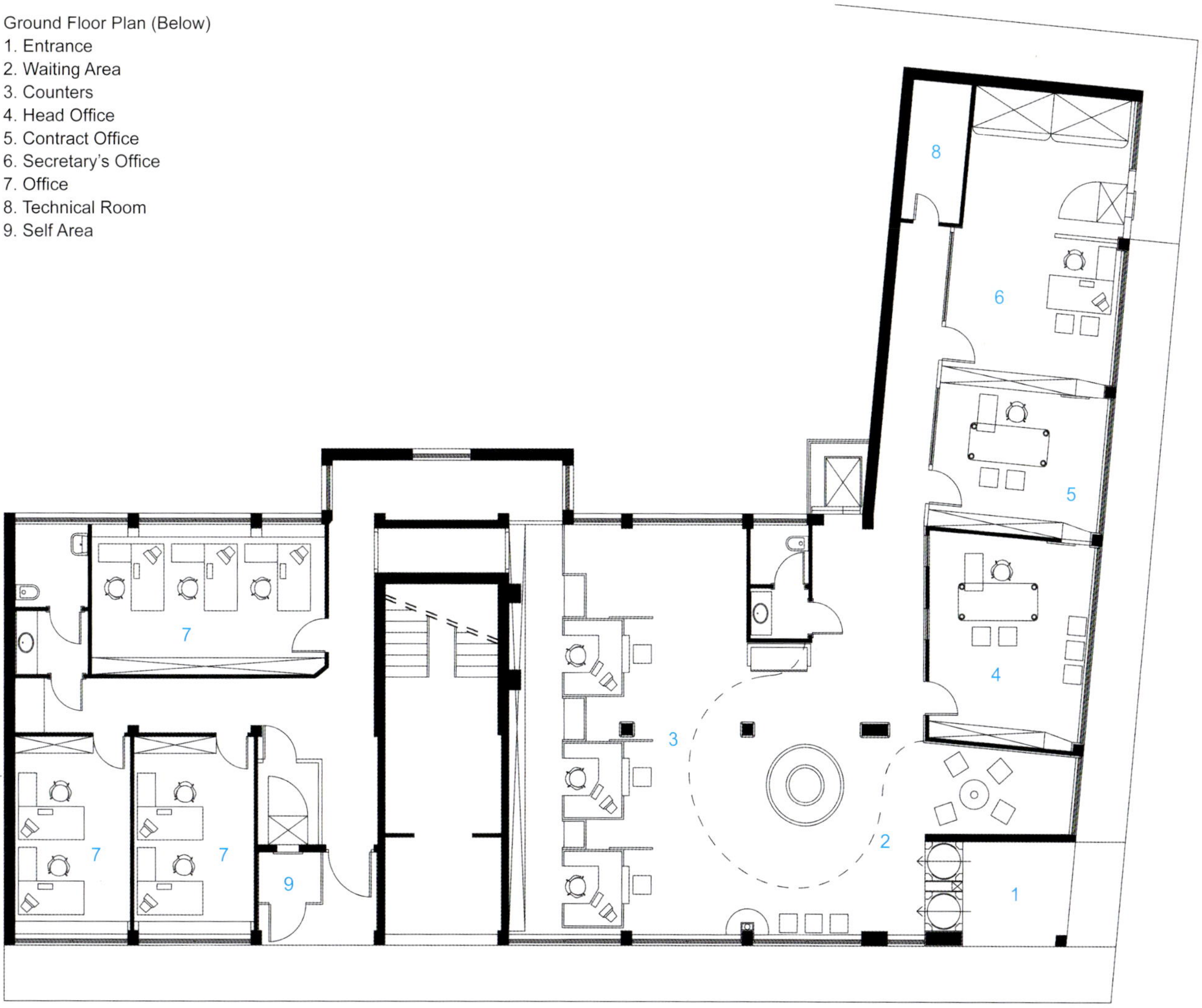
8
6
5
4
7
3
2
7
7
1
9

how can
we help?
bankwest

bankwest
OUR NEW YEAR'S RESOLUTION:
MAKE THOUSANDS
OF PEOPLE RICHER.
7.50

2

BankWest

Location: Sydney, Australia
Completion Year: 2008
Designer: Design Clarity
Photographer: Design Clarity

With minimal presence on the east coast of Australia, BankWest wanted to create a new bold retail banking experience. Previously presenting as a "traditional" bank, the bank wanted to avoid any of the cliché dark Mahogany timber veneers & usual long waiting queues associated with banks.

The methodology behind the project was to develop a physical presence that would take banking to the next level. The clients wanted to create bold, attractive stores rather than typical branches. The shopfront zone had to grab people's attention and display the non-financial products on offer.

The initial concept was based on the idea of concealing and revealing. By creating custom-made joinery items with stark, white exteriors and bright bold orange interiors, the design team could control the use of colours and forms. Display units throughout the space have an exposed plywood detail and rounded corners to add warmth and texture to the overall space. Break-out lounge spaces are decorated with designer furniture; moveable ottomans, plasma screens and funky orange "Hoppy" lights create an inviting mood. To reinforce the project methodology, a bright orange runway floor and floating ceiling were developed in the shape of the BankWest lozenge logo, to highlight the key customer transaction zone.

The materials specified by the design team, not only had to withstand the general wear and tear associated with busy retail environments, but also remain fresh and contemporary for at least 5 years. For this reason the number of materials in the BankWest store concept palette was deliberately limited.

The controlled use of texture, colours and lighting were paramount to the appeal and success of the new BankWest concept. A limited palette of materials was selected to create an uncluttered, bright, contemporary interior space. Vinyl timber floor was selected to add warmth to the overall space and for its durability & cost effectiveness. Transparent orange acrylic was used on the meeting room partitions to create subtle visual privacy.

1. The interior is designed with bright and bold orange, together with the orange lighting, creating a warm atmosphere
2. Exterior

MAKE THOUSANDS
OF PEOPLE RICHER
MAKE THOUSANDS
OF PEOPLE RICHER
internet
express deposit
important notice to all customers
phone
bankwest
3

3. ATMs
4. Rest area, the ceiling is designed with BankWest's diamond logo
5. Movable screens make the space more flexible

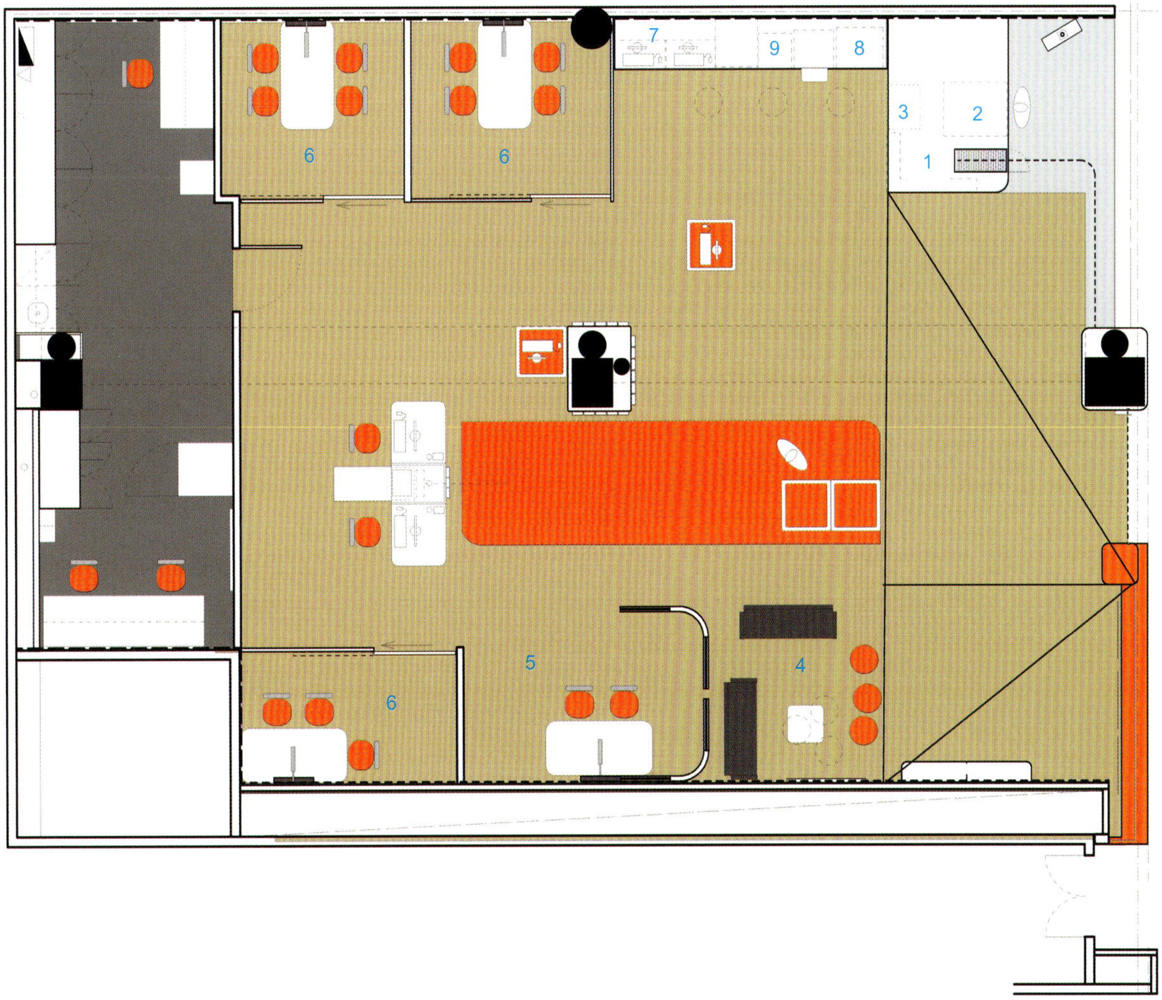
7
9
8
3
2
1
6
6
5
4
6

Ground Floor Plan (Left)
1. Display
2. ATM
3. Coffee
4. Break Out Space
5. Semi-Private Igloo
6. Private Igloo
7. Internet
8. Coin Counting Machine
9. Multi-Function Printer

BCP
S
Gerente
de Oficina
Carlos Seminario
Banca
Exclusiva
1

BCP
Banca Empresa

Banco de Crédito del Perú (BCP)

Location: Lima, Peru
Completion Year: 2009
Designer: José Orrego
Photographer: Juan Solano
Area: 3,200 m²

A brand new concept was developed for one of the most important banks in Peru. The institution, named for its first 52 Years' Bank of Italy, began operations on April 9th, 1889, adopted a credit policy based on the principles that would guide their institutional behaviour in the future. On February 1st, 1942, it was agreed to replace the name, by the Banco de Crédito del Perú (BCP).

In order to achieve greater international clout, BCP opened branch offices in Nassau and New York, a fact that BCP became the only Peruvian Bank present in two of the most important financial centres worldwide. The expansion of BCP's activities created the need for a new headquarters for central management. To this end BCP built a building of 30,000 square metres, approximately, in the district of La Molina. Then, with the aim of improving the services, BCP established the National Network of Tele process, which in late 1988, connecting almost every office in the country with the central computer of Lima, also created the Current Account and National Savings Book, and installed an extensive network of ATMs.

Contemporary work requires new adjustable spaces, which were the centre of the research made by the design team. Based on that, the project tries to optimise the system, interaction and work team: every working spot was integrated to each other so that a central multi-proposal space would appear. The intention at BCP was to reduce the occupation ratio without neglecting the quiality of the office environment.

1. Counter area and waiting area
2. Reception, the rounded ceiling makes the space more elegant and decent

The concept of lighting includes management systems that synchronise artificial and natural light at the same time to create a comfortable atmosphere. The design bet on inner perspectives to gain visual range and amplitude. The project is supposed to recreate the sensation of an Urban Café in an office context.

3

3. Rest area, the curved ceiling and rounded pendants make the space look like a café
4. Informal meeting place

Banca
Empresa
GOE
4

5

5. Background office space
6. Conference room

6

EXTRABANCA

1

2

EXTRABANCA
EXTRABANCA

EXTRABANCA
3

Extrabanca

Location: Milan, Italy
Completion Year: 2010
Designer: Crea International
Photographer: Daniela Di Rosa (Crea International)
Area: 175 m²

Extrabanca's opening represents the first retail banking concept ever conceived which addresses as main clientele target to the immigrants. The leading idea lies itself on the poetic concept distinguishing the remarkable identity of Extrabanca: the will to act as linking bridge towards a new different world, where dreams can come true.

The project metaphor of this new retail design concept is represented by the bridge which is the distinctive architectural feature of the place. It is seen as a sinuous portal of wood which spaces out the overall surface, articulating the operational desks and welcoming customers to a new reassuring retail banking experience. A powerful dynamic sign which decisively translates the sense of continuity of the project, and breaks up at same time the most conformist retail banking design layouts.

From outside a peculiar stylistic role is played by the window system which is made of "Canaletto" walnut wood reporting the backlit logo of Extrabanca, while the flag ones located in the interior enhance the visibility through the deep red colour of the logotype. The visual impact is furthermore enhanced by a sophisticated dynamic lighting system of Led RGB.

As for the finishing and the colour palette, it has been made an institutional choice through an elegant chromatic mood transferring inside the retail design concept the corporate colours: red, white and barrel grey. Finally the white architectural box results to be scanned by an entrance portal distinguished by a deep lacquered red, pointing out the meaningful presence of the brand since the first step into the branch.

Once again Crea International succeeded in conceiving such an innovative retail banking design concept able to communicate through design a series of values related to the respect of listening, pride and customised service. Once again a step ahead in the conception of meaningful retail design concepts.

1. Exterior
2. Windows with deep red patterns showcase the meaning of the brand
3. Reception and waiting area

WE BRIDGE
YOUR DREAMS

WE BRIDGE
YOUR DREAMS

4. Dynamic logos on the interior walls
5. Meeting room, deep red logo adds energy for the space
6. Bridge is the concept of interior design
7. Winding wood doors connect different desks

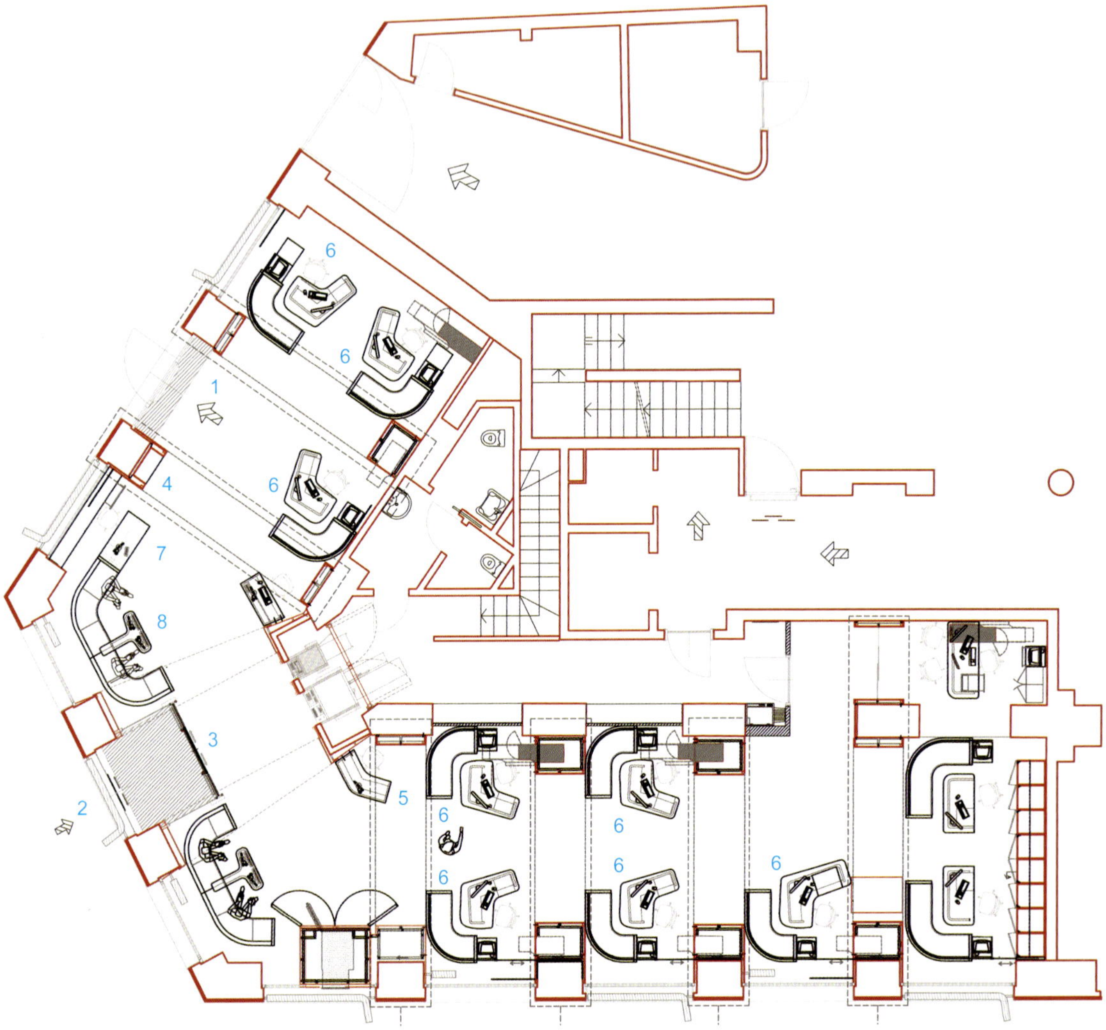
1
2
3
4
5
6
7
8

Ground Floor Plan (Left)
1. Emergency Exit
2. Entrance
3. Compact Portal With Nocturnal Locking System Gate
4. Coffee Area
5. Welcome Butler Desk
6. Consultancy Working Desk and Cashier
7. Home Banking Working Desk
8. Waiting Area

7

1

2

Bank of Fornacette in San Romano

Location: San Romano, Italy
Completion Year: 2009
Designer: Massimo Mariani, Jurji Filieri, Alessandro Mariani
Photographer: Alessandro Ciampi
Area: 370 m²

From Bank of Fornacette the designers were asked for introducing a new branch office on the ground floor, and partly on the first floor for a total area of 370 square metres, of a building built in 1980s which before was a storehouse. The designers had to keep right functions and distributional ways. The ground floor was a free plan just once interrupted by the oversize staircase in the centre of the room. The designers decided to collect all the features which came out from the context, trying to transform them into design guidelines. So the staircase became the main axis of the entire project; the exterior has been covered with wooden panels in brown warm coffee colours Abet Laminati series Fibre rimmed with natural beechwood. This coating is designed like a giant brick wall.

Like a cutter the staircase divides the ground floor into two areas: from one side the hall with counters and services for customers; on the other side there are directional offices, the secretary's office, the caveau, the meeting room and an archive room. On the upper floor there are few other operative offices. Like in a cave everything is brown (furniture, floor, ect.); sometimes colours arise like flowers: the waiting bench is red, tables are yellow, columns are blue and directional office walls are green, only the modular false ceiling is white. Also important is the lighting project; sometimes there are carpentry work elements which accomodate the light fixtures, or sometimes like in meeting room the lighting is fixed as sunbeams.

Everything seems like not conventional room and each working area looks fine. Every furniture is custom designed and realised by carpentry work, including tables, partition walls, doors and benches, and sometimes laquered or natural. Also in this project the colours and materials characterise the space giving it a look unconventional, looking for a new definition of "bank" more cheerful and friendly.

1. General view of the teller area
2. View of the waiting area

3

4

3. External view of the box office
4. View of the head office

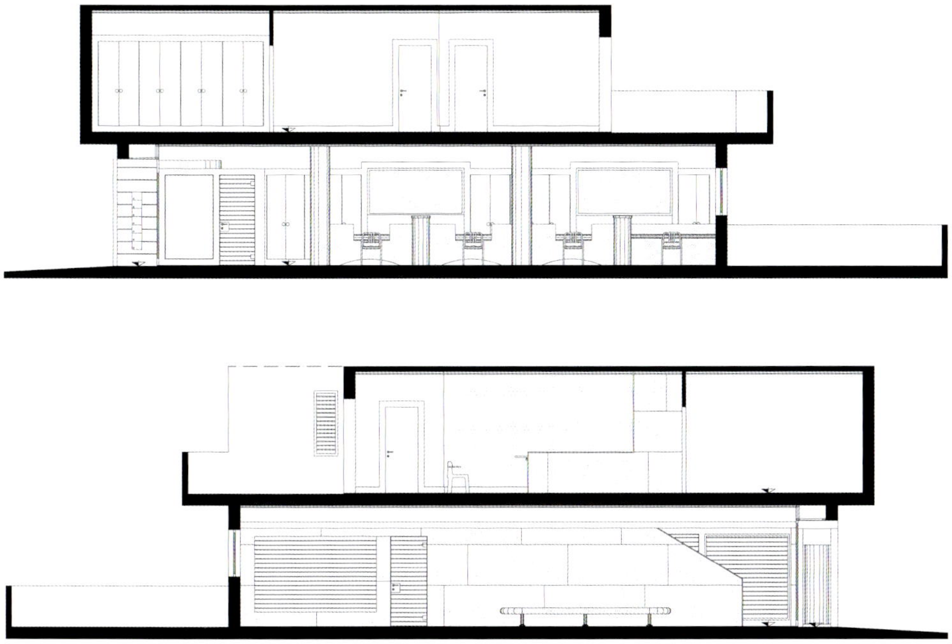

Sections

5

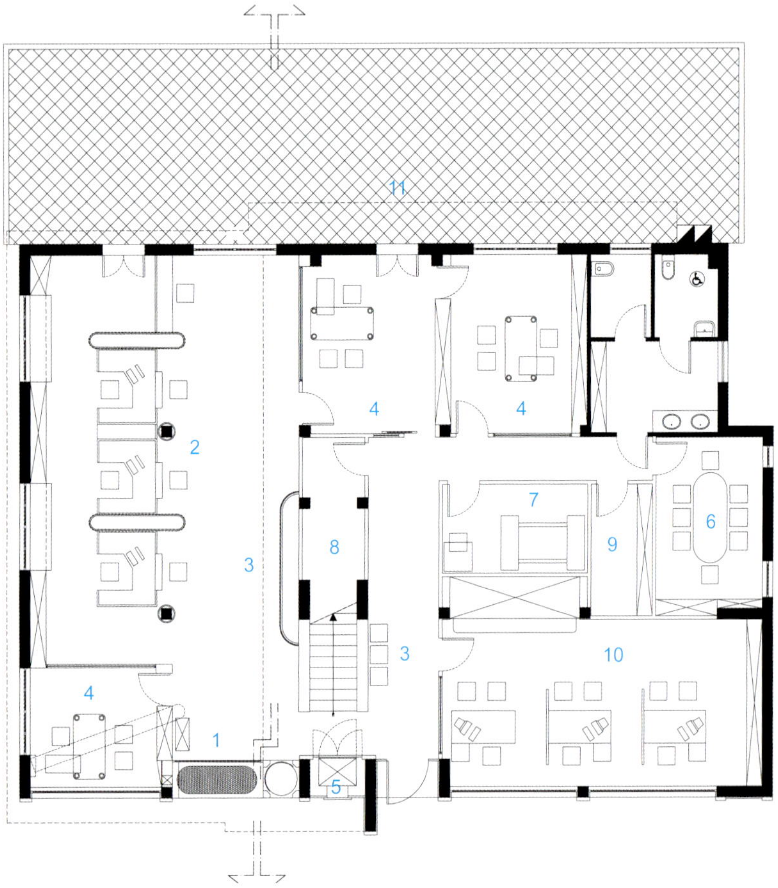
11
2
3
4
4
4
7
6
8
9
3
10
1
5

5. View of the secretariat
6. Meeting room
7. Waiting area

Ground Floor Plan (Left)
1. Entrance
2. Counters
3. Waiting Area
4. Office
5. Self-service Area
6. Meeting Room
7. Caveau
8. Store Room
9. Technical Room
10. Secretariat
11. Terrace

First Floor Plan (Right)
1. Waiting Area
2. Office
3. Terrace

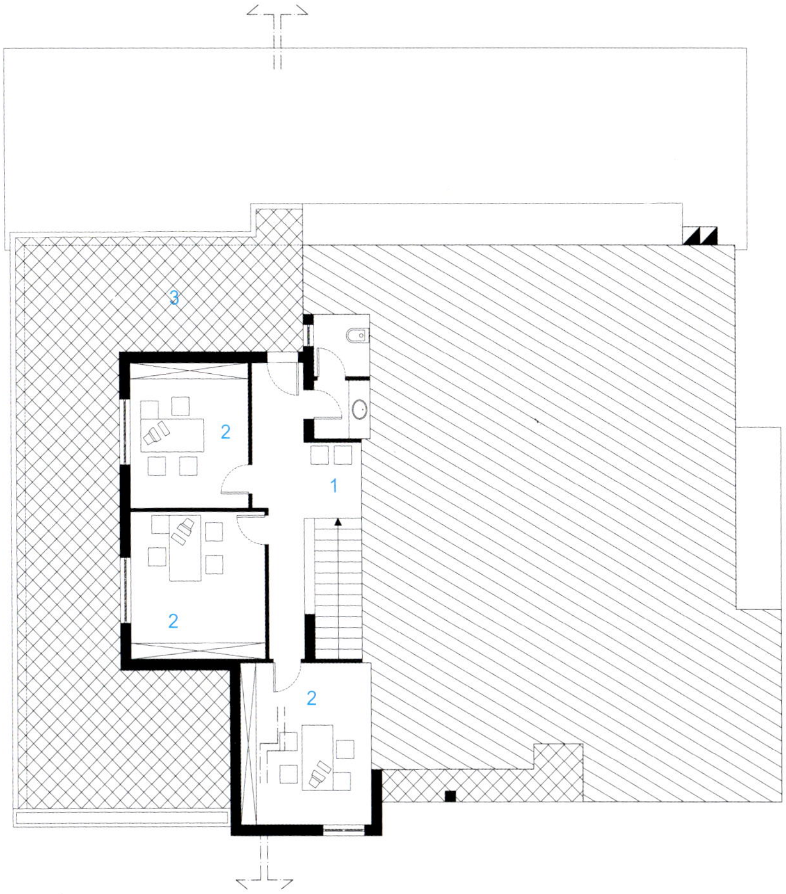
3
2
1
2
2

2

Bank in Pontedera

Location: Pontedera, Italy
Completion Year: 2005
Designer: Roseda Gentile, Alessandro Mariani, Massimo Mariani
Photographer: Alessandro Ciampi
Area: 600 m²

The bank is placed inside the historical centre of the town; it occupies the ground floor and the first floor of a building which had been erected in nineteenth century; it is developed on a total surface of 600 square metres. The building was already occupied by another bank and it is opened on the internal bamboo garden, designed in pure Japanese style. The designers worked only on architectural elements and existing walls changing contents and global image of the interior.

On the ground floor a big lobby introduces at the operative area enlighted by a big skylight, which houses four open counters designed as "newsstand", a private counter, some offices and waiting benches. The ground floor also houses a caveau and service rooms; on the left of the lobby, near head office there is a softly-shaped green staircase leading to the first floor where visitors can find several offices, a secretariate, archives, meeting room, etc.

The existing coating "travertino" stone of the lobby has been partly demolished and partly painted in white varnish. The staircase has been encapsulated in a green plasterboard husk; only the wood steps were kept. All green-colour tones present almost everywhere are part of a green palette which derives from the different green tones of bamboo garden, each one used in a strategic way on the staircase, on niches and lighting boxes of the lobby and passageways.

All furnishings are custom designed and realised by carpentry work, treated with warm colours and various wooden essences like Abet laminates (Fibre) are repeated in the interior design; decoration with circular reliefs is a recurrent pattern of all white laquered cupboards both of the ground and the first floor. Other finishes like concrete marble floor on the ground level and rubber floor on the first level complete the variety of materials used.

1. Counters on the ground floor
2. Private counter

3

4

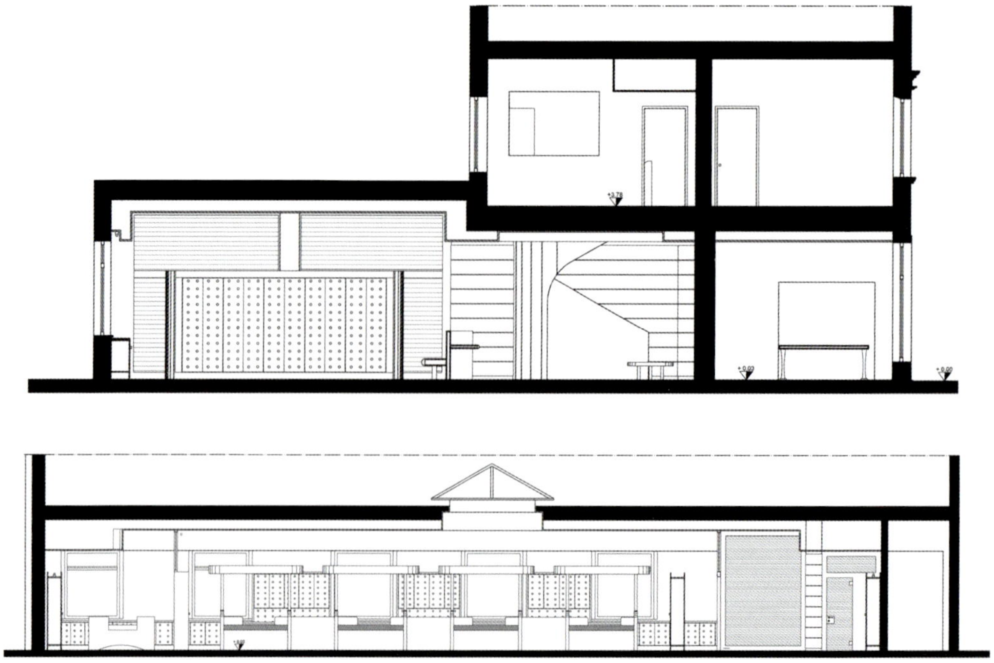

Sections

5

6

3. Partitions details
4. General view of office
5-6. Head office

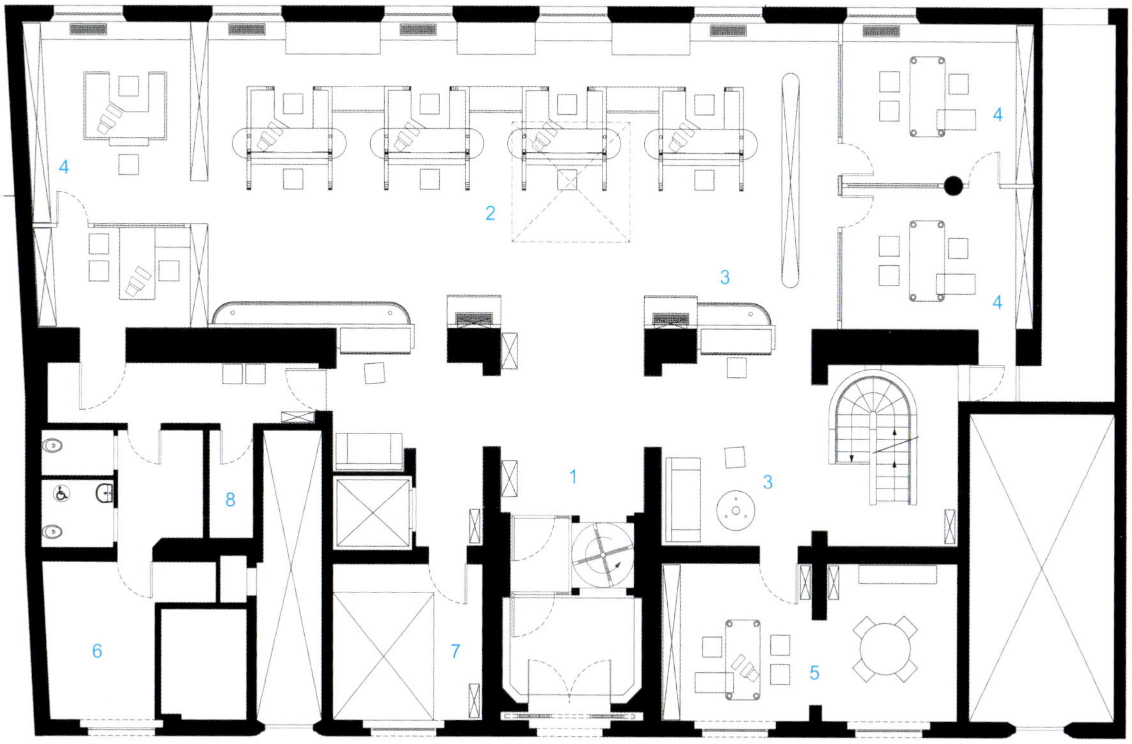
1
2
3
3
3
4
4
4
4
5
6
7
8

Ground Floor Plan (Right)
1. Entrance
2. Counters
3. Waiting Area
4. Office
5. Head Office
6. Cash Machine
7. Caveau
8. Technical Room

2

AGCI Bank

Location: Bologna, Italy
Completion Year: 2008
Designer: Elda Bellone, Roseda Gentile, Alessandro Mariani/Massimo Mariani
Photographer: Alessandro Ciampi
Area: 650 m²

The project concerns the design of a building located in the centre of Bologna, recently taken over as the headquarters of a new bank, Banca AGCI. The building is on three levels, two above and one partly below ground, with a total surface area of 650 square metres. On the outside, the façade has been left as it was prior to the work, while inside a systematic series of modifications have been carried out partly to adapt the building to better suit its purpose as a bank.

In particular, the staircase is the only big intervention made to provide vertical communication between floors. The lift block has been realised in reinforced concrete with a special black protective acrylic coating with a semi-opaque effect, in contrast with green pantone of the walls; the staircase is also characterised by a coloured carpentry work element to support lighting fixtures.

From the functional point of view, the ground floor houses the areas most strictly connected with the banking business: the hall houses two open counters and a private one characterised by a glass wall and a red carpentry work element which houses the light fixture, lay above the partition wall. In the hall there are also advisory services for customers, the branch management, an office, a waiting area and naturally the main entrance. The management and administrative offices as well as the loan management and services offices are on the first floor, while the meeting rooms, a number of other banking offices, safe deposits and service areas are in the basement.

The basement is characterised by a ramp which connects the lower level to external level for security escape way. This ramp is designed with a white iron net parapet and natural beechwood handrail. Also here the contrast between green pantone and grey creates a unique space, more joyful than other spaces, with the scattered light on the ceiling. In fact colours of the walls, green and grey, are given the task to liven up the space and emphasise the furniture elements, all custom designed and generally treated with warm colours and wood materials.

1. Private space on the ground floor, the semi-transparent partitions ensure privacy
2. Counters on the ground floor, the contrast of green and grey creates a unique space

3

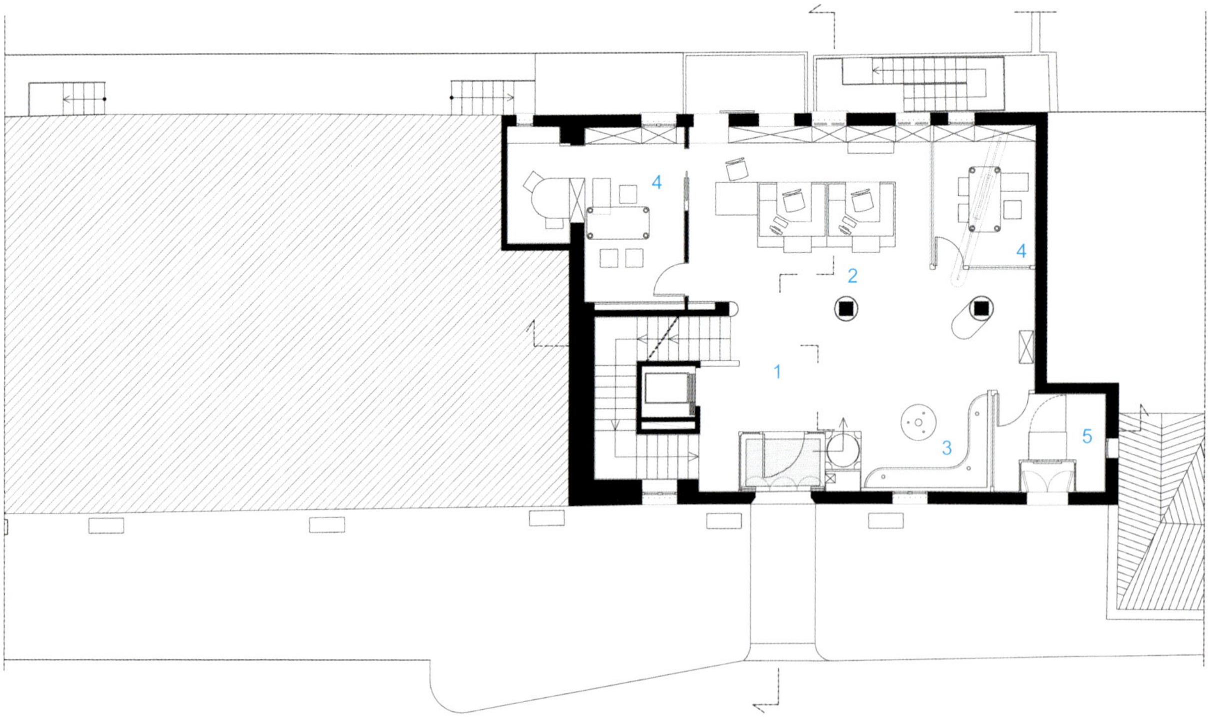

4
2
4
1
3
5

Ground Floor Plan (Left)
1. Entrance
2. Counters
3. Waiting Area
4. Office
5. Self-service Area

3. Waiting area on the ground floor
4. Underground meeting room
5. Underground waiting area

Sections

THIERS
idepi
ADVERTENCIA

1

idepi
CRÉDITO ES
CREER EN TI
EL
BANCO DE
UNO

2

Banco Deuno

Location: Mexico City, Mexico
Completion Year: 2007
Designer: Usoarquitectura
Gabriel Salazar, Fernando Castañón
Photographer: Tygre

1. Customer service area
2. Exterior
3. Graphic and word information is used in the interior design
4. The interior uses bold colour palettes
5. Lounge
6. Counter details

Banco Deuno (Your-own Bank) is a new concept of the Mexican IXE Grupo Financiero where communication among the client and the bank is very open and always the same. Under the concept of renovating the bank institutions, Banco Deuno confided in usoarquitectura to transform all the institutional precepts and corporate image into an interior design where the main core is the client's experience.

Colour is the central element of the design concept. All the elements, from the collaborators uniforms to the front pieces integrated to the different buildings where the branches are located, are part of the daring colour palette. The spatial language generated by this selection of colours, not common for bank institutions in Mexico, contains all the clients needs stipulated in the programme. Every branch is different from the others representing a very big challenge for usoarquitectura who translated it into the integration of the general concept for each one.

The different spaces are standardised by the correct selection of finishes and colour application, being this last one the personal signature of each branch. The bank's dynamic culture is interpreted through this ample colour palette. The combinations are flexible and can be adapted according to each space needs. What architects Gabriel Salazar and Fernando Castañón applied are their knowledge and experiences in commercial interior architecture developing adequate areas for both the internal operation of the bank and customer service.

Each branch is different but everyone has the same shape and colour language. No matter which branch the client is in, he will feel in Banco Deuno. The communication campaign and the new bank concept were also translated in a series of text and image messages that combined with the colour palette complement the dynamic of the bank.

BIENVENIDO
QUE
TENGAS
UN BUE
DÍA
3

4

EL
BAN
CO DE
UNO
ADIÓS A LO
TRADICIONAL.
HOLA A LO
AUTÉNTICO
¡HOLA!
A LO PERSONAL

¡QUE TENGAS
UN BUEN DÍA!
5

QUE
TENGAS
UN BUEN
DÍA
BIENVENIDO
6

Ground Floor Plan (Below)
1. Entrance
2. Reception
3. Counter
4. Customers Service Centre

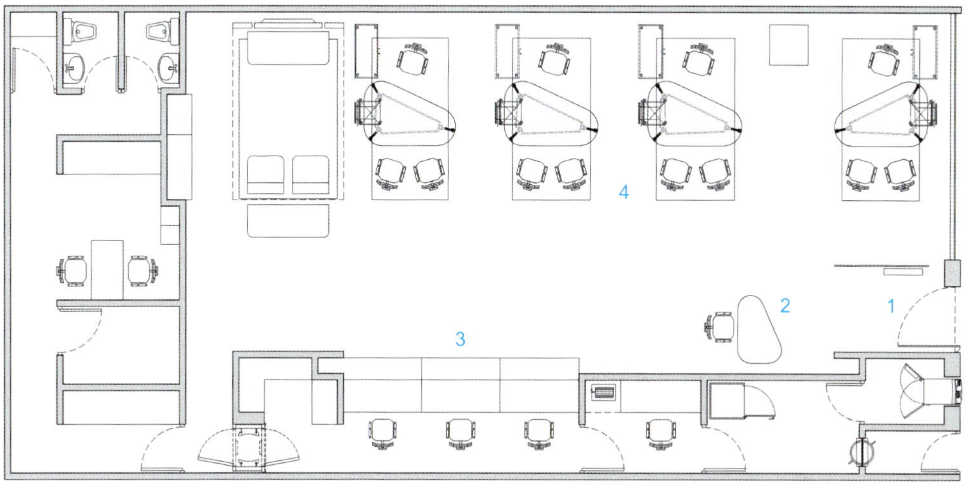
4
2
1
3

1

Bank in Collesalvetti

Location: Collesalvetti, Italy
Completion Year: 2009
Designer: Massimo Mariani
Photographer: Alessandro Ciampi
Area: 200 m²

The project concerns the renovation of a building placed inside the historical centre of Collesalvetti, to use as bank branch. This branch occupies approximately an area of 200 square metres. The main elevation (on Roma Road) keeps invaried, so now you can identify the bank only by the signboard or the logos on the windows.

From the functional point of view the bank is developed on two storeys: the ground floor houses the hall with counters, the branch management, the secretary's office and a small deposit; while archives and a deposit are in the basement. Along all the perimeter, the walls of the hall, the branch management and the secretary's office are characterised by finishes with a Locatelli perforated wooden cladding painted in light blue underlined by white frames.

The project of this space is quite clear. It's a small space so the designers have adopted a sort of circular holes pattern as a coating of the entire walls, furniture and doors. The result is an atmosphere unique and precious at the same time. In fact the coating of the hall is detached from the wall to create a vacuum and the colour of the behind wall is visible from the small holes of the pattern; in other cases this coating is mounted directly on a surface with the same colour, producing a relief effect (doors).

There are only two colours that define the entire spaces, which are light blue and white. These colours are present everywhere; even the two seats located in front of the counters have been painted in light blue.

Everything is custom designed and made by carpentry work: counters, wall coverings, cupboards, tables, knobs, except only few seats of the waiting area and offices (executive chairs), floors, lighting and modular false ceiling.

1. Waiting area in the hall, the colours of the wall can be shown through the holes on the panel
2. Counter zone, the interior is combined with blue and white

3

4

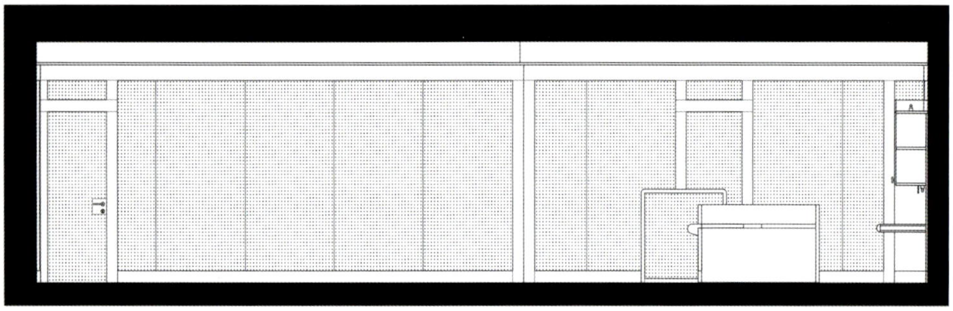

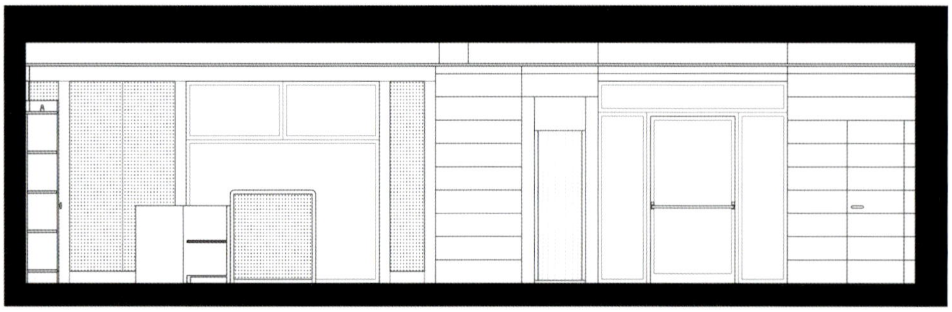

Sections

5

6

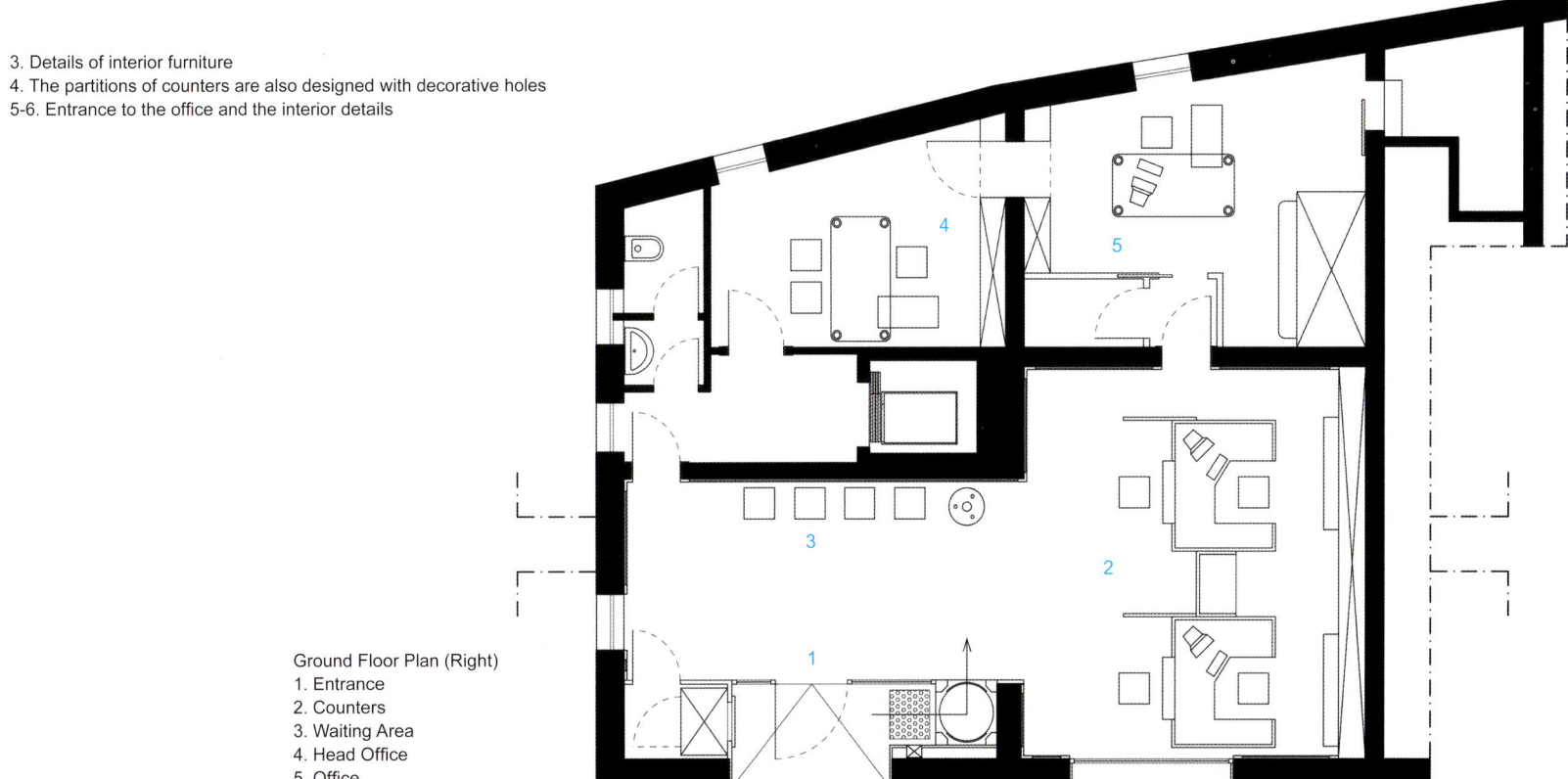

3. Details of interior furniture
4. The partitions of counters are also designed with decorative holes
5-6. Entrance to the office and the interior details

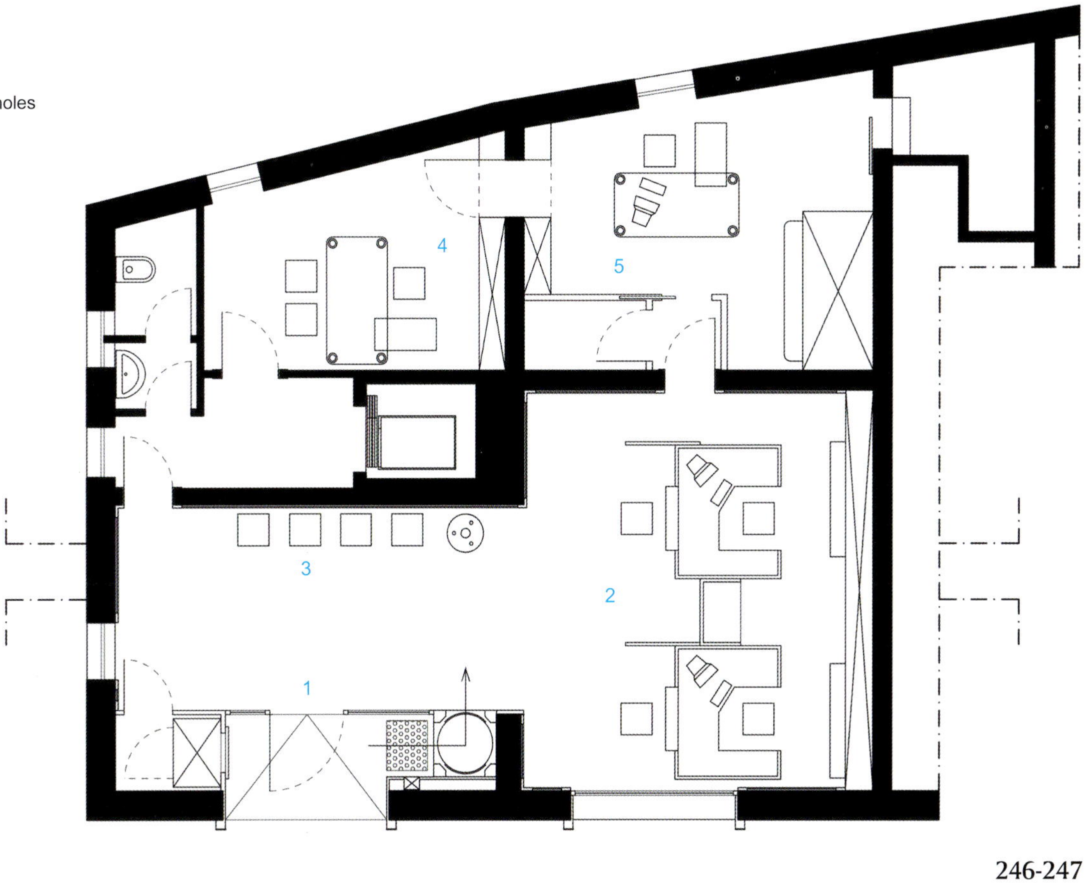
1
2
3
4
5

Ground Floor Plan (Right)
1. Entrance
2. Counters
3. Waiting Area
4. Head Office
5. Office

MIDFIRST
BANK
3030

2

MidFirst Bank 3030 Camelback

Location: Phoenix, USA
Completion Year: 2007
Designer: Lauren Rottet
Photographer: Eric Laignel
Area: 2,230 m²

MidFirst Bank, an established Oklahoma City bank, sought to enter the competitive Arizona market and commissioned the Rottet Studio's design team to create a brand for the company in order to set MidFirst Bank apart from the local competition. 3030 Camelback was the first MidFirst branch introduced to the Arizona culture. It serves as a branch location for MidFirst as well as a corporate office.

All local materials were used in the design process; however, the natural materials of the Arizona desert tend to vary greatly in their colours and finish, which is why the design team used a hand selection process to ensure uniformity amongst the materials. These warm, natural materials are accented by rustic orange colours resulting in a masculine yet sophisticated and hospitable style.

Controlling heat gain while simultaneously achieving the look of light-filled space in the desert climate always poses a problem; however, the Rottet Studio design team was able to overcome this obstacle by adding overhangs to the south and west sides of the building and installing automatic Mecho shades on the windows which draw and repel themselves based on the time of day and the amount of sun entering the space. Also, glass-enclosed rooms were oriented inboard with circulation adjacent to the wall of windows and internal atrium, which maximises access to natural light and enhances the sense of space as well.

Amenities include private offices, visitor offices, video conference rooms, break rooms, a mail room, and a full service bank security including a vault and security monitoring into the design process.

Creating a comfortable, hospitable environment on a branch bank budget is always a challenge; however, it was achieved by using local vendors and materials to keep costs down while supporting the local community at the same time.

1. Rest area, natural materials with different colours and textures add elegance and decency for the space
2. Exterior

3

3. Reception
4. Waiting area, the hard lines of wall paintings and sofas emphasise the corporate image

4

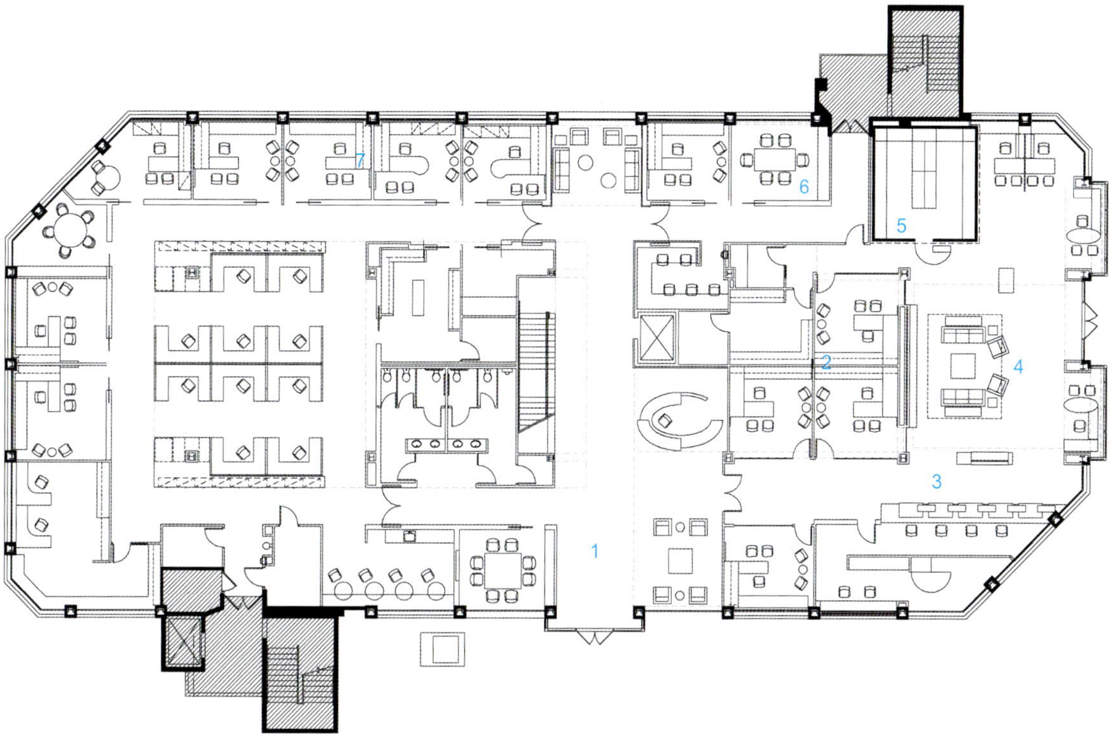
7
6
5
2
4
3
1

Ground Floor Plan (Left)
1. Entry & Reception
2. Private Offices
3. Teller Stations
4. Lounge with Fireplace
5. Vault
6. Conference Room
7. Open Work Stations

5

6

7

8

5. Private office, warm colour palette and natural materials present a comfortable and luxurious atmosphere
6-7. Meeting room
8. The executive level sitting room and the reception

1

2

MidFirst Bank One Renaissance

Location: Phoenix, USA
Completion Year: 2008
Designer: Lauren Rottet
Photographer: Eric Laignel
Area: 372 m²

One Renaissance is a unique MidFirst Bank branch. While most branches are free-standing buildings located around the city, One Renaissance is the only MidFirst location to date sited in the lobby of a high-rise building in downtown Phoenix. Since this particular location is not free-standing, it initially lacked the individuality of the other branches. This became the design team's biggest challenge - making this branch stand out from the building lobby itself to attract the downtown business clientele all while upholding the MidFirst brand image.

Despite the fact One Renaissance is a unique branch bank and was designed with MidFirst's larger, corporate locations in mind. In fact, it utilises wood and leather to accentuate the masculine, yet hospitable image of the brand but appears a little more contemporary and formal than other branches in order to appeal to the downtown clientele. The private bank incorporates less warm-coloured natural Arizona stone into the design and more woods and cool colours.

One Renaissance has all the amenities you would find in a branch bank and more, including: private offices, open workstations, teller booths, a conference room, the break room, the visitor lounge, a mail room, and a full service bank security monitoring system.

1. Lounge, smart lighting design provides orange glow
2. Reception and counters

3. Perspective of counters and open workstations, the whole space is designed with wood and leather, quite modern
4. Meeting room

4

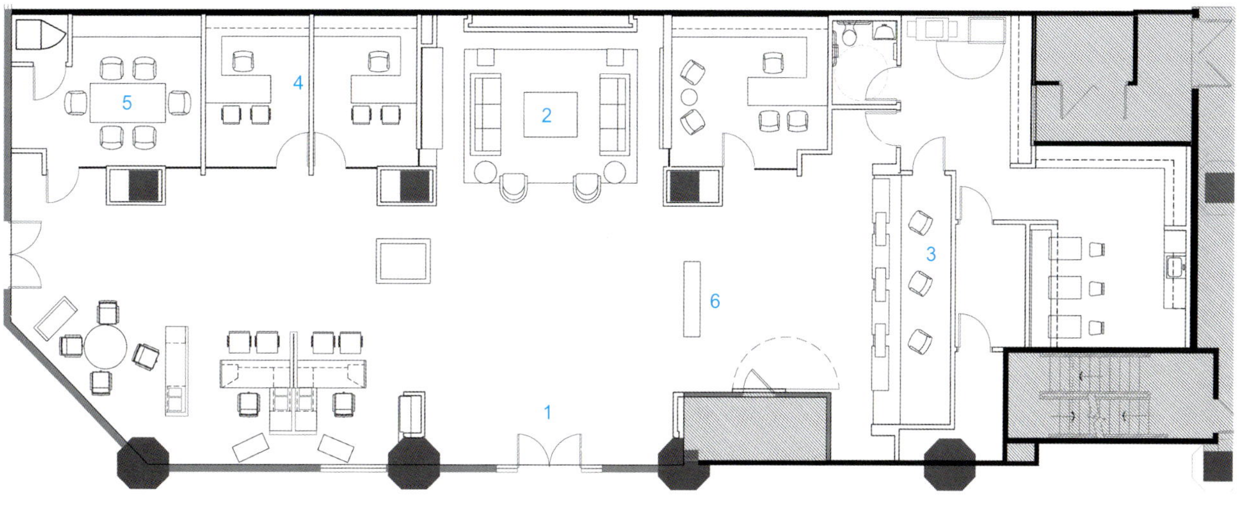
5
4
2
6
3
1

Ground Floor Plan (Left)
1. Entrance
2. Lounge
3. Teller Booth
4. Private Offices
5. Conference Room
6. Reception

2

MidFirst Bank Market Street (Private Bank)

Location: Scottsdale, USA
Completion Year: 2008
Designer: Lauren Rottet
Photographer: Eric Laignel
Area: 929 m²

Rottet Studio successfully created a brand and image for MidFirst Bank in the Arizona market and carried that image on to their Market Street location, which serves as corporate offices for the President and CEO as well as a private branch location for high-deposit clients who require more personal service.

Compared to the rustic and traditional image of other MidFirst branch locations, the private bank, as it has become known, is much more contemporary in design and is intended to appeal to the specific clientele frequent to the location. The lounge area is the centre point of the project with a large fireplace and suede-panelled walls. The fireplace is not functional due to the fact the bank is located within a high-rise building but clever lighting design which casts a warm fire-like glow from the lounge. This orange glow can be seen through the exterior glass walls of the space from the lobby and helps draw attention to the bank from outsiders. The clever lighting design attracts attention to the architectural design of the space and the impressive art collection, which was hand selected by Rottet Studio such as the two Mie Olise paintings that hang in the first floor "idea room" and the Chuck Close photograph in the conference room.

Amenities include private offices, visitor offices, large conference rooms (open and private), break rooms, a mail room, and a full service bank security which incorporate security monitoring into the design process.

Warm, natural materials are contrasted by cool metals and stone resulting in a bold yet refined aura that is welcoming to all customers.

1. Conference room, the whole space takes wood as its decoration materials
2. Reception

3

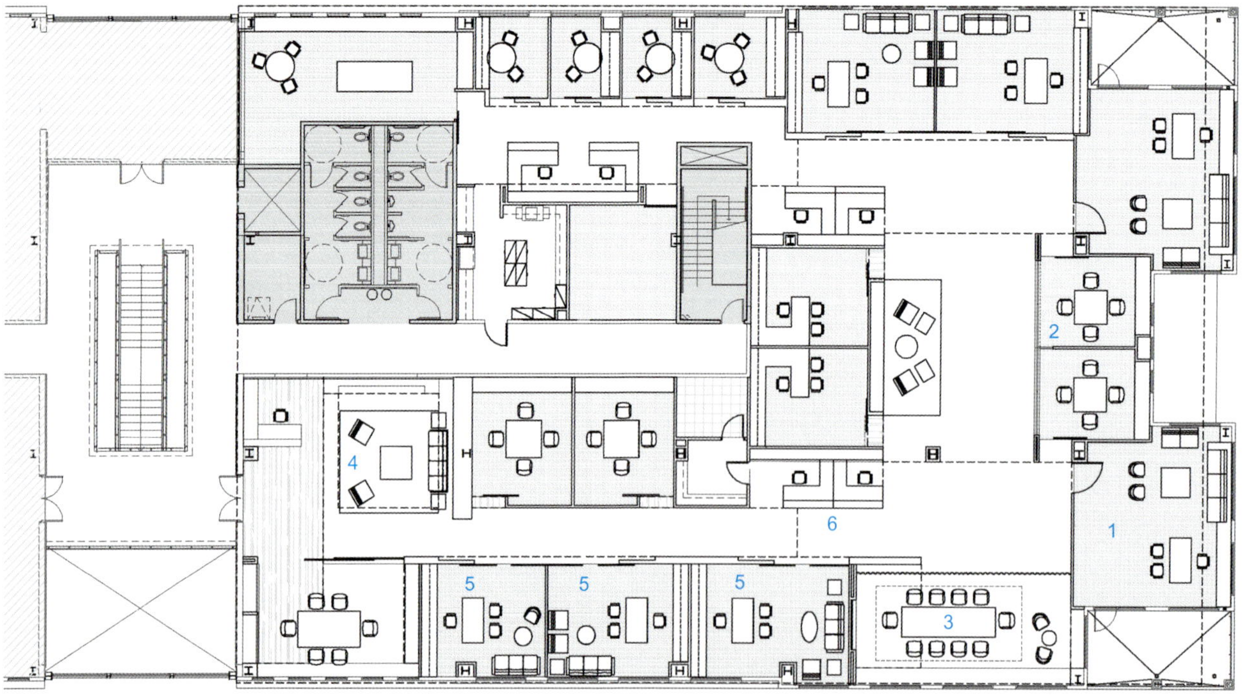

Ground Floor Plan (Left)
1. President's Office
2. Meeting Rooms
3. Conference Room
4. Lounge
5. Private Offices
6. Reception

3. Lounge, with large flannel walls and fireplace
4. President's office

1

2

BCI Private Bank

Location: Santiago, Chile
Completion Year: 2008
Designer: Felipe Assadi+Francisca Pulido
Photographer: Eric Laignel
Area: 1,309 m²

Banco de Crédito e Inversiones (BCI) is a Chilean bank specialising in savings and deposits, securities brokerage, asset management and insurance. This BCI Private Banking branch, located in Santiago, Chile, is one of the BCI branches for VIP and designed by the Chilean architectural studio ASSADI + PULIDO (Felipe Assadi + Francisca Pulido).

The term "private" refers to the customer service being rendered on a more personal basis than in mass-market retail banking, usually via dedicated bank advisers. So the design must be dedicated for the VIP customers and bank officers, with the design concept "All for people".

The reception desk is very simple but with particular lighting which forms the wall borders of the reception. The waiting area is very near to the reception area, composing of two pairs of sofas and a table. The two sides of this area are in sharp contrast, one side in black colour and the other side white. The main hall and the passageway are specially designed for the VIP members, with grand glass wall and human sculptures of typical Chilean style. While passing by, the customers will feel free as at home.

The whole area of 1,309 square metres is mainly in the two natural colours, black and white, which make this bank design simple and classical. This is also the design concept of the studio ASSADI + PULIDO.

1. Reception, smart lighting design adds depth for the space
2. Reception

3

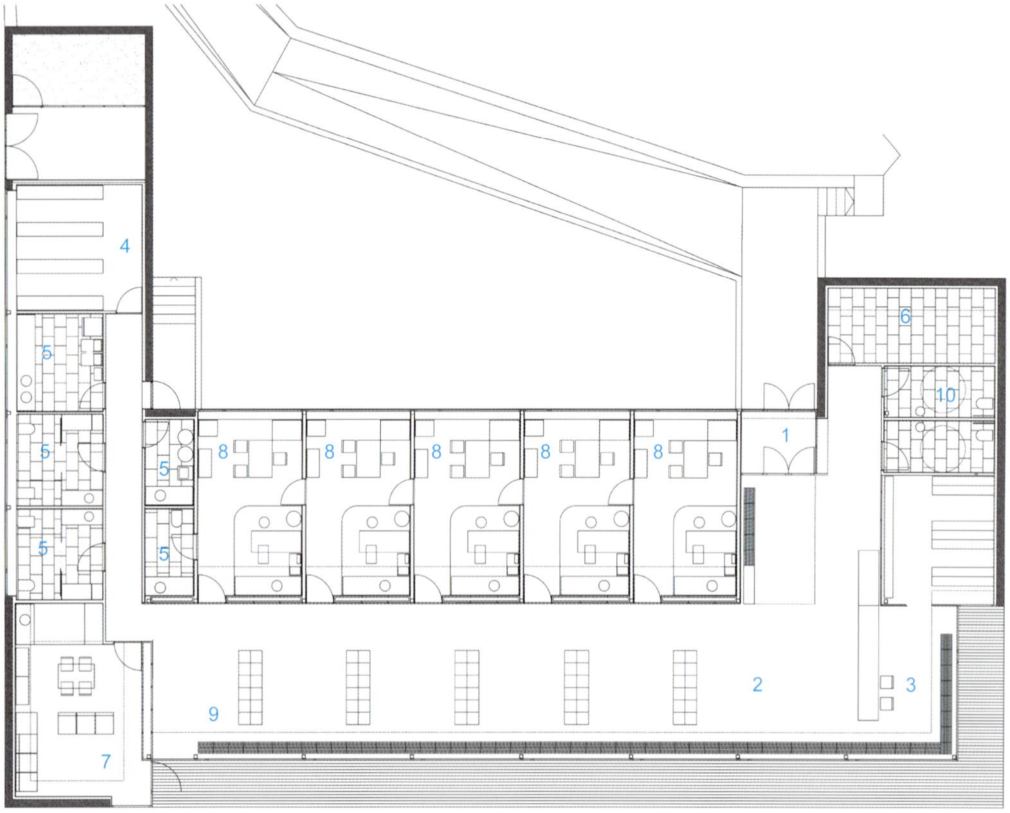
4
5
5
5
5
5
8
8
8
8
8
1
6
10
2
3
9
7

Ground Floor Plan (Left)
1. Entrance
2. Main Hall
3. Reception
4. Safety Office
5. Office
6. Washing Room
7. Café Room
8. Room for Private Banking
9. Waiting Area
10. Lavatory

3. Passage
4. Private office, with contracted decorations

2

One California Bank

Location: Oakland, USA
Completion Year: 2007
Designer: Mark Horton
Photographer: Ethan Kaplan
Area: 641 m²

In an empty tenant space in a struggling neighbourhood, One California has filled a vacancy in an area with many empty storefronts. Boosting financial literacy is an important component of the bank's mission. Recognising that banks can be intimidating to first-time users in this tight, urban setting, design lends to a place that is comfortable and inclusive. The layout allows movement to the teller and banker stations, while creating an intimate waiting area. Broad views to the street outside give a greater sense of security to the neighbourhood and encourage other businesses to set up shop there.

1. The semi-separate design of private offices ensures the privacy of the space
2. Perspective of counters
3. Perspective of private offices, the curved partitions provide the space with diversity and aesthetic
4. Private offices view from the waiting area

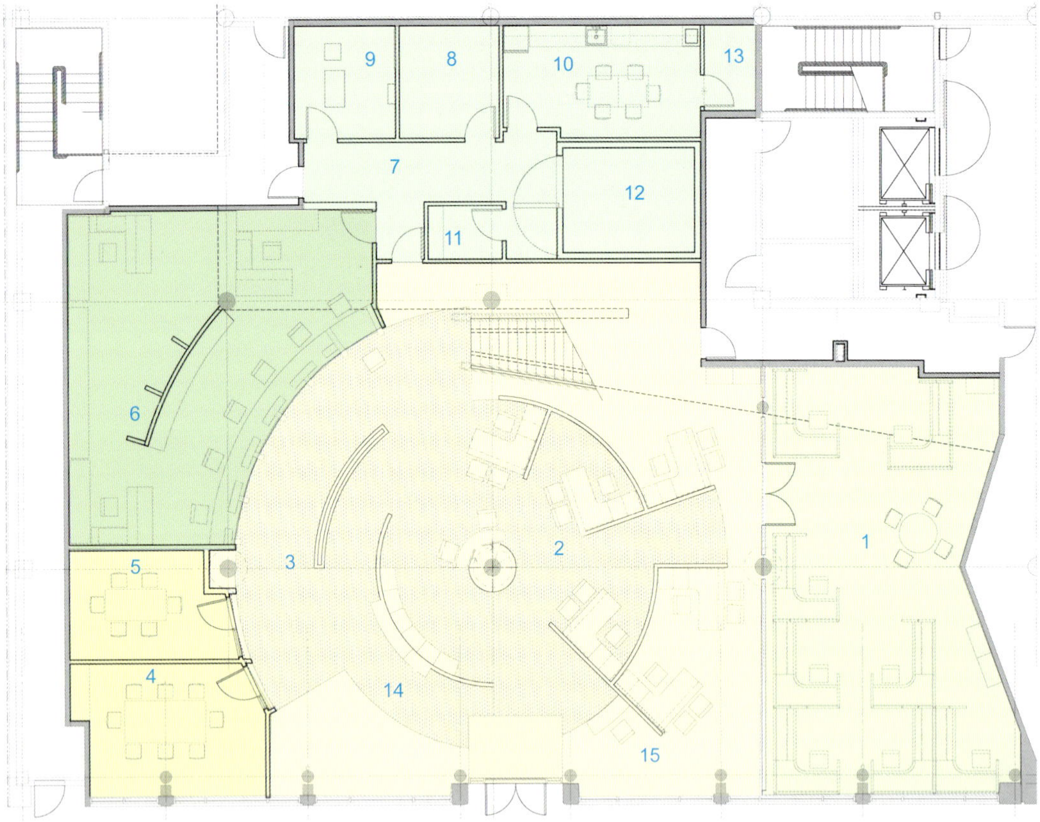

9
8
10
13
7
12
11
6
1
2
5
3
4
14
15

Ground Floor Plan (Left)
1. Office Area
2. Private Banking
3. Cue Area
4. Conference Room 1
5. Conference Room 2
6. Teller Area
7. Hall
8. Storage
9. Server Room
10. Employee Area
11. Coupon Booth
12. Vault
13. Closet
14. Check-writing Counter
15. Guard Booth

3

EXIT

4

INDEX

3XN
Strandgade 73, DK-1401 Copenhagen K, Denmark
Tel: +45 7026 2648
Fax: +45 7026 2649

Albera Monti & Associati
Milano
Via Meravigli, 14
Tel: +39 02 8699 6670 6574
Fax: +39 02 8699 3527

Audrius Ambrasas Architects
Architektų biuras, Teatro Str. 12, LT-03107 Vilnius Lithuania
Tel: +370 5 2620670

Bolwin Wulf Architekten
Nürnberger Strasse 8, 10787 Berlin
Tel: +49 30 887 280 90
Fax: +49 30 887 280 920

Clive Wilkinson Architects
144 North Robertson Boulevard, West Hollywood, CA 90048 USA
Tel: +1 310 358 2200
Fax: +1 310 358 2205

Crea International
Milano
Via Voghera, 7
20144 milano, Italy
Tel: +39 0245487558
Fax: +39 0245487669

Design Clarity
Studio 204, 61 Marlborough St, Surry Hills NSW, 2010, Australia
Tel: +61 0 2 9319 0933

Ecker Architekten
Lglaver Straße 13, 74722 Buchen, Germany
Tel: +49 62 81-56 56 54
Fax: +49 62 81-56 35 70

Eisfeld Engel Architekten
Ander Alster 11,20099 Hamburg
Tel: 040 555 02 977 0
Fax: 040 555 02 977 20

emmanuelle moureaux architecture + design
Tounkyo Bldg 3F, 1-14-14 Uchikanda, Chiyoda-ku, Tokyo 101-0047
Tel: +81 3 3293 0323
Fax: +81 3 3293 0322

Felipe Assadi+Francisca Pulido
Santiago, Chile
Tel: +56 2 2345558 /2 8979720

Gray Puksand
Brisbane
4 / 26 Commercial Road, Fortitude Valley, QLD 4006
Tel: 07 3839 5600
Fax: 07 3839 5622

HASSELL
Level 5, 70 Hindmarsh Square, Adelaide SA, Australia 5000
Tel: +61 8 8220 5000

Herrmann + Bosch
Teckstraße 56, DE-70190 Stuttgart
Tel: +49 0 711 268 41 11 0
Fax: +49 0 711 / 268 41 11 29

Ingenhoven Architects
Plange Mühle 1, 40221 Düsseldorf, Germany
Tel: +49 0 211 30101 01
Fax: +49 0 211 30101 31

Jay is Working. Co., Ltd.
#421,HIT bldg, Hanyang Univ, 222 Wangsimni-ro, Seongong-gu,
Seoul, Korea
Tel: +82 2 597 5902
Fax: +82 2 597 5903

Kauffmann Theilig & Partner Freie Architekten BDA
Zeppelinstr. 10, 73760 Ostfildern/Kemnat
Tel: 0711 45 122 0
Fax: 0711 45 122 40

kub a / Karl und Bremhorst Architekten
Linke Wienzeile 4 / 2 / 4, A-1060 Wien
Tel: +43 0 1 526 22 86
Fax: +43 0 1 524 88 20

Mark Horton Architecture
101 South Park, San Francisco, CA 94107
Tel: 415 543 3347
Fax: 415 543 1440

Massimo Mariani Architetto
Via Aldo Rossi 15, 51016, Montecatini Terme (PT)
Tel: +39 0572 766 324
Fax: +39 0572 912 742

METROPOLIS PERU
Calle Boulevard 162 Oficina 501 (espalda edificio CRONOS)
Santiago de Surco, Lima - Perú
Tel: 511 4375635 / 4376542 / 4376538

NAU Architecture
Riedtlistrasse 27, 8006 Zurich, Switzerland
Tel: +41 44 271 0680
Fax: +41 44 271 0678

Ott Architekten
Konrad-Adenauer-Allee 35
86150 Augsburg
Tel: 0821 20757 0
Fax: 0821 20757 22

Petra Consultants Architects Ltd.
Zaimi 1, Athens, 10682
Tel: +30 210 3604345
Fax: +30 210 3604250

Pichler& Traupmann Architekten ZT GmbH
Kundmanngasse 39 / 12, 1030 Wien
Tel: +43 0 1 7133203
Fax: +43 0 1 713320313

Planet 3 Studios Architecture Pvt. Ltd
505, Tanishka, Next to Big Bazaar, Off Western Express Highway,
Akurli Road, Kandivali (E), Mumbai - 400 101.
Tel: 022 6699 5442 / 2870 5454
Fax: 022 6699 5443

Rottet Studio
808 Travis Street, Suite 100, Houston, TX 77002
Tel: +1 713 221 1830

Spore Architecture
94 Pike St #30, Seattle, WA, 98101
Tel: 206 940 2146

Studio Kuadra
P.za Galimberti 6, 12100 Cuneo Italy
Tel: +39 0171 691778
Fax: +39 0171 691778

Usoarquitectura
Av. Contreras 246-201 col. Sanjeronimo lidice 10200, Mexico d.f.
Tel: +5255 1520 1765